GOD AT THE GRASS ROOTS

Religious Forces in the Modern Political World
General Editor Allen D. Hertzke, The Carl Albert Center,
University of Oklahoma at Norman

Religious Forces in the Modern Political World features books on religious forces in politics, both in the United States and abroad. The authors examine the complex interplay between religious faith and politics in the modern world, emphasizing its impact on contemporary political developments. This new series spans a diverse range of methodological interpretations, philosophical approaches, and substantive concerns. Forthcoming titles include:

God at the Grass Roots: The Christian Right in the 1994 Elections (1995)
    edited by Mark J. Rozell, Mary Washington College, and Clyde
    Wilcox, Georgetown University
Churches of the Poor: The Pentecostal Church in Central America
    by Anne M. Hallum, Stetson University
*The Right and the Righteous: The Christian Right Confronts the
    Republican Party*
    by Duane Oldfield, Boston College
The Prophetic Mode and Challenge in Religion, Politics, and Society
    edited by Neil Riemer, Drew University, editor

GOD AT THE GRASS ROOTS

The Christian Right in the 1994 Elections

Edited by Mark J. Rozell and Clyde Wilcox

Rowman & Littlefield Publishers, Inc.

ROWMAN & LITTLEFIELD PUBLISHERS, INC.

Published in the United States of America
by Rowman & Littlefield Publishers, Inc.
4720 Boston Way, Lanham, Maryland 20706

3 Henrietta Street
London WC2E 8LU, England

British Cataloging in Publication Information Available

Library of Congress Cataloging-in-Publication Data

God at the grass roots : the Christian right in the 1994 elections /
edited by Mark J. Rozell and Clyde Wilcox.
p.   cm.
Includes bibliographical references and index.
1. Conservatism—Religious aspects—Christianity—History—20th
century.   2. Elections—United States.   3. United States—Politics
and government—1993–   4. United States—Church history—20th
century.   I. Rozell, Mark J.   II. Wilcox, Clyde, 1953–   .
BR526.G63   1995   324.973'0929'0882—dc20   95-30671   CIP

ISBN 0-8476-8097-5 (cloth: alk. paper)
ISBN 0-8476-8098-3 (pbk.: alk. paper)

Printed in the United States of America

∞ ™ The paper used in this publication meets the minimum requirements of
American National Standard for Information Sciences—Permanence of
Paper for Printed Library Materials, ANSI Z39.48–1984.

Contents

Preface

This book examines an important facet of the watershed 1994 national elections: the role of the Christian Right in the so-called Republican Revolution. After the Republican landslide, Reverend Pat Robertson's Christian Coalition advertised that it had helped to elect a large number of the GOP congressional candidates and therefore claimed the right to promote its version of policy change in the 104th Congress. Taking its cues from the Republican "Contract with America," the Christian Coalition put forth its own "Contract with the American Family"—an agenda of social policies reflecting the goals of many Christian social conservatives.

The Christian Coalition and other Christian Right groups have certainly succeeded in getting the rest of the country to listen to their call for social policy reform. News media accounts frequently describe the Christian Coalition's young executive director Ralph Reed as one of the country's most influential political operatives. A *Time* magazine cover story went so far as to tell readers that Reed's plan of "taking over" the political process was "working." With such popular media attention, the Christian Right has attained a degree of political legitimacy among both political elites and the public that it could never before claim.

Further testimony is provided by the efforts of the current crop of GOP presidential aspirants to reach out to the Christian Right. Such moderate conservatives as Senator Robert Dole and economic conservatives as Senator Phil Gramm have gone to extraordinary lengths to show that they support the Christian Right's agenda. Political analysts consider such efforts crucial to the nomination quests of these candidates. So sure are these pundits of the Christian Right's impact on the GOP nominating process that they have routinely dismissed the chances of Senator Arlen Specter—the only candidate to date openly opposed to the Christian Right agenda—and declared his candidacy merely an effort to make a statement about the GOP's captivity to the Christian Right.

To be sure, the Christian Right did not achieve this unprecedented degree of respectability and influence in one election. Rather, influential leaders in the movement have fashioned a long-term strategy of gathering strength from the grass roots across the country. For example, the Christian Coalition sponsors seminars and trains Christian social conservatives nationwide in the techniques of political activity at the grass roots. The organization has chapters in all 50 states and has shown itself highly effective at lobbying at the state and local levels. Although the Christian Coalition is clearly the most prominent, it is just one of many grassroots Christian Right organizations promoting social policy change in the United States today.

This book provides the first state-by-state analysis of the role of the Christian Right in an election year. Our objective is to illuminate the role the Christian Right played in various states in the 1994 elections. We selected a number of states—particularly in the South, Midwest, and West—in which the Christian Right's influence was most strongly felt. Given the change of focus by the Christian Right away from the national level and increasingly toward the grass roots, a state-level analysis allows for a greater understanding of the movement's goals, strategies, successes, and failures.

As we hope to make clear, it is inaccurate to describe the Christian Right—as many have—either as a nationwide organization "taking over" the Republican Party or as merely a pesky fringe group. Just as many prematurely declared the death of the Christian Right after Robertson's failed presidential campaign and the dismantling of the Moral Majority, many today overstate the grassroots strength of the movement.

A state-by-state survey reveals that the story is much more complex than that conveyed by many popular analyses. In some states, the Christian Right has formed a healthy partnership with traditional conservative groups in the GOP and ultimately strengthened the party. In other states, the Christian Right is engaged in open warfare with other GOP factions that resist what they consider to be an unwelcome encroachment in their party's politics. The state-level analyses explain much about why the Christian Right has been able to work so well in the GOP in some states but so poorly in others.

The following chapters reveal a political movement that has begun to enter the mainstream, yet is suffering many of the transitional problems associated with trying to achieve political maturity. Leaders of such organizations as the Christian Coalition show a high level of political sophistication, yet they often find it difficult to convince supporters to accommodate the realities of the political process. The true test of the Christian Right's growth in influence will be whether its leaders can indeed mobilize supporters at the grass roots to work within a political system characterized by compromise and incremental change.

We are grateful for the assistance and support of a number of individuals and organizations. Our colleague John Green not only contributed the introductory essay for this book, but also carefully read and commented on every chapter. His many suggestions were invaluable to this project.

The following individuals provided research assistance on particular chapters: Amy Foley, Tom Lipscomb, Kristen Lee Carter, Julie Newell, Sachin Shah, and Zachary Ward.

The American Political Science Association and the Earhart Foundation provided support for our in-depth study of the Christian Right in Virginia, from which chapter 6 is drawn.

We appreciate the permission granted by the American Political Science Association to reprint portions of the six essays on the Christian Right and the 1994 elections that appeared in the March 1995 issue of *PS: Political Science and Politics*.

1

The Christian Right and the 1994 Elections:
An Overview

John C. Green

In 1994, the news media rediscovered the Christian Right, and came away perplexed. The movement seemed to contradict conventional wisdom at every turn. First, many observers were surprised that it was still strong and active, given the responsibility assigned to it for past Republican failures, including the presidential loss in 1992. Second, its activities were neither all successes nor all failures, making the story line difficult to follow. How could a relatively small group with a controversial agenda contribute to unexpected Republican gains in places like Minnesota, while at the same time candidates prominently identified with it, such as Oliver North, were defeated? Why was the Christian Right at once so strong and so weak?

No doubt much of this confusion results from well-known proclivities of journalists, including a penchant for "horse race" coverage, a focus on controversy, and a poor sense of history. There is, however, a deeper misunderstanding at work as well. It is widely assumed that religion is on the wane in modern societies. Thus, its repeated expressions in public affairs, such as the Christian Right, come as a great surprise. In response, many observers are ready to interpret such expressions as temporary aberrations that will quickly fade away. In fact, the Christian Right has been discovered and dismissed in the press at least four times since it emerged on the national scene with the Moral Majority in 1979.

Fifteen years of research by political scientists offers a broader perspective: the real story of the Christian Right is the steady growth in size and sophistication of a political movement that, like other movements, has both strengths and weaknesses. Key to clarifying the movement's role in 1994 is understanding that religion can be an important factor in American politics but that there are also limits to its influence.

1

The essays in this volume are state-level case studies of the Christian Right in the 1994 elections, and taken together they catalogue the movement's strengths and weaknesses in a variety of situations. In some states, such as South Carolina and Oklahoma (and to a lesser extent, California, Michigan, and Texas), the Christian Right made the best use of its strengths, operated within a united Republican Party, and contributed to electoral victory. However, in other states, such as Virginia (and to a lesser extent Oregon, Georgia, and Florida), the movement's weaknesses were evident, producing a divided GOP and contributing to defeat on election day. And in still other states, such as Iowa and Minnesota, both patterns operated at once.

Understanding the Christian Right

Much of the confusion surrounding the Christian Right is revealed in the ways it is labeled. The most common label, the "religious right," is much too broad. This term most usefully refers to an alliance of religious conservatives from many different backgrounds, including evangelical Protestants, conservative mainline Protestants, traditionalist Catholics, orthodox Jews, and so forth. Long a dream of some conservative leaders—and a nightmare for their liberal counterparts—this kind of alliance has appeared only sporadically among movement organizations and activists, although the potential is real enough (Kellstedt et al. 1994; Guth and Green 1992). However, to date most of the political action has been limited to one segment of this unrealized alliance, evangelical Protestants. On the other hand, a term used by many apologists, the "pro-family" movement, is much too narrow. The Christian Right's goals extend beyond concern for families, and such concerns are common to a wide range of groups, including many on the left. While far from perfect, the term "Christian Right" best describes the phenomenon in question: a movement that seeks to restore "traditional values" in public policy by means of mobilizing evangelical Protestants, many of whom self-consciously identify themselves as "Christians" in the sectarian usage of the term.[1] (See the South Carolina case for a sensitive discussion of the varieties of evangelicals.)

Another source of confusion stems from the different aspects of the movement. Like other movements, the Christian Right can be usefully described by different strata of activity, with leaders and movement organizations at the "top," sets of activists in the "middle," and a group of potential voters at the "bottom." This division is useful because it parallels the strata of the religious communities that serve as the basis for the movement: religious leaders, active lay persons, and the rank-and-file congregants (Wald and Smidt 1993). From this perspective, the Christian Right, properly so called, is all three of these types of actors set in "movement" politically, and not just prominent leaders, isolated activists, or potential followers.

Yet another source of confusion is the dynamic nature of the movement. The Christian Right represents just the most recent involvement of evangelical Protestants in American politics and dates from the late 1970s (which is why many of the early studies of the movement referred to it as the "new" Christian Right) (Wilcox 1992). The movement first came to national attention with the founding of the Moral Majority by the Reverend Jerry Falwell, a prominent televangelist, in 1979 and its subsequent support of Ronald Reagan in the 1980 presidential election. Since then it has had an uneven path: many of the original leaders, organizations, and activities have faded away and have been replaced by new ones, which are on balance more sophisticated (Moen 1992). (See the Florida case on this history.) In addition, the Christian Right has considerable internal diversity and is frequently characterized by conflict and disagreement.

All of these misunderstandings have tended to obscure the Christian Right's considerable strengths and parallel weaknesses. (See the Minnesota case for an excellent discussion of how the media cover religion in campaigns.) There is, in fact, some warrant for describing the movement as strong and effective, and an equal warrant for describing it as divisive and ineffective. To avoid the temptation to overstate either tendency, it is useful to briefly describe these strengths and weaknesses, and then how they might play out in politics.

Strengths

The Christian Right's strengths derive primarily from the vitality of evangelical Protestantism (Jorstad 1993). Of particular importance is the internal structure of evangelicalism: this tradition combines orthodox Christian beliefs with intense individualism, resulting in a highly decentralized set of organizations, including thousands of small denominations, parachurch groups, and independent churches. Even the largest bodies, such as the giant Southern Baptist Convention (the largest Protestant denomination in the country), are actually voluntary alliances of their component institutions. This environment puts a premium on aggressive, entrepreneurial leaders who can successfully compete for money, followers, and publicity with the world—and with each other. Such leaders become adept at recognizing discontent among religious people, identifying opportunities to respond to such discontents, and organizing the resources to bring the two together. They also become familiar with the latest communications, fundraising, and organizing techniques. And many are part of religious movements, such as fundamentalism, that are based on explicit and repeated challenges to religious authorities. Thus, the evangelical subculture is closer to the rough and tumble of American electoral politics than many other religious traditions.

Although by no means inevitable, these leadership skills can be effectively applied to politics if the opportunity presents itself. And the contemporary experience of the evangelical subculture has done just that. Over the last generation, social and economic forces have increasingly brought evangelicals into contact with lifestyles and worldviews they find abhorrent. Government policies directed at protecting, extending, and even enforcing these rival values were particularly galling, and all the more so when they dealt with matters easily linked to traditional, religiously based morality: sexual conduct, abortion, women's roles, family arrangements, education, crime, and the legal status of religion itself. Many observers have been tempted to ascribe such complaints to personality problems or to the sublimation of economic stress, but the bulk of research on the evangelicals and the Christian Right finds little support for such explanations (cf. Wilcox 1992). Instead, social issue discontent arises directly from the deeply held religious beliefs of evangelicals, much as similar discontents among social issue liberals come from their beliefs (Hertzke 1993). In fact, many of the complaints of evangelicals are widely shared by other religious people. (See the Oregon case on these discontents.)

These discontents have generated a corps of zealous activists that could be tapped by entrepreneurial leaders to, on the one hand, provide the resources for movement organizations and, on the other, engage in politics directly (Leege 1992). Like other politically involved Americans, these activists are drawn largely from the ranks of the middle class, are relatively well educated, and have professional jobs and good incomes; a large proportion of them are women, and many reside in suburban portions of major metropolitan areas (Smidt et al. 1994; Guth et al. 1994). In fact, the major distinguishing feature between these activists and other kinds of conservative activists is their high degree of religious commitment: they are very orthodox theologically and very active in church. While churches themselves are rarely a formal part of the movement's organization, they are key to its success: the close-knit, face-to-face communities and the communication networks that tie them together are a fertile source of activists (Gilbert 1993). Because of these activists' religious commitments, social issues are usually at the top of their agenda, but many have consistently conservative views of economic and foreign policy as well.

One of the principal goals of the movement organizations and member activists is to mobilize rank-and-file evangelicals for political purposes, which points to a final movement strength: the relative size and cohesiveness of evangelicalism in the mass public (Green et al. 1994a; Smidt 1993). Nationally, white evangelicals make up about one-quarter of the adult American population, and are even more numerous in southern and midwestern states. The high degree of religious commitment among them allows for effective mobilization on the basis of religious networks and moral appeals. Such a group is a good place to begin building an electoral coalition. By way of reference, evangelicals are about as numerous as Roman Catholics, and a larger group than mainline Protestants or the secular population. Although they are hardly a political monolith, mobilizing just one-half of this large tradition would produce a voting bloc more numerous than African American voters, and roughly ten times larger than Jews or Episcopalians (cf. Leege and Kellstedt 1993; Smidt 1993; Wilcox 1992).

Weaknesses

The strengths of this religious-based mobilization—entrepreneurial leaders, committed activists, and dedicated voters—give the Christian Right considerable potential in politics. But such mobilization has parallel weaknesses as well. For one thing, evangelicals have been very difficult to organize, even at the elite level. One special problem has been the otherworldly orientation of deeply religious people; many of them have had little interest in politics and others have been downright hostile to it. Another equally serious problem is religious particularism, where long-standing theological differences have seriously inhibited political cooperation. It has been even harder to reach out beyond evangelicalism to members of other traditions who might share political concerns, particularly Catholics and African Americans. And the entrepreneurial tendencies among evangelical leaders have been a further drag on cooperation, as each leader looks out for his or her own interests. Thus, movement leaders must spend a great deal of effort mobilizing their own constituencies (cf. Wilcox 1992; Jelen 1991).

Another weakness is the intense and sometimes extreme views of movement activists (Guth and Green 1987). The very opinions that motivate these people to engage in movement politics often make them difficult to work with. This problem has seriously interfered with political alliances with secular conservatives. Central to these difficulties is the movement's social issue agenda, which is quite controversial in many quarters. Attempts to set priorities, broaden the movement's goals, or compromise on such issues can become a source of conflict. The division between purists and pragmatists is common in movement politics, of course, but may be all the more problematic because of the movement's religious dimension (Green et al. 1994b). Indeed, Christian Right organizers must spend considerable effort managing the movement's own constituencies.

Finally, the Christian Right's organizing activity and controversial agenda can produce equally intense countermobilization by opponents, particularly liberal movements, many of whom draw on the natural rivals of evangelicals, religious liberals and the secular population (Wilcox 1994; Green and Guth 1990). Many important social institutions are also often critical of the Christian Right's agenda, including the news media, the entertainment industry, public and higher education, and the professions. In addition, key elements of the movement's agenda are not popular with the public, making it possible to mobilize large blocs of voters opposed to the movement. When combined, these factors can present quite formidable opposition.

Potential Results

Not surprisingly, then, the weaknesses of religious-based mobilization—internal conflicts, uncooperative activists, and countermobilization by opponents—also limit the movement's influence. The relative importance of these strengths and weaknesses in any particular situation, and thus the Christian Right's likely impact, depends on how the movement responds to the electoral opportunities it confronts. The case studies that follow reveal two general tendencies in each regard, each of which has important implications for the future of the movement (cf. Green and Guth 1988).

The first tendency is what might be called the "bleak scenario" (cf. Nesmith 1994; see the Iowa case), where the movement's weaknesses overwhelm its strengths. Here internal dissension, a controversial agenda, and countermobilization, together or separately, produce a divided party, an unelectable candidate, or an ineffective campaign, and as a result contribute to defeat at the polls. In these circumstances the movement operates primarily as a form of protest, expressing strongly felt opinions and in the process alienating large portions of the electorate. While there may be some value in such protests (building the movement, for example), they do not directly change elected officials or public policy. If the bleak scenario is followed to its logical conclusion, the Christian Right will eventually fade from the scene—a pattern that has already occurred with some early expressions of the movement (see the Virginia and Michigan cases for examples). Forms of the bleak scenario occurred in nearly every state studied here, but the most notable examples include the Senate races in Virginia and California, the governors' races in Minnesota, Florida, and Georgia, and the initiative campaigns in Oregon.

The second tendency is the "rosy scenario," where the movement's strengths overcome its weaknesses. Here entrepreneurial leadership, committed activists, and mobilized voters, together or separately, generate a united party, a competitive candidate, and an effective campaign, and as a result contribute to victory on election day. In these circumstances the movement operates primarily as an interest group, furthering a set of narrow goals and in the process cooperating with a broader coalition. There may be some value in this approach as well (tangible accomplishments, for example), but it means tempering the movement's demands. If the rosy scenario is followed to its logical conclusion, the Christian Right will eventually become integrated into the Republican Party, a pattern that is far advanced in some places (see the California and Georgia cases on this point). The irony, of course, is that such integration is as likely to cause the movement to fade from the scene as failed protests (see the Oklahoma case on the dynamics of movements). Forms of the rosy scenario also occurred in nearly all of the states studied, but the most notable examples included the Senate races in Minnesota, Michigan, and Oklahoma, and the governors races in Iowa, South Carolina, Texas, and California.

The Movement's Strengths and Weaknesses in 1994

What did the Christian Right actually do in the 1994 campaign? A good place to begin is with the movement leaders and organizations at the national level and in the various states. Overall, the "big three" Christian Right organizations were quite active: the Christian Coalition, Concerned Women for America, and Focus on the Family. Founded by televangelist Pat Robertson after his 1988 presidential campaign, the

Christian Coalition is the largest of these organizations, and because of its focus on grassroots organizing, it was the most prominent in the campaign. The Coalition claimed some 1.5 million members, 48 state chapters, and some 1,400 local chapters in 1994. Ralph Reed, the Coalition's executive director, is one of the most sophisticated movement leaders and has recruited an equally adept national staff. Concerned Women for America is an evangelical women's group founded in 1978 by Beverly LaHaye, wife of Rev. Tim LaHaye, a longtime movement leader. Concerned Women had a strong headquarters staff, some 1,200 local affiliates, and a membership several hundred thousand strong in 1994. Focus on the Family is a large pro-family group founded by radio psychologist James Dobson. Its political arm, the Family Research Council, directed by another savvy leader, Gary Bauer, had 26 state affiliates and more than a hundred thousand local activists in 1994. The grassroots work of all three organizations was supplemented by their regular print and electronic media efforts. In addition, there were numerous smaller organizations, such as the Christian Action Network, built out of the remnants of the Moral Majority.

The state case studies reveal this organizational diversity and then some. The Christian Coalition was prominent in nearly all the states covered, but stronger in some places (South Carolina and Oklahoma) and weaker in others (Michigan and Oregon). Concerned Women and the Focus on the Family affiliates were the next most common, followed by several organizations associated with schools, such as Citizens for Excellence in Education and home schooling groups. Prominent regional or state groups also received attention. The American Family Association was active in South Carolina, the Traditional Values Coalition in California, and Citizens for Traditional Values in Michigan; the Citizens Alliances in Oregon, Washington, and Idaho were as important as the national groups. Dozens of purely local groups were quite active as well. The case studies also identified organizations routinely allied with Christian Right groups, including the Eagle Forum, the Right to Life Committees, and several secular conservative groups.

This mix of organizations allowed the movement to deploy a large number of resources, but at the risk of conflict and confusion. While there was only limited formal cooperation between these diverse groups, there was also an absence of the bitter infighting that has often characterized the movement. There were some important exceptions, however. On one hand, the leaders of Christian Right groups and allied organizations in Texas met routinely—as they continue to today—to coordinate their activities (a meeting known as "The Gathering"). On the other hand, the lack of coordination between the Michigan Right to Life Committee and the Christian Right groups may have reduced Republican gains in Michigan, and various Christian Right groups sparred in some southern primaries. The availability of training materials and campaign literature from the major national groups did provide some minimal uniformity to these disparate efforts, however.

But how many resources did the movement actually deploy? While no official figures are available, informed observers estimate that the major national groups probably expended at least $25 million on their grass-roots efforts, mostly in the form of campaign literature and its distribution. The case studies suggest that several million dollars were also raised for similar purposes at the state and local level. But the muscle of the movement was clearly its activist corps. A careful review of the membership claims of the national organizations and "Christian" fundraising lists suggests that in 1994, the total movement membership may have been as large as four million. Many of these were surely nominal or "checkbook" members, but if as few as 5 percent were dedicated activists (an assumption supported by poll evidence as well as interviews), the corps would have numbered 200,000 nationwide. The case studies report similar numbers: the active membership of Christian Right organizations is reported in the tens of thousands, and dedicated activists in the thousands.

All told, these are quite impressive resources, particularly in the context of a midterm rather than a presidential election. Although there is no systematic evidence available at the national level or in the case studies, it appears that efforts by the Christian Right's opponents were more limited. Led by People for the American Way, a host of liberal organizations loudly sounded the alarm about the Christian Right and attempted to encourage countermobilization. As part of this effort, a new "religious left" organization was founded, the Interfaith Alliance, and leaders of the Democratic Party vigorously attacked the Christian Right. There is some evidence of effective countermobilization in Virginia, Florida, Georgia, Oregon, and Iowa; the other cases suggest much less success.

Nevertheless, disputes between Christian Right activists and their more moderate counterparts in Republican circles were the stuff of the campaign: every case study reports conflict surrounding the movement's controversial agenda. It is clear that these problems are widely recognized by candidates, party leaders, and movement activists alike. Republicans handled these problems successfully in some cases (South Carolina, Oklahoma, California, and Iowa) and unsuccessfully in others

(Minnesota and Virginia), with mixed results occurring in other places. Data on convention delegates in the Virginia case reveal the dimensions of these conflicts. While Christian Rightists and more moderate Republicans actually agreed on many issues and had similar demographic characteristics, there were stark differences on key social issues such as abortion, pornography, and education. These differences were exacerbated by the conflict over party nominations. While more moderate Republicans surely must bear part of the blame for these divisions, the movement's activist corps showed much less pragmatism and sophistication than its leadership.

What about the electorate in the 1994 campaign? Media surveys taken during the campaign showed that the Christian Right faced both opportunities and challenges with the mass public. First, an index of support for the movement revealed a nearly two-to-one bias in favor of the Christian Right among white evangelical Protestants (52 to 26 percent). In contrast, the population as a whole was evenly divided (33 to 33 percent), and the secular population showed nearly a two-to-one bias in the opposite direction (19 to 43 percent). Similarly polarized patterns occurred on many of the movement's core concerns, including abortion. However, the more general notion that religious values should play a greater role in political decisions was much more popular than the Christian Right or its agenda, with 57 percent of the public wanting a greater role for religion and 17 percent wanting a lesser role. This pattern was very strong for evangelicals (74 to 10 percent) and was found even among seculars (35 to 25 percent). Crosscutting economic issues reveal the potential for a broad conservative coalition: equal numbers of evangelicals and seculars favored fewer government services and fewer taxes over more of both (60 percent). Many of the case studies found a similar pattern of opinion.[2]

The Christian Right and Candidate-Centered Politics

One of the great truisms of contemporary politics is that American elections are "candidate centered," meaning that candidates themselves are the most dynamic elements in campaigns and their quality is a decisive factor (cf. Salmore and Salmore 1989). The influence of movements such as the Christian Right comes chiefly from their association with candidates: strong candidacies make it possible for the movement to "succeed" and poor ones produce high rates of "failure." Movements can influence candidacies in at least three ways: through the recruitment of candidates themselves, the provision of campaign resources to them, and the direct mobilization of voters on their behalf. In 1994, the Christian Right was active in all three ways with varying degrees of success. The movement's weaknesses are most evident at the level of candidate recruitment and its strengths most evident in direct voter mobilization.

There is no great mystery to electoral success in candidate-centered politics: recruit good candidates and target support for them according to their chance of winning. Of course, this is easier said than done, even for political organizations that are more cohesive than the Christian Right. And the perennial choice between the most electable candidates and candidates with the best agenda is particularly difficult for the movement to handle. Candidate recruitment offers the Christian Right the broadest range of influence over elections through the selection of candidates, but it also brings to the fore its internal divisions, its controversial agenda, and some strong rivals.

Movement Self-Starters

The problems involved in candidate recruitment are most obvious when candidacies arise from within the Christian Right itself. Such candidates are usually energetic proponents of the movement's core agenda and are often more conservative than other movement activists. In addition, they frequently lack other credentials, such as previous political experience or government service and a well-developed agenda on other issues of concern to voters. Not surprisingly, such candidates are rarely successful. Few obtain major party nominations and those that do tend to lose by large margins, producing one or another form of the bleak scenario. These candidates also provide the best targets for criticism (although it seems that opponents of the movement rarely like more pragmatic candidates any better). The stereotype of the "extremist" religious candidate has some basis in fact. Indeed, too close an identification with the Christian Right can be devastating with voters. Minnesota's Allen Quist is a good example of all these features, as were William Dannemeyer in California, Henry Jordan in South Carolina, and Tom Feeney in Florida. And there were countless other examples for lower-level offices, even in places such as Georgia and Texas, where the Christian Right's agenda is more popular.

For these reasons, more pragmatic Christian Right leaders often discourage such "self-starters" and sometimes actually work against them. However, movement leaders do not control their activist followers, and they can find themselves swept along in support of popular candidates who have no real chance of success. Opposing such candidates can damage the movement's local organization and, worse yet, produce independent candidacies that complicate the general election. A good example of the latter occurred in the third congressional district in Kentucky, and similar efforts were reported in several other states. (Ironically, the most important independent campaign occurred among party moderates in Virginia, and it might well have helped Oliver North had it been more successful.) The number of movement self-starters in 1994 appears to have been comparable to previous years, and overall they fared poorly (Green, Guth, and Hill 1993).

As the cases of Oregon and Iowa reveal, the Christian Right has been very active in ballot issues as well. Politically, a referendum on a single controversial issue, such as gay rights, resembles the situation of a self-starting movement candidate. And as with self-starters, such efforts frequently fail, largely because they present an unpopular issue in isolation. Of course, liberal movements can have much the same problem, as revealed by the successful Stop ERA campaign reported in Iowa. Broader-based referenda, such as California's Proposition 187, are more likely to pass even when enthusiastically backed by the movement in much the same way as broader-based conservative candidates do better at the polls.

Good candidates do arise from time to time from within the movement, however, and under the right circumstances they can do very well; Steve Largent and J.C. Watts in Oklahoma are examples. In addition, self-starters can sometimes acquire sufficient experience and credibility to be successful. James Inhofe in Oklahoma is an example, and Mike Farris in Virginia and John Knox in Georgia might be examples in the making. In fact, one of the reasons the Christian Right has placed emphasis on winning local offices is to develop a pool of good candidates for the future (Guth and Green 1992). In fact, the Christian Right appears to have recruited a few more successful candidates from within its own ranks than in previous years. It is unclear, however, if this represents a trend or the unique circumstances of 1994.

Nomination Politics

Christian Right leaders have sought to minimize the problems of self-starters by becoming involved in the rough-and-tumble of nomination politics. In some cases, movement activists have helped recruit credible candidates who shared their goals, but mostly they have supported or opposed candidates recruited by other means. This process is quite informal and mostly local, involving three-way contacts between candidates, activists, and leaders. Under the best circumstances, this kind of involvement reduces the risks to the movement since the disagreements between purists and pragmatists can be negotiated around a particular candidate. This seems to have happened with David Beasley in South Carolina, Tom Coburn in Oklahoma, and Rod Grams in Minnesota.

There is no guarantee, of course, that such a process will succeed: not only can movement activists refuse to support the eventual nominee, as happened in Minnesota with Governor Carlson, but the movement can be saddled with a popular but flawed candidate, as with Oliver North in Virginia or Michael Huffington in California. In 1994, the Christian Right appears to have been involved in more contested nominations than in the past, and seems to have fared better. Clearly, the rules of such contests had an effect: nominating conventions encourage movement activists to follow their purist inclinations (as in Minnesota and Virginia), whereas primaries tend to encourage pragmatism (as in South Carolina and Oklahoma). Indeed, Christian Rightists showed a remarkable degree of pragmatism in many state primaries, often backing candidates in the general election who defeated their favorites, such as in South Carolina and Georgia, or supporting a ticket balanced by a favorite candidate, as in Florida.

The Christian Right's involvement in nomination politics parallels its involvement in Republican Party organizations. Some of this interest reflects the natural affinity of conservative activists for the more conservative party, but there is much more at stake. Participation in the GOP offers the Christian Right two important benefits: direct access to the process of candidate recruitment and, more important, a forum in which to build coalitions. Given the movement's weaknesses, much negotiation and collaboration must take place outside the movement organizations themselves, and parties are well suited for these purposes. Involvement in the GOP reduces the risks to the movement one step further by insulating the rank-and-file activists from other coalition partners and even the eventual nominees. As before, however, there is no guarantee that such a process will be successful. South Carolina, Texas, California, Michigan, and Oklahoma are examples of this strategy working, whereas Minnesota, Virginia, and Oregon show the opposite. The cases of Iowa, Florida, and Georgia reveal just how tenuous even successful party alliances can be.

There is some systematic evidence that the Christian Right is participating more fully in the GOP. A recent survey by *Campaigns and Elections* magazine (Persinos 1994) finds that the movement and related social issue allies are a "dominant" influence in some eighteen state Republican organizations and a "substantial" influence in thirteen more. Most of these states are located in the South, Midwest and West where anecdotal evidence suggests that the movement may be even stronger in local Republican organizations. Interestingly, all of the states covered in the following essays were listed in the "dominant" category. (See the Texas case for a good account of the movement in party politics.) As with the selection of candidates, a key to success seems to be an element of restraint on movement activists. In California, for example, the movement activists have adapted to their minority status within their state's secular culture, whereas in Texas and Georgia, Christian Rightists made necessary adjustments with secular conservative allies. But once again, the Virginia and Oregon cases show how unrestrained activism can help polarize the party. The case of Iowa shows how restraint on the part of moderates is important as well.

The role of "coalition broker" is critical for a rosy scenario to emerge. This role was rarely played by movement leaders themselves, although in Texas, Georgia, and California movement pragmatists surely helped. More often than not, the brokers were the candidates themselves, who assembled a following of Christian Rightists and other conservatives that was sufficient to win. John Engler in Michigan, Pete Wilson in California, Kay Bailey Hutchison and George Bush in Texas, Terry Branstad in Iowa, and George Allen in Virginia in 1993 are all examples of more moderate Republicans who successfully wooed the movement as well as its rivals into a winning coalition. The role of coalition broker was performed with great skill by party leaders in Oklahoma.

Campaign Support

Once candidates are nominated, the Christian Right can help provide resources for their campaigns, which plays to the movement's strengths. Unlike other political groups, the Christian Right organizations have never been particularly involved in supplying material aid to campaigns, such as financial donations, and 1994 followed this pattern (California was the only important exception). What the movement has generated instead is "person power" in the form of grassroots activists, which, as we have seen, were quite numerous in 1994. As the case studies suggest, such efforts range from serving as campaign officials, organizers, or fundraisers to more menial campaign work. These activists were not evenly distributed, of course. The 800 to 900 volunteers reported in Largent's campaign in Oklahoma was probably unusually high; the re-

ports of 600 activists in one part of Georgia might have been more typical. Movement activists were clearly part of many of the campaigns covered in the following essays, sometimes to great effect.

It is here, however, that pragmatism in the recruitment of candidates
can be very costly: local activists run on enthusiasm, which can be throt-
tled by moderation and compromise. In Minnesota, it was difficult to
transfer the enthusiasm of Quist's backers to his rival Carlson, just as it
may be difficult for many of North's Virginia followers to support more
moderate Republicans in the future. The Oregon case reveals just how
hard reconciliation can be, even if the rival groups are willing. The Iowa
and Oklahoma cases point to the importance of the actual conduct of
the campaign: if candidates avoid divisive issues and stress consensual
ones within the local context, even delicate coalitions can hold together.

Finally, the Christian Right specializes in the direct mobilization of
voters on behalf of candidates, activities that play most completely to
the movement's strengths. The tactic of choice is the production and
distribution of nonpartisan "voter guides." This literature usually com-
pares the candidates on a set of issues of interest to the movement,
where an effort is made to draw differences between them. Although
there is rarely any kind of explicit endorsement, an attentive reader can
easily determine where the movement stands. (The Oklahoma and
Georgia cases contain excellent descriptions of the voter guides.) The
voter guides are distributed by mail to organization members, by hand
via local organizations, and through churches. Indeed, a favorite operation is to "leaflet" evangelical churches the Sunday before the election.
Most of the case studies mention the voter guides and related activities,
and all the authors see them as having been effective. The reason for
this positive impact is straightforward: the voter guides provide action-
able information to predisposed voters from a trusted source.

The number of voter guides produced and distributed in 1994 was
quite large, and on the par with similar efforts in 1992. For example, the
Christian Coalition claims to have distributed some 33 million during
the campaign, and other organizations, many quite local, may have contributed several million more. The Christian Coalition issued guides in
all competitive congressional and gubernatorial elections, and their
state and local affiliates did the same in many areas. The Coalition also
boasted of an impressive local workforce for these efforts alone, perhaps
numbering 75,000 nationwide; in some states, numerous evangelical
churches were involved in these efforts (comprising perhaps one-third
of the effort in South Carolina). Much more modest efforts were directed at getting local activists to the polls and stimulating them to rouse

their friends, neighbors, and co-parishioners. The power of these efforts comes in part from generating support for many candidates simultaneously. It is less clear how well the movement could target these efforts; the Oklahoma case may be the exception rather than the rule.

How productive were these efforts on election day? Overall, the impact seems to have been positive. Nationally, exit polls reveal that white evangelical voters constituted more than 20 percent of the House vote, three-quarters of which went Republican, probably an all-time high. Other more generous estimates of conservative religious voters suggest that the number may be over 30 percent (but with less than two-thirds voting Republican), whereas a narrower estimate of voters identifying with the movement is 14 percent (with four-fifths backing the GOP). All such estimates suggest that turnout among the movement's target base was higher than in 1990.[3] The case studies support these national numbers, although the size and impact of evangelicals varied from state to state. Evangelicals were the most numerous in the southern states, and thus had the most impact, but they made up significant blocs in other states as well. And their voting behavior was the same everywhere: substantial backing for Republican candidates up and down the ticket.

Thus, evangelical Protestants, however defined, were one of the core Republican constituencies in 1994. It is worth noting, however, that in none of the case studies did the evangelical vote constitute a majority of the votes cast for Republicans. Even in successful primary bids, evangelical votes were but one element of a broad conservative coalition. But as such, the Christian Right contributed to a host of Republican victories, including the takeover of both houses of Congress for the first time in forty years, control of a majority of governorships, and major gains at the state and local levels. Indeed, the case studies reveal the importance of the movement to dozens of very close elections in all regions of the country. These gains might have been even greater if the rosy scenario had prevailed in more states.

In general, the 1994 elections were a success for the Christian Right, comparable in many respects to the boost the civil rights movement received in 1964 and the gains made by the labor movement in 1948. Will this situation persist in the future, particularly when the political environment is less conducive to the movement's activities? The answer is unclear. The case studies reveal that both the bleak and rosy scenarios can obtain, depending on the interplay of national trends, local circumstances, and movement activities. Given its many strengths, the Christian Right can be a major player in electoral politics and a cornerstone of a resurgent Republican Party. At the same time, the movement's many weaknesses may impose stern limits on its influence and complicate Republican fortunes. With any luck, however, the Christian Right will cease to be misunderstood by professional observers of politics; the essays in this volume represent a step in that direction.

Notes

1. One of the central tenets of evangelicalism is that individuals become Christians by means of personal acceptance of Jesus Christ as savior. Thus, being a "Christian" is an achieved rather than ascribed status, and it cuts across denominational backgrounds. Hence, Patrick Buchanan is described as a "Catholic Christian" in movement literature, while Methodist Hillary Rodham Clinton's status as a "Christian" is suspect.

2. These data come from a *Newsweek* survey conducted 26 August to 1 September 1994 by Princeton Survey Research Associates. The index of support for the Christian Right had two items: knowledge and evaluation of the Christian Coalition and evaluation of Pat Robertson.

3. These data were taken from network exit polls and propriety polls conducted by campaign consultants. A good source of these polls and related information is Ladd (1995).

References

Gilbert, Christopher P. 1993. *The Impact of Churches on Political Behavior.* Westport, Conn.: Greenwood Press.

Green, John C., and James L. Guth. 1988. "The Christian Right in the Republican Party: The Case of Pat Robertson's Supporters." *Journal of Politics* 50:150–65.

———. 1990. "Politics in a New Key: Religiosity and Participation Among Political Activists." *Western Political Quarterly* 43:153–79.

———. 1993. "Politics in the Promised Land: The Christian Right at the Grassroots." Pp. 219–34 in *Research in the Social Scientific Study of Religion,* ed. Monty L. Lynn and David O. Moberg. Greenwich, Conn.: JAI Press.

Green, John C., James L. Guth, and Kevin Hill. 1993. "Faith and Election: The Christian Right in Congressional Campaigns 1978–1988." *Journal of Politics* 55:80–91.

Green, John C., James L. Guth, Lyman A. Kellstedt, and Corwin E. Smidt. 1994a. "Murphy Brown Revisited: The Social Issues in the 1992 Election." In *Disciples and Democracy,* ed. Michael Cromartie. Grand Rapids, Mich.: Eerdmans.

———. 1994b. "Uncivil Challenges? Support for Civil Liberties among Religious Activists." *Journal of Political Science* 22:25–50.

Guth, James L., and John C. Green. 1987. "The Moralizing Minority: Christian Right Support among Political Contributors." *Social Science Quarterly* 67:598–610.

———, eds. 1992. *The Bible and the Ballot.* Boulder, Colo.: Westview Press.

Guth, James L., John C. Green, Lyman A. Kellstedt, and Corwin E. Smidt. 1994. "Onward Christian Soldiers: Religious Interest Group Activists." Pp. 55–76 in *Interest Group Politics,* 4th edition, ed. Allan Cigler and Burdett Loomis. Washington, D.C.: CQ Press.

Hertzke, Allen D. 1993. *Echoes of Discontent.* Washington, D.C.: CQ Press.

Jelen, Ted G. 1991. *The Political Mobilization of Religious Belief.* Westport, Conn.: Praeger.

Jorstad, Erling. 1993. *Popular Religion in America.* Westport, Conn.: Greenwood Press.

Kellstedt, Lyman A., John C. Green, James L. Guth, and Corwin E. Smidt. 1994. "Religious Voting Blocs in the 1992 Election: The Year of the Evangelical?" *Sociology of Religion* 55:307–26.

Ladd, Carll Everett, ed. 1995. *America at the Polls 1994.* Storrs, Conn.: The Roper Center for Public Opinion Research.

Leege, David C. 1992. "Coalitions, Cues, Strategic Politics, and the Staying Power of the Religious Right." *Political Science* 25:198–204.

Leege, David C., and Lyman A. Kellstedt, eds. 1993. *Rediscovering the Religious Factor in American Politics.* Armonk, N.Y.: M.E. Sharpe.

Moen, Matthew C. 1992. *The Transformation of the Christian Right.* Tuscaloosa, Ala.: University of Alabama Press.

Nesmith, Bruce. 1994. *The New Republican Coalition.* New York: Peter Lang.

Persinos, John F. 1994. "Has the Christian Right Taken over the Republican Party?" *Campaigns and Elections* 15 (September):21–24.

Salmore, Barbara G., and Stephen A. Salmore. 1989. *Candidates, Parties and Campaigns,* 2nd edition. Washington DC: CQ Press.

Smidt, Corwin E. 1993. "Evangelical Voting Patterns: 1976–1988." Pp. 85–117 in *No Longer Exiles,* ed. Michael Cromartie. Washington, D.C.: Ethics and Public Policy Center.

Smidt, Corwin E., Lyman A. Kellstedt, John C. Green, and James L. Guth. 1994. "The Characteristics of Religious Group Activists: An Interest Group Analysis." Pp. 133–71 in *Christian Political Activism at the Crossroads,* ed. William Stevenson. Lanham, Md.: University Press of America.

Wald, Kenneth D., and Corwin E. Smidt. 1993. "Measurement Strategies in the Study of Religion and Politics." Pp. 26–49 in *Rediscovering the Religious Factor in American Politics,* ed. David C. Leege and Lyman A. Kellstedt. Armonk, N.Y.: M.E. Sharpe.

Wilcox, Clyde. 1992. *God's Warriors.* Baltimore, Md.: Johns Hopkins University Press.

———. 1994. "Premillenialists at the Millennium: Some Reflections on the Christian Right in the Twenty-first Century." *Sociology of Religion* 55:243–62.

2

Florida: Running Globally and Winning Locally

Kenneth D. Wald

In the November elections, the Florida GOP took control of the state senate for the first time since Reconstruction, pushed up its minority share of the state house to the highest level in the twentieth century, gained a net of one cabinet seat to forge a tie with the Democrats in that crucial executive body, and augmented its majority on the Florida congressional delegation. Republicans were also heartened by the landslide reelection of U.S. Senator Connie Mack, who had eked out the barest of victory margins in his 1986 race.

There was considerable disappointment at the GOP's failure to recapture the governorship, to dislodge a number of supposedly vulnerable first-term Democratic congressional representatives, to win control of the lower house of the legislature, or to obtain a larger majority of the state senate. Nonetheless, the GOP gains marked 1994 as a banner year, signaling the emergence of the Republican Party as an equal partner in Florida government and the transformation of the state from a modified one-party to a full-fledged two-party competitive system. If the rise of Florida Republicanism seemed less impressive than the GOP electoral surges in some other southern states, that was simply because there was a pattern of gradual electoral growth to build upon (Craig 1991; Parker 1992). With only incremental gains in votes and seats in 1994, the Florida GOP could nonetheless cross the threshold from opposition to political power.

The successes and failures of the state GOP call attention to the role of the Christian Right in Florida politics. Across the nation, commentators were quick to attribute a significant share of the massive Republican gains of 1994 to the mobilizing role of Christian conservatives (Berke 1994). Although it was perhaps predictable that a liberal organization like People for the American Way would emphasize the contribution of

19

the Christian Right to the dramatic growth of Republican political power, other commentators shared the opinion that Christian conservatives had helped fuel the Republican landslide.[1] Perhaps symbolically putting the seal on the connection, *Newsweek*'s pictorial gallery of the new Republican power structure included a full-page portrait of Ralph Reed, chief organizer for the Christian Coalition. The Florida commentary also mentioned the important role of Christian activists in the Republican breakthrough at the state level.

The experience of the Christian Right in Florida largely mirrors developments in the nation as a whole. When the Christian Right surged to national prominence during the 1980 election, its power seemed potentially unlimited. Liberal commentators drew ominous parallels between the Islamic revolution in Iran and the resurgence of Protestant fundamentalism in the United States. Ironically, the movement appears to have peaked nationally at the precise moment when it was first recognized by the mass media. Rank and file Christian conservatives moved in force to the core of Republican Party politics and assumed a role similar to that which organized labor had long enjoyed among the Democrats. Yet for all their loyalty and intense commitment during the Reagan-Bush years, the Christian conservatives had precious little to show for their efforts, electorally or in terms of public policy (Moen 1992). In reaction to its limited gains, the Christian Right embarked in the late 1980s on a new strategy that emphasized local concerns and a style of campaigning that avoided strong religious language. This second coming of the Christian Right appears to have scored some notable policy successes which eluded the movement during its brief period of national attention.

The same trajectory is evident in Florida. That is, while the movement has shown itself adept at penetrating the organization of the statewide Republican Party, giving it a key voice in the selection of Republican nominees, its mass electoral power is considerably less impressive than its organizational role would suggest. Indeed, close identification with the movement has more often proven itself a liability than an electoral asset to candidates for statewide office. Furthermore, the policy initiatives sponsored by Christian Right advocates have run up against intense opposition in Tallahassee and have gone down to defeat. In Florida, as in the United States, the movement has shown its greatest successes under three conditions—when it concentrates on the local level, when the issue is not partisan but rather poses a clear question of traditional morality, and when its own role and involvement are downplayed through "stealth" campaigns. In reviewing the 1994 midterm elections in Florida, this chapter suggests that patterns in Florida offer, in microcosm, a nice model of what has happened to the Christian Right movement nationally.

Background

If we are to appraise the successes and failures of the Christian Right in Florida politics, it is important to remember that the movement began as an effort to mobilize religious conservatives under Republican auspices. To what extent have the religious conservatives become a major component of the Republican Party in Florida and to what degree have they impressed their political priorities on the party? If we look separately at the three major components of parties identified by V. O. Key, Jr.—the party in the electorate, the party as organization, and the party in government—the answer varies with each component. Those who emphasize the significance of the Christian Right point to the gains it has made in the first two realms, whereas skeptics tend to focus on the failure to translate these resources into policy outputs.

Organizationally, the Christian Right is clearly an integral part of the Florida Republican hierarchy. *Campaigns & Elections*, a trade journal for political consultants, classifies Florida as one of eighteen states where the Christian Right has gained a dominant voice in the state GOP organization (Persinos 1994). This means, according to the experts consulted by the magazine, that Christian conservatives have a working majority in the decision-making organs of the state party. Yet this success may amount to less than it first seems because of the chronic disorganization that afflicts the Republican Party apparatus at state level. Almost fifty years after V. O. Key described Florida politics with the slogan "Every Man for Himself," the state's parties, Republican no less than Democratic, remain "weak, fragmented, factionalized, underfunded, underorganized and non-policy-oriented" (Scher 1994, 50). While individual Republican candidates are quite capable of mounting effective and well-organized campaigns for office, the party organization itself has not been equally professional or particularly important in the battle for party control (Scher 1992, 176–83). In Florida, as elsewhere, the Republican Party is defined by its candidates, and aspirants for party nomination seldom emerge from the party organization or even pay it much heed. The controlling voice the Christian Right is presumed to possess within the party may not carry much weight outside party circles.

At the mass level of the so-called party in the electorate, the Christian

Right has also become an important conduit by which the Republican Party has encroached on traditional Democratic constituencies and fueled its rise to parity. In middle-class and solidly working-class neighborhoods—formerly reliable Democratic strongholds and still majority Democratic in voter registration—the Republican embrace of moral conservatism has helped GOP candidates carve out solid voting majorities (March 1994). The Christian conservatives, though hardly a majority at the grass roots, are now said to account for a sizable share—perhaps as high as a third—of Republican primary voters in Florida (Dunkelberger 1994).

Almost twenty years after they set out to forge a partisan realignment by attracting fundamentalist Christians to the Republican banner, conservative activists can point to Florida as one state where considerable progress has been made. What has the Christian Right obtained for its assent to this bargain? What has been the impact on the third face of the Republican Party, the party in government? Has the social movement capitalized on its partisan potential to change the state and enshrine cultural conservatism in public policy? Here the story is quite different. While some members of the state party in the legislature have worked to realize the Christian Right agenda, it is hard to identify any successes. During the 1994 session of the Florida legislature, a small group of Christian conservatives launched an ambitious effort to pass a number of bills dealing with public nudity, prayer in school, educational curricula, corporal punishment, and similar subjects (Mitchell 1994). Even though these bills enjoyed sympathy from a number of highly placed legislative leaders, they were not promoted as a matter of high priority— precisely the scenario that confronted the leaders of the national Christian Right organizations when they pressed their claims on Congress after the 1980 election. Consequently, in Florida as in the nation's capital, most bills introduced in the service of the Christian Right program died in committee or were quietly buried in conference, the same fate that traditionally befell such legislation. Thus, while the Christian Right has undeniably become a critical element in the Florida Republican Party, organizationally and as an electoral force, there is significant doubt that its reach has extended much beyond that. While the religious conservatives have received some symbolic recognition from Republican elites, they have yet to capture the commanding heights of party authority. Moreover, the electoral success of state office candidates elected with Christian Right support has thus far failed to yield the dramatic policy changes called for by Christian Right organizations.

This pattern was reaffirmed in the 1994 Florida midterm elections. As we shall see, the Christian Right could legitimately claim little in the way of statewide success and had to be content with a few glimmers of accomplishment primarily at the local level.

The Gubernatorial Race: Fear of Feeney?

In the highest-profile race on the Florida ballot, the contest for the governorship, Republican Jeb Bush failed to unseat Democratic incumbent Lawton Chiles. Chiles won a narrow victory despite Bush's popularity and name recognition, the very well-financed and tightly organized Republican campaign, broad public dissatisfaction with Chiles's record of accomplishment, and the general pro-Republican tide that swept the nation. Jeb Bush's defeat was all the more striking given the ability of his older brother, a comparative political neophyte, to oust a much more popular Democratic incumbent in Texas.

This race seems to illustrate the argument that Christian Right influence is inversely proportional to the degree of public awareness of its role. The principal contribution of the Christian Right in electoral terms occurred during the Republican gubernatorial primary. Anticipating a strong Republican year and with the state still recovering from recession, five major candidates sought the Republican gubernatorial nomination in Florida. By virtue of his name recognition and access to campaign contributions, Jeb Bush became the front-runner almost upon his announcement of candidacy. Bush had never held elective office, serving only in the low-profile appointive office of Secretary of Commerce under Republican Bob Martinez, but he was well known as the son of the former president, a prosperous south Florida businessman, and an active member of the state GOP. Nonetheless, few predicted an easy route to nomination for Bush. His two most formidable rivals for the nomination were sitting cabinet members, Secretary of State Jim Smith and Treasurer–Insurance Commissioner Tom Gallagher. Smith had been a popular Democrat who left the party when he lost its gubernatorial nomination in 1986 and had subsequently won handily in statewide races as a Republican. Gallagher, a former state legislator known for his youthful exuberance and freewheeling ways, had achieved a high public profile due to his aggressive actions against errant insurance companies in the wake of Hurricane Andrew. The race also attracted former state senator and Republican leader Ander Crenshaw as well as Ken Connor, a Tallahassee attorney. It was the strongest Republican gubernatorial field in years and posed the definite prospect of a bitter and divisive primary.

Both Smith and Gallagher represented the more libertarian wing of the GOP that regards moral regulation, like economic regulation, as a suspect venue for state activity. Neither attempted to identify himself closely with the antiabortion sentiment that animated many Christian conservatives, and they took similarly libertarian views toward homosexual conduct, an issue of some importance during the early stages of the campaign.

The battle for Christian conservative voters thus engaged only three of the five Republican candidates, the three who described themselves as born-again Christians (Dunkelberger 1994). Of the three, Ken Connor perhaps had the best claim for support based on past activity in the cause of moral traditionalism. Connor was a past president of Florida Right to Life, the major antiabortion organization, and made his pro-life views a centerpiece of his gubernatorial platform. Though Connor offered a comprehensive vision for the state, he was consistently portrayed as a single-issue candidate focused almost exclusively on abortion. Ander Crenshaw could also make an appeal for support on similar grounds. Though known primarily for his objection to increasing state revenue, arguing that Florida must learn to live within the fiscal constraints imposed by its sole reliance on sales and tourist taxes, Crenshaw was also an outspoken advocate of "traditional family values." He was known for his sympathies to Christian conservatives during his term as state senate president and publicly assured Republicans that he would never knowingly hire homosexuals (Debenport 1994b). Crenshaw was also staunchly pro-life and had led efforts to strengthen state limits on abortion following the *Webster* decision by the U.S. Supreme Court in 1989.

Like his father, who rather awkwardly defined himself as a born-again Episcopalian, Jeb Bush had an ambiguous public image on the issues that tend most to engage Christian conservatives. During the campaign, Bush portrayed himself as a social conservative: he emphasized his support for private school tuition tax credits and restoring prayer to the schools, announced his opposition to abortion on demand, and indicated that he supported a unsuccessful petition drive to put a Colorado-style anti–gay rights initiative on the November ballot. These issue positions did not dramatically distinguish him from most other Republican nominees, but Bush reached out more aggressively to the Christian Right by anointing as his running mate one of the most socially conservative members of the state legislature (*Palm Beach Post* 1994).

Tom Feeney, a second-term state representative from Orlando, was the Christian Coalition's legislator of the year. A core member of the so-called God Squad in the legislature, he had emerged as the point man in advocating the group's social agenda during the 1994 session. Reportedly elected to the legislature with the backing of the Christian Right, Feeney had argued passionately for many of the causes dear to the heart of the right-wing fundamentalists. Like Bush, Feeney endorsed tuition tax credits for private schools, school prayer, strict limits on abortion, and reduction of welfare benefits to unmarried women who had children while on state support. But he went well beyond his running mate's conservatism with several controversial issue stands. Feeney was a leader in House efforts to guard the right of parents to spank their children, ban nude beaches, require parental consent before students could participate in activities like yoga, hypnosis, and meditation, and require hospitals to inform the state about the characteristics of abortion patients. He was publicly aligned with a movement to limit the power of the state to intervene against parents in cases of suspected child abuse.

The nominee for lieutenant governor also made headlines, none of them favorable, with provocative statements about the value of teaching children the superiority of American culture and claims that Haitians came to America in order to collect welfare benefits. The extreme style of his rhetoric was evident when he characterized Governor Chiles, a moderate pro-choice advocate, as part of an antifamily coalition "trying to execute as many unborn as you can get away with" (Debenport 1994b). By introducing proposals to alter the teaching of the Holocaust and to permit public school teachers to include religious references in historical documents, he aroused the concern of the Jewish community about his sensitivity to them and to the separation of church and state. His support for a motion that Florida secede from the United States if the national debt exceeded $6 trillion was cited as evidence that he was out of the mainstream. Yet if these positions seemed unreasonable to journalists or campaign commentators, they may not have seemed extreme or even exceptional to many fundamentalists. Indeed, when he condemned yoga and hypnotism as "satanic," Feeney demonstrated common cause with the worldview of fundamentalist Christianity.

Though respected by his Republican house colleagues for his work ethic and debating skills, it is clear that Feeney's selection was primarily a way for Jeb Bush to signal the Christian Right that he was on their side of the culture wars. Feeney was young, relatively inexperienced, and hardly a statewide name. Indeed, Feeney's home in the Republican "Interstate 4 corridor" of central Florida, the party's base of support where it hardly required shoring up in statewide elections, meant he would add little to the ticket where it most needed help in November. The choice of Feeney was significant because it reflected Bush's recognition that he needed to appeal to Christian conservatives in order to secure nomination in a crowded primary field.

On two counts, the strategy appears to have worked. It helped secure for the Bush-Feeney ticket the endorsement of the American Family Association (AFA) headquartered in Tampa. Though less well known nationally than the Christian Coalition, the Florida AFA had gained considerable prestige in conservative Christian circles for spearheading the referendum defeat of Hillsborough County's gay rights ordinance and was receiving substantial publicity for its efforts to promote a statewide constitutional amendment that would enjoin cities and counties from providing legal protection to gays, lesbians, and bisexuals (see page 36). AFA had been expected to support Connor because of his years of yeoman's service to the antiabortion cause but the organization instead recommended that Republican primary voters endorse Bush. While praising Connor, the organization apparently preferred to go with a sympathetic candidate favored to win over one of its own who was deemed likely to finish in the back of the pack. The strategy of embracing the conservative Christians also helped Bush amass 46 percent of the vote in the Republican primary, pushing Crenshaw and Connor into fourth and fifth place, respectively, and persuading the second-place finisher, Secretary of State Jim Smith, to withdraw. This enabled Jeb Bush to avoid a costly and disruptive runoff primary. If Feeney did not make Christian conservatives enthusiastic about Jeb Bush, his inclusion at least made Bush more palatable to them.

The choice of Feeney thus reinforces the notion of the centrality of the Christian Right in both the Republican organization and its mass electoral coalition. But it also demonstrates that securing the support of the Christian Right in a very public way may eventually exact a heavy price in the general election. In that sense, Bush's strategy of enamoring himself to Christian conservatives may have succeeded too well (Ash and Goldschmidt 1994).

In a state where gubernatorial and lieutenant governor candidates run as a team, Feeney was generally judged to have been an electoral liability for the Bush campaign and seems to have been kept out of the general election campaign limelight. To be fair to Feeney, most potential Republican running mates would not have compared favorably to the incumbent, "Buddy" MacKay, a widely respected moderate with a reputation for decency, competence, and good judgment. But the Democrats used the comparison to good advantage throughout the fall campaign (Kleindienst 1994). Governor Chiles seized on some of Feeney's statements, calling them "spooky" and labeling the Republican legislator as "sort of the David Duke of Florida politics." The Democratic campaign issued daily "Feeney facts" calling attention to the candidate's more outlandish positions and statements. (Getting into the alliteration game, Jeb Bush tried to turn the issue against Chiles by asking the governor in radio debate why he had such a "Feeney fetish.")

The Democrats used Feeney's selection to raise public doubts about what the inexperienced Jeb Bush would do in office. As part of a strategy to paint Bush "as a poster boy for the Christian Right" (Willon, 1994a), Chiles argued that Bush's selection of Feeney meant that the Republican gubernatorial candidate shared Feeney's agenda and belied his moderate image. Playing on the same theme of Bush as a stealth candidate of the Christian Right, other Democratic speakers warned that Bush would follow suit by appointing extreme right-wingers to judgeships and other positions of government authority. They warned about the dangers of putting an extremist just a heartbeat away from the governor's mansion. Claims that Bush and Feeney wanted to impose religion and their Christian values were publicized through private mailings to Jewish voters, a key constituency in South Florida where the Chiles-MacKay ticket needed a high turnout (Nevins 1994b).

The conventional wisdom among political scientists is that vice presidential nominees seldom determine an election because most voters make their choice on the basis of presidential candidates. But it has also been recognized that the choice of a particular individual as a vice presidential candidate may itself affect how voters assess the judgment of presidential nominees. In that same manner, Bush's selection of Feeney played into and probably helped determine the major theme of the Chiles campaign—that Bush was too unknown and inexperienced to run the state of Florida. Chiles was the elder statesman of Florida politics, a former state legislator and U.S. senator and the incumbent governor. He was a familiar face and a reassuring presence, attractive even to many Christian conservatives. He had promulgated a clear theme as governor, pioneering the "reinventing government" movement that was later seized by the national Democratic administration. Chiles was also identified with popular causes such as reducing infant mortality, stopping illegal immigration, increasing literacy, and improving local control of education. These resources hardly guaranteed his reelection but they gave him a wellspring of public recognition to draw upon. By contrast, Bush was a relative newcomer who had only moved to Florida in

1980. His lack of governmental experience may have been an asset in a year when "career politicians" were under assault but it could also be exploited as a weakness. That was precisely the overriding theme of Chiles's campaign, exemplified by the tag line of television commercials that "We just can't trust Jeb Bush as governor." The choice of Feeney as a running mate gave Democrats additional ammunition in their effort to raise public doubts about Jeb Bush.

The evidence from the polls and election results suggests that Feeney—either on his own or as a factor that raised questions about Bush's judgment in making the selection—did some damage to Bush in what was a very close race. Democrats had hoped that fear about Feeney and his extremely conservative agenda would provoke a countermobilization of liberals, religious minorities, African Americans, and other Democratic constituencies in large urban areas, neutralizing the Republican advantage among Christian conservatives (Nevins 1994a). On election day, the Chiles-MacKay ticket did indeed amass large margins in south Florida, the Tampa area, and Palm Beach County, precisely where the campaign had placed its hopes. How much did Bush's association with the Christian Right matter? A Democratic Party tracking poll in mid-October showed south Florida voters much more concerned than probable voters elsewhere about Bush's "extreme right-wing positions."[2] According to election day exit polls, only about 7 percent of the electorate cited a candidate's extremism as a factor in the vote decision, but among those who did, four out of five voted for Lawton Chiles. The finding that Jewish voters were twice as likely to cite the extremism factor to explain their vote suggests that the Chiles strategy succeeded in its targeting. The evidence also points to the wisdom of Democratic strategists in contrasting the veteran governor with the unknown and untested challenger. The "candidate's experience" was cited as a reason for voting more often than any other single factor and it cut overwhelmingly—95 to 5 percent—in Chiles's favor.[3]

Apart from the Feeney factor, what role did the Christian Right or its policy agenda play in the 1994 gubernatorial campaign? On balance, it is hard to find evidence that the core social issues—things like abortion, school prayer, and homosexuality—moved many voters one way or another. Crime was the major topic of discussion. Florida has long been a high crime state, a status attributed by most criminologists to poverty, a high dropout rate, and the weak social ties of its many migrant inhabitants. Florida is already among the states with the largest proportion of its residents behind bars and has made considerable use of the death penalty. Nonetheless, in the context of the gubernatorial election, the two candidates competed to show who could be tougher. Chiles was well placed to deflect criticisms that he was soft on crime. He had presided over numerous executions, put in place an aggressive expansion of the prison system, and endorsed harsher penalties for career criminals.

It is tempting to portray crime as an issue, like economics, essentially unrelated to cultural conservatism, a separate dimension in the voters' calculus that overrides concern about the core issues on the Christian Right agenda. Although that may be so for some voters, many others do see crime as a reflection of underlying moral decay. The link between spiritual decay and illegal behavior was one of the most potent themes used in the late 1970s by the secular conservatives who, as noted above, were instrumental in recruiting several Protestant pastors into Republican politics. It was also a major theme of Pat Robertson in his unsuccessful campaign for the Republican presidential nomination in 1988. According to polling data, many Americans do perceive the roots of violent crime in "declining moral values" and believe that a return to tradition will help stem the tide (Tomkins 1994). This means that crime is "available" to candidates who wish to appeal to Christian conservatives by framing it as a problem that can be solved by building "family values." But as the Florida results demonstrated, there is a way for candidates not associated with the Christian Right to co-opt concern for crime. The strategic problem facing Christian conservatives (and secular liberals) is that diagnosing crime as a moral malady with deep social causes does not promise quick solutions. A large majority of Americans believe that the policies of school prayer and character development advocated by Christian conservatives are good for children, but few are convinced they would quickly lessen the threat of violent crime. As Chiles showed, it is probably more effective to offer concerned voters stricter laws, harsher conditions, and more and bigger prisons, rather than to fight crime at its "root" by building up traditional family values. Thus, despite Americans' belief in the contribution of deficient morality to a high crime rate, the issue is often framed in ways that have little to do with Christian Right policies on education, child care, or other problems. Chiles seems to have neutralized the issue by precisely that approach.[4]

Bush's major attempt to undermine Chiles's image as a crime-fighter appears to have backfired in a spectacular way. Late in the campaign, after a series of Chiles advertisements had wounded Bush with charges of shady business practices, the challenger counterattacked with a powerful advertisement that featured the angry mother of a young murder victim. She told an interviewer of her frustration with Chiles's unwillingness to hasten the execution of her daughter's murderer and declared that the governor would not punish murder aggressively. Despite the undeniable emotional power of the advertisement, it became a serious liability to the Bush campaign when the Chiles campaign reported that the governor *had* signed a death warrant in the case but the convicted murderer's appeal of the death sentence effectively took the matter out of Chiles's hands. The media focus on the apparent untruthfulness of the Bush claims overshadowed the issue and helped direct attention to Bush's trustworthiness rather than Chiles's credentials as a crime-fighter. For some commentators, this was the decisive factor that swung a narrow majority to Chiles just before election day (Willon 1994b).

The abortion issue does not seem to have been much of a factor in the election outcome, and to the extent it played a role, the advantage appears to have gone to the Democrats. Bush and especially Feeney were known as pro-life. While this issue has attracted Christian conservatives to Republican candidates, it has not been an especially potent electoral factor in Florida. In the aftermath of the 1989 *Webster* decision that allowed states more room to regulate abortion, then-governor Bob Martinez convened a special session of the legislature to tighten Florida's laws. When the session failed to produce any legislation of consequence, it became another piece of evidence casting doubt on Martinez's acumen and contributed to his landslide defeat by Chiles in 1990 (Cook, Jelen, and Wilcox 1994). The perception that the pro-life position had hurt Martinez may have accounted for Bush's limited use of the theme in 1994. Indeed, Bush seemed to go to great lengths to avoid the impression that he would disturb the status quo, telling the debate audience that he thought the issue was effectively closed by the position of the U.S. Supreme Court (Quindlen 1994). For his part, Chiles accepted the role of pro-choice spokesman and told female voters that Bush was out to curtail their reproductive freedom. But he also soft-pedaled the issue, pulling assertive pro-choice television ads after a trial run. Both candidates thus downplayed the issue, suggesting that it may be useful as a way of differentiating among Republican primary candidates but works against the Republican nominee in the general election. Indeed, among the 10 percent of the electorate that cited abortion as a reason for choosing one candidate, Chiles had a 10 percent margin over Bush.

Elsewhere . . .

If we look elsewhere on the ballot for the influence of the Christian Right, we tend to find several patterns. On some issues the leaders of the Christian Right took strong positions that won handily, but the very breadth of the victory suggests that the Christian Right was but one element of a much larger coalition and not necessarily critical to success. On other issues, the activists associated with conservative Christianity took unique stands, which went down to stinging defeat. In a few instances, when the Christian Right was itself the focus of an issue, it seems to have been repudiated. That leaves only a few cases on which the religious conservatives were reputed to constitute a swing vote.[5] We shall consider each scenario in order.

The 1994 ballot included a statewide initiative for limited casino gambling. Despite spending over $16 million, ten times the sum spent by opponents and by far the most ever spent on a state referendum, the initiative was roundly defeated (Lavelle 1994). Christian organizations were among the most persistent critics of the plan. Rather than attacking the morality of gambling itself—a strategy that had failed to dissuade Floridians from implementing a state lottery several years earlier—the campaign against casino gambling focused on the social costs of gambling and its deleterious economic and physical impact on the state. In addition to emphasizing gambling addiction and the link to criminal activity, it was argued that gambling would discourage people from visiting a state that had built its tourism around "family" entertainment. The strategy worked because the initiative was defeated heavily, the only statewide initiative *not* to succeed in 1994. Despite their unanimity against the initiative, the Christian conservatives could not credibly take responsibility for the outcome. The casino gambling initiative lost almost everywhere and would have done so whether the Christian Right denounced it or not. In a year when they were concerned above all else with crime, particularly crime against tourists, Floridians did not want to gamble on a risky new enterprise that could exacerbate the problem of crime.

Illustrating a different pattern, the 1994 midterm election featured a vote on the retention of two sitting members of the state supreme court. Neither of the justices had received much publicity and there was no organized campaign against them. This contrasted with retention elections in the recent past when both religious and secular conservatives had campaigned aggressively against two other members of the supreme court. Beneath the horizon of media coverage, however, some religious conservatives did mobilize against the incumbents and urged members of their organizations to vote against retention (March 1994). In the voter guides distributed by the Christian Coalition, the two incumbents were labeled as hostile to family values. Even those who agreed with this characterization and voted against retention did not have many specific items in the bill of indictment, relying on vague images to make their case. Perhaps for that reason, the two justices kept their seats but by narrower margins than had been expected. Nonetheless, the Christian Right had to acknowledge defeat.

In at least one case, the Christian Right itself became the central focus of attention and was lambasted at the polls. In 1990, using the stealth strategy of concealing their agenda beneath rather vague campaign pledges about teaching "basics" and restoring discipline, two candidates associated with the Christian Right were elected as Republicans to the school board of Lake County, near Orlando. The rural county was soon rocked by controversy as the two new members aligned with an incumbent to form a controlling bloc, dubbed "the religious right majority," and pressed for implementation of a number of extremely conservative policies (States News Service 1994; Duryea 1994). These included attempts to promote a sex education curriculum that stressed abstinence, opposition to the use of the "guided imagery" technique, and claims that the self-esteem movement was a cover for teaching "Eastern religions" (Badie 1994). The Lake County School Board eventually garnered national attention when in May 1994 it passed a policy statement instructing teachers to teach the superiority of American culture over other systems of thought and social practice. Despite its vagueness and the probability that the directive would be a dead letter, the board's clumsy assault on multiculturalism inspired a lawsuit by the local education association and brought the board and Lake County both ridicule and condemnation. There was even an attempt by a countermovement, describing itself as a coalition for "mainstream values," to have the governor dismiss the three members for violating the state's policy on multicultural education.

Though defended by religious conservatives and promoted as a model for other communities by Tom Feeney (Kim 1994), the school board majority inspired a determined countermobilization by mainstream Republicans in the primary. With three seats up for grabs, including one previously held by the retiring senior member of the Christian Right bloc, they focused particular attention on candidates who used statements and slogans similar to the programs offered by the religious conservatives when they first ran in 1992. Using the language of radical homosexuals, one Republican candidate gleefully decided to "out" three other rivals for the Republican nomination whom she described as "clones" of the current majority. While the targeted nominees denied the linkage to the existing majority, these claims seemed hollow when it was revealed that two of them endorsed teaching "creation science"—an alternative to evolution that claims the world was created in a manner compatible with a literal reading of Genesis—and a third refused to take a stand. The readiness of the organizer for the Florida Christian Coalition to describe the three nominees as "our" candidates further undercut their claim of independence (Weber 1994). Throughout the primary, the religious agenda of the dominant bloc and the divisiveness that ensued upon its formation in 1992 became the center of the debate and the three aspirants who had been associated with the Christian Right eventually paid the price. Though the three "clones" survived the first primary to make a runoff, they were drubbed by two-to-one margins in the primary runoff against candidates described as "moderate." On election day in November, the moderate Republican nominees all won their seats, depriving the Christian Right of its voting majority. One of the first acts of the new board majority was to repeal the "American culture is superior" policy. Besides their own defeat, the Lake County Christian conservatives helped raise concerns about school board candidates with similar agendas elsewhere, usually putting such candidates on the defensive and prompting many to deny the likeness (Barszewski 1994).

Perhaps the best case for Christian Right influence was the election for commissioner of education, a cabinet-level position. The race featured two relative newcomers to statewide attention who both had impressive credentials and, in keeping with the tenor of the election, both pledged to slash the state education bureaucracy and restore local control of schools. The incumbent, former state representative Doug Jamerson of St. Petersburg, had been appointed to the office only a few months earlier when the previous commissioner resigned to accept a university presidency. A former teacher and administrator, Jamerson campaigned in defense of Chiles's program of local empowerment and as an advocate of increased spending. His opponent, Republican Frank Brogan of Martin County, was a former superintendent of schools. Brogan largely echoed the concerns of religious conservatives about the perilous state of public schools and called for the restoration of discipline, prayer, and traditional values (Rado 1994). He also advocated tuition tax credits for private school tuition, a position anathema to the teachers' union and many advocates of public education. Brogan won the endorsement of voter guides for conservative Christians and won his race on election day.

Given their longstanding concern with the molding of young minds, Christian conservatives have always regarded education as a major concern and took strong actions in favor of Brogan (Gillis 1994; Kaplan 1994). Did they account for his victory? It is hard to know how much the religious conservatives mattered. On one hand, it can be said that Democratic incumbents seldom lose reelection to unknown Republicans unless the incumbent has suffered bad press from a scandal. Jamerson was plagued by no such scandals and enjoyed the enthusiastic endorsement of both Governor Chiles and the education unions. On the other hand, there were several circumstances that favored Brogan other than his support from Christian conservatives. First, despite Jamerson's status as an incumbent, the race for education commissioner was essentially an open seat contest. Jamerson had never before run for statewide office and had occupied the position for a short time. While they have seldom defeated entrenched Democratic incumbents for cabinet office, Republicans have been winning most of the open seat cabinet contests of late. Indeed, Jamerson was joined in defeat by the Democratic candidate for secretary of state, a well-known conservative Democrat who was not facing a candidate so strongly embraced by the Christian Right. Second, and probably more significant, Jamerson was black and no African American has won a statewide election in Florida since the end of Reconstruction. It is likely that race played a substantial role in the outcome. Brogan's televised ads, running extensively in the more conservative north Florida area, took the unusual tack of featuring a long video segment of Jamerson addressing a meeting. Most candidates do not feature their opponents so centrally in television advertisements unless they simultaneously attack their integrity, competence, or fitness. Thus it is likely that the latent function of these ads was to emphasize Jamerson's blackness, a presumed electoral liability. While his support from the Christian Right undoubtedly played a role in his victory, Brogan's principal success seems to have issued from other factors.

In other races for state office, particularly at the state legislative level, the Christian Right was sometimes implicated in defeat and occasionally accredited with a major role in victory (Rose 1994). There was considerable speculation in the aftermath of the election about how changes in the composition of the Florida legislature would bear on the capacity of social conservatives to carry the day. Would the Christian Right be able to claim enough credit for the Republican house and senate gains that it could overcome previous resistance to the passage of various socially conservative programs? If so, conservative policies on abortion, school prayer and the like might finally make it into law. One could find arguments either way. On one hand, the defeat of stalwarts like Crenshaw in the senate and Feeney in the house had deprived the Republican "God

Squad" of some of its most effective legislators, diminishing its legislative clout. Yet, on the other hand, their absence might well be offset by the election of other social conservatives on the Republican ticket, the enhanced clout that would accrue to all Republicans from the high tide that lifted the party's fortunes, and the knowledge that the new house Republican leader was part of the social conservative bloc. Moreover, the Republicans would not have to carry the initiative by themselves. From time to time, a number of conservative Democrats had joined with their Republican colleagues to support various motions reflecting the aims of religious conservatives. During the 1994 session, for example, liberal groups lobbied heavily against a senate bill permitting silent and voluntary school prayer. This particular piece of legislation had been introduced and championed by a conservative Democrat from north Florida. A senator from an Orlando suburb, also a Democrat, had jumped on the same bandwagon by introducing legislation to promote character development lessons in the public school curriculum. These trends prompted some strong statements about the intention of religious conservatives to capitalize on the more "family-friendly" environment in Tallahassee.

Despite the hopefulness of Christian activists, most commentators doubted that the situation in Tallahassee would change significantly. In the past, Democratic leaders had usually found a way to contain proposals that would energize religious conservatives but outrage their opponents. That prospect remained with a Democrat as governor and another Democrat holding the speakership in the state house. But it was the newly empowered Republicans who seemed likely to constitute a major roadblock to the agenda of cultural conservatism. In a manner reminiscent of their counterparts in Washington, D.C., Florida Republican leaders emphasized that their principal goal was fighting crime and cutting the size of government. True to their word, the early weeks of the 1995 legislative session focused on various anticrime initiatives and a welter of proposals to cut the state budget. Amid these efforts, movements for school prayer and other forms of cultural conservatism got short shrift. Once again, it seems, the Christian Right has been a victim of its own (limited) success. The perception that the movement was gaining strength prompted a countermobilization by opponents and raised public awareness of the "dangers" lurking in the shadows of the movement. Those who had been identified with the Christian Right, either as members or as supporters who enjoyed the patronage of the movement, often had to go to great lengths to deny their involvement or downplay its significance. The net effect was to make the issues that prompted Christian Right mobilization more salient to the general public—or at least those opinion leaders who monitored legislative developments—and thus to limit their opportunities to act on the agenda.

Gay Rights

Perhaps no other policy debate, not even abortion, can match gay rights as a hot-button issue for religious conservatives. Since the 1970s, many American communities have debated proposals to extend antidiscrimination laws beyond categories of race, ethnicity, gender, and disability status to encompass what is variously called "sexual orientation" or "sexual preference." Eight states and approximately 130 local jurisdictions now maintain some form of legal protection for gays, lesbians, and bisexuals (Button, Wald, and Rienzo 1994). In a ferocious countermobilization, several communities have passed and then repealed such ordinances and a number of states have considered legislation to either promote or prohibit such legislation statewide. In 1992, Colorado took the step of prohibiting its jurisdictions from extending antidiscrimination protection on the basis of sexual orientation. This controversial amendment, which was later invalidated on constitutional grounds by the Colorado Supreme Court, effectively repealed several previously enacted city and county ordinances.

As the 1994 election approached, it appeared that Florida would be the next major frontier in this battle, a fitting situation because Florida had been the place where the issue had first received national attention. In 1977, Dad4e County in south Florida had drawn national attention when a campaign led by the singer Anita Bryant successfully overturned a gay rights ordinance in a spirited local referendum. The Dade County referendum, championed by a number of fundamentalist pastors, was one of the major incidents that focused the attention of conservative organizers on the latent electoral power of religious conservatives. By 1994, however, seven Florida local jurisdictions had passed laws that provided legal protection for gays, lesbians, and bisexuals. Despite the bitter memories of 1977, the south Florida gay community was substantial and the state's northwest panhandle area was known to attract a substantial number of gay vacationers, earning it the (unwanted) reputation as the "Gay Riviera."

Against this background, the American Family Association announced a petition drive to put on the November ballot a statewide initiative that would preempt local legislation. The Tampa-based organization, which had previously succeeded in promoting a referendum to repeal Hillsborough County's gay rights ordinance, sought to repeat that success across the entire state. To put the proposal before the voters required that organizers obtain more than 400,000 signatures from registered voters. They did so with apparent ease, although the effort required a considerable mobilization at the local level. By midyear, the amendment was certified as having attracted sufficient valid signatures to appear on the ballot.

The "religious" nature of this controversy is interesting. The leaders of the Colorado initiative have strongly favored a kind of stealth campaign in which the moral argument against homosexuality is downplayed publicly. There is no doubt that the organizing power behind the campaign for signatures was rooted in fundamentalist churches and that religious doctrine was the principal factor motivating the campaign. Fundamentalists have taken the lead in such efforts nationwide (Roberts 1994), and the leader of the Florida petition movement, David Caton, was a born-again Christian who made no secret of his moral abhorrence of homosexuality and the religious basis of his objections to legal protection (*Orlando Sentinel* 1993).

But rather than attack gay rights legislation on the grounds that it violates God's word, they instead framed their attack in the secular language of American individualism. Gay rights were condemned as "special rights," as the demand by a militant group for legal privileges not accorded other minorities. Ironically, while gay advocates typically perceived the laws as defensive measures to shield them from retribution should their sexual orientation be revealed, the opponents argued that these laws were aggressive initiatives demanded by gays to assert the legitimacy of their lifestyle. There was a kind of sad resignation to the tone taken by many supporters of the petition drive, arguing that they had no objection to gays per se but didn't see why they wanted to publicize and promote their sexuality. This strategy had been prevalent in Colorado and in several successful campaigns to repeal local ordinances around the country, and it was adopted in the Florida campaign.

Much to the chagrin of the petition organizers, the initiative was disallowed by the Florida Supreme Court before it could get on the state ballot. Under a Florida statute, state ballot initiatives must be restricted to a "single subject" to meet constitutional muster. This was designed to prevent the passage of omnibus legislation which might affect the functioning of the state in many domains. Without ruling on the constitutionality of the legislation, the court ruled that it touched upon too many functions of government and thus could not meet the legal standard.

What had promised to be a major issue statewide was eventually reduced to one county referendum in north Florida. Alachua County, the
home of the University of Florida, had in 1993 narrowly passed legislation extending antidiscrimination law to sexual orientation. The law itself was symbolic because it provided that incorporated areas could opt
out of the ordinance by a vote of their local legislative body, and all the
municipalities of the county exercised that option. Hence the ordinance
applied only to unincorporated areas, predominantly rural and lacking
in much employment or rental housing. Nonetheless, the gay rights ordinance had inspired intense opposition from a number of conservative
churches, and they announced a plan to put the ordinance on the ballot
in 1994. They succeeded in obtaining enough signatures to force a public vote on two proposals, a straightforward repeal of the ordinance and
charter language prohibiting the county from ever legislating on the
basis of sexual orientation. These proposals survived a legal challenge
and appeared on the Alachua County ballot.

Like their statewide counterparts, the local organizers tried hard to
avoid the appearance of a religious crusade. The ordinance was criticized not so much on moral grounds but rather as a dangerous prece-
dent that would allow gays access to the hearts and minds of the county's
children. The organizers stressed the differences between minorities
that warranted protection because of widespread discrimination based
on criteria that were indelible—race, gender, and the like—and spuri-
ous claims for protection from groups that did not suffer discrimination
or that based their claim on behavior chosen voluntarily. A theme that
is a staple of fundamentalist discussion of homosexuality—that AIDS is a
form of divine retribution for behavior that offends God—was nowhere
publicly in evidence. Privately, it was a different matter. The organizers
of the petition campaign were drawn overwhelmingly from evangelical
congregations, and those congregations also provided the shock troops
for the petition campaign—donors, precinct workers, lawyers, poll
watchers, and so on. But virtually the only public recognition of the
religious nature of the campaign was on the side that urged retention
of the gay rights law. In order to counter the impression that the
churches were lined up solidly against the ordinance, a group of local
clergy drafted a statement calling for citizens to vote against the two
petition initiatives. Though much was made of the ecumenical nature of
the ordinance supporters, the truth was that many were from historically
liberal traditions such as Judaism, Congregationalism, and Unitarian-
ism, and that most of the other signatories were from campus ministries
that have long been much more politically liberal than their traditions

as a whole. The religious fault lines were clear to observers but seldom discussed openly.

Alachua County has a liberal reputation, so the petition organizers argued that a repeal there would show that gay rights ordinances were not viable anywhere in Florida. That liberal reputation is largely undeserved, the product primarily of Alachua County being one of only two Florida counties to cast a majority of its presidential vote for George McGovern in 1972. However, the county has a number of small country towns and many rural areas appreciably less liberal than the city of Gainesville, and even that community is less liberal today than it was during the heyday of student political activism two decades ago. Moreover, one of the most liberal forces, the African American community, was seriously divided on the issue, and the sole black member of the county commission had cast one of the two votes against the ordinance in 1993. Hence it was no surprise that the two petition initiatives passed handily. The vote in favor of the repeal and preemption was highest in the outlying rural areas but passed as well in the more liberal city of Gainesville.

The Alachua County gay rights referendum was the clearest and least ambiguous instance of Christian Right achievement in the 1994 election. As such, it illustrates both the conditions that magnify the prospects for Christian conservative success and the limiting factors. First, Christian Right success is most likely when it is exercised at the local level. Florida is a large state with a diverse population. Statewide efforts are difficult and tend to run up against the opposition of well-organized liberal groups that have the capacity to counteract the Christian Right. In contrast, the Christian Right is most able to mount a sustained effort at the local level where its organizational base—evangelical churches—is concentrated. Second, the movement is most likely to win when it concentrates on questions of fundamental moral values. Homosexuals are one of the most negatively regarded groups in public life and seldom enjoy influential allies—even among people who are otherwise sympathetic to minority causes. Arguments against gay rights laws— particularly if they are seen to facilitate intimate contact with gays or give them access to children—can draw on a widespread if unarticulated revulsion against homosexuality. A willingness to "tolerate" gays by decriminalizing homosexual acts by consenting adults does not translate easily into a belief that homosexuality is morally equivalent to heterosexuality and deserves legal protection. By contrast, the practice of abortion is less repugnant simply because most people can easily envision circumstances where they might want to exercise reproductive choice. The abortion decision also seems more "private" than homosexuality, which raises fears of harassment and deviant behavior in public places. From the viewpoint of practical politics, gay rights is a good issue upon which to mobilize, abortion and other Christian right priorities less so. Third and finally, the Christian Right is more likely to win when it is not itself the issue. Lake County is undoubtedly more conservative than Alachua County, yet it defeated the representatives of the Christian Right while the latter accepted their policy recommendations. The difference is that the role of the Christian Right was less salient in Alachua County than in the Lake County school board. The Christian Right tends to fail when it is recognized as the prime mover and to succeed when it disguises its leading role. Hence the popularity of the stealth approach in various campaigns.

The importance of these factors is further underlined by the congressional election in the Sixth District, which includes Alachua County and some additional conservative and rural areas to the south and east. The first-term Democratic congressional representative, Karen Thurman, faced a spirited challenge from a Republican candidate who was closely identified with the Christian Right. Don "Big Daddy" Garlits was a famous retired drag racer recruited by the Republicans to face Thurman. With his natural name recognition and ample finances, he seemed well placed to capitalize on the Republican tide and dislodge Thurman. Yet in the end, Garlits went down to a decisive defeat. To some degree, it is important to acknowledge that Thurman was a moderate to conservative Democrat much in tune with the rural parts of the district and that Garlits showed himself to be woefully ignorant about some basic features of the district.[6] Yet other such Democrats were successfully portrayed as "tax and spend" liberals and defeated. Garlits's poor showing in such a favorable Republican climate is largely attributable to his Feeney-like qualities—a fervent evangelicalism that exemplifies the fundamentalist style and a penchant for offering what struck many thoughtful voters of moderate outlook as outrageous statements about women, gays, blacks, and other subjects. Because the issue was partisan and the focus of debate was the fundamentalist worldview of Garlits, he was unable to replicate the success of the more circumspect Christian Right in the Alachua County referendum.

The Impact

This chapter has taken a skeptical view of the electoral influence of the Christian Right in Florida's 1994 midterm election. While recognizing the strategic importance of the movement in Florida Republican circles and its occasional successes locally, it seems hard to envision the movement as a juggernaut destined to change the shape of Florida politics. While it has taken a significant role in the organizational and electoral life of the Republican Party, the Christian Right has not translated those resources into political power. Apart from the strategic factors cited in this chapter, the limitations of the movement as a statewide factor can be reduced to demography and geography. Looked at as an agglomeration of voting blocs, Florida is less congenial to the Christian Right than many southern states where the movement has been more successful. By common consent among scholars of the Christian Right, the movement makes its greatest appeal to Protestant evangelicals who are deeply enmeshed in their local churches. It has done least well among the irreligious, gays, and those population groups associated with the old Roosevelt coalition—Jews, blacks, and union members. Based on the exit poll data, there were a great many more Florida voters from the opposing camp (a third of the entire electorate) than there were church-attending, born-again Protestants (13 percent of the electorate).[7] Though the latter group voted almost four to one for Jeb Bush, they were offset statistically by the two-to-one margin for Lawton Chiles among the much larger share of voters who were unlikely converts to Republican candidates embracing Christian conservatism. The geography of the state poses an additional barrier. In Florida, politics is media-driven. With seven major media markets and so much population turnover, it is hard to mobilize a strong statewide movement. The face-to-face contacts and grassroots activism that work in smaller locales do not translate easily to the larger canvass of a statewide election. These barriers can more easily be overcome when the movement concentrates on local level concerns, takes policy positions that draw support from a wide range of voters, and avoids making the sponsoring role of the movement the basis for public debate.

Has the Christian Right learned from its experience? In the movement's earlier flirtation with national power during the Reagan era, it often hamstrung itself by a penchant for political purism and a tendency to alienate moderates with intemperate speech. Has it proven capable of moderating its position and learned to avoid inflammatory language? We find in Florida the same tendency to greater political sophistication that Matthew Moen (1992) discovered in his study of the evolving national movement. Among several signs of increased political maturity in the 1994 Florida midterm elections, the most significant was the decision of Christian Right organizations to endorse the gubernatorial candidacy of Jeb Bush over his four Republican rivals. By rights, Ken Connor and Ander Crenshaw had stronger claims on endorsements because they had fought the good fight in the trenches and Bush was essentially a newcomer to the battle. Yet it was decided that Bush's likely electability made him preferable to candidates who otherwise were closer to heart. The decision to endorse Bush, coupled with similar evidence of pragmatism in other states, suggests that at least some of the movement's leaders are willing to trade doctrinal purity for political power.

As observed elsewhere, there were clear signs that Christian conservative activists tried to avoid becoming the center of public debate. Although some activists could not resist using inflammatory language, the muzzling of Tom Feeney by the Bush campaign, the scrupulous avoidance of religious language in the gay rights conflict, and the occasional use of stealth campaign strategy all reflect a recognition that success may require soft-pedaling and dissimulation. Any number of candidates with strong ties to the Christian Coalition and personal histories of political mobilization based on religious beliefs tried to downplay those connections, highlighting instead their fiscal conservatism and insisting on the right to claim the "mainstream" mantle (Holmberg 1994; Shanahan 1994). Borrowing a page from Pat Robertson's 1988 campaign plan, Christian activists tried to portray their opponents as the true religious bigots in the 1994 election. When the national Democratic Party or its Florida candidates raised public fears about the agenda of the Christian Right, Christian conservatives quickly responded by accusing the Democrats of insulting religious people and churchgoers. There is more than a hint of hypocrisy in these charges because critics of the Christian Right often go to great lengths to distinguish between the political agenda of self-appointed religious spokesmen and the rank-and-file churchgoers in whose name they profess to speak. Indeed, the critics argue that statements represented by the Christian Right as "the Christian position" do not in fact reflect the views of people in the pews. Whatever its intellectual honesty, this strategy of portraying themselves as the victims of religious oppression suggests that Christian conservatives recognize a need to moderate their aggressive image.

Looking beyond 1994, the best prospects for the Christian Right in Florida emerged from a relatively obscure constitutional amendment that passed virtually without comment and without any apparent organized contribution from religious conservatives. Voters approved a constitutional amendment that will make it easier for future petition drives to place referenda on the ballot by discarding the old single subject standard. As noted above, the judicial limits on ballot initiatives had been a significant barrier to the Christian Right, most recently derailing the American Family Association's petition drive for a constitutional amendment barring gay rights laws. In future elections, there will be no such hurdle facing advocates of social change. The removal of the single subject rule is permissive rather than definitive; proposals that appear on the ballot via the petition route will still have to earn the support of a majority of voters. Florida voters have periodically shown themselves to be more willing than the Florida legislature is to pass radical legislation, and they might very well have embraced the anti-gay rights amendment. Yet even with an easier petition process, the Christian Right still faces barriers rooted in demography, geography, and political strategy. If the playing field has become more level thanks to structural changes in Florida law, the power of the competing teams remains stacked against the Christian Right. Winning the occasional local battle does not mean that Christian conservatives have won the Florida culture war.

Notes

I appreciate the research assistance of Angela Peppe and the suggestions of Richard K. Scher. Persons interested in spotting potential bias should know that the author was tangentially involved in some of the developments described in the chapter. He provided research for a legislative opponent of the bill to include religious references in school curricula, contributed a bit of time and money to the campaign to preserve the expanded human rights ordinance in Alachua County, and was a signatory on a Democratic letter to Jewish voters in the Sixth Congressional District.

1. I use the terms *religious right, Christian Right, Christian conservatism,* and their variants interchangeably to refer to the main subject of this essay. I understand that these terms are limited, suggesting wrongly that only Christians subscribe to the agenda of social and moral conservatism or that all Christians do so. Neither statement is accurate. There are non-Christians who approve the "family values" platform and people who regard themselves as conservative and Christian but do not share the beliefs of groups like the Christian Coalition. We need some shorthand way to refer to the object of interest and, for all their limitations, these terms do seem to pinpoint the target.

2. I am grateful to Wally Mealiea of Hamilton and Staff for making this tabulation available to me.

3. The exit poll data were collected by Mitofsky International and provided to me by Clyde Wilcox.

4. The exit polls revealed that voters who cited crime as one of the two major

factors in their gubernatorial vote choice split pretty evenly between the two candidates.

5. Because the two newly elected Republican congressional representatives both emphasized their strong religious traditionalism, it may be tempting to credit their success to the religious right. However, both victories were in open seats that had long been trending Republican. Indeed, the seats had previously been filled by Democrats who voted extremely conservatively on social issues, one of whom had been doing so for years before there was a religious right. The seats would probably have gone Republican regardless of the social conservatism of the candidates.

6. Indeed, when he first announced his intentions to run for Congress, Garlits indicated his intention to run in a district already represented by a conservative Republican. Party leaders had to encourage him to change his plans and run against an incumbent Democrat in an adjoining district.

7. By restricting the core constituency to whites and Protestants, I do not mean to suggest that blacks and Catholics who share evangelical religious traits are unsympathetic to the agenda of the religious right. However, these groups are generally considered allies rather than integral members of the movement. Including blacks and Catholics who fit the Christian Right profile based on born-again/evangelical status and weekly churchgoing raises the core constituency to 17 percent of the electorate but diminishes its political cohesion because the African American evangelical churchgoers voted heavily for Chiles and Catholic "evangelicals" voted less heavily for Bush than their Protestant counterparts. This analysis is intended to be illustrative rather than definitive. It does not settle the complicated question of who should be counted as part of the Christian Right but rather indicates that those who fit the sociological definition of the likeliest supporters are far from a dominant electoral force. That conclusion holds regardless of the precise cutoff points used in the analysis.

References

Ash, Jim, and Keith Goldschmidt. 1994. Untitled dispatch issued by Gannett News Service (4 November).

Badie, Rick. 1994. "Candidates Target Hart 'Clones'." *Orlando Sentinel* (21 August): 1.

Barszewski, Larry. 1994. "Labels Hang on Hopefuls: Schools Candidates Discuss 'Right' Issue." *Fort Lauderdale Sun-Sentinel* (16 October): 1B.

Berke, Richard L. 1994. "The 1994 Election: The Voters." *New York Times* (12 November): 10.

Bruce, Steve. 1988. *The Rise and Fall of the New Christian Right.* Oxford, England: Oxford University Press.

Button, James, Kenneth D. Wald, and Barbara Rienzo. 1994. "The Politics of Gay Rights in American Communities." Paper presented to the annual meeting of the American Political Science Association, New York.

Cook, Elizabeth Adell, Ted G. Jelen, and Clyde Wilcox. 1994. "Issue Voting in Gubernatorial Elections: Abortion and Post-*Webster* Politics." *Journal of Politics* 56: 187–99.

Craig, Stephen C. 1991. "Politics and Elections." Pp. 77–110 in *Government and Politics in Florida*, ed. Robert Huckshorn. Gainesville: University of Florida Press.

Crawford, Alan. 1981. *Thunder on the Right.* New York: Pantheon.

Debenport, Ellen. 1994a. "Crenshaw Says He Would Not Hire Gays." *St. Petersburg Times* (17 June): 1B.

———. 1994b. "He Intensifies Bush's Message." *St. Petersburg Times* (23 August): 4a.

Dunkelberger, Lloyd. 1994. "Christian Conservatives Voting on Morals, Values." *Gainesville Sun* (6 September): 1B.

Duryea, Bill. 1994. "A Swing Back to the Middle." *St. Petersburg Times* (24 November): 1D.

FitzGerald, Frances. 1986. *Cities On a Hill.* New York: Simon and Schuster.

Gillis, Anna Maria. 1994. "Keeping Creationism Out of the Classroom." *BioScience* 44: 650.

Holmberg, David. 1994. " 'Traditional Values' Candidate Walsh Quietly Confident on Issues." *Palm Beach Post* (5 November): 1B.

Kaplan, George R. 1994. "Shotgun Wedding: Notes on Public Education's Encounter with the New Christian Right." *Phi Delta Kappan* 75: K1.

Kim, Rose. 1994. "Board Eyes Emphasis on American Values." *Newsday* (Queens edition) (23 June): 7B.

Kleindienst, Linda. 1994. "Feeney Unfazed by Name-Calling." *Fort Lauderdale Sun-Sentinel* (3 November): 24A.

Lavelle, Louis. 1994. "Backer Says Casino Drive Odds Stacked." *Tampa Tribune* (13 November): 2, 6.

March, William. 1994. "Religion, Culture, Income Influence Voting Patterns." *Tampa Tribune* (13 November): 1.

Mitchell, Peter. 1994. "Legislature's Future Leaders May Come from 'God Squad'." *Orlando Sentinel* (10 April): 1B.

Moen, Matthew. 1992. *Transformation of the Christian Right.* Tuscaloosa, Ala.: University of Alabama Press.

Nevins, Buddy. 1994a. "Bush Running Mate Stirs Chiles' Hope." *Fort Lauderdale Sun-Sentinel* (28 October): 8B.

———. 1994b. "Voter Letter for Chiles Upsets Some." *Fort Lauderdale Sun-Sentinel* (4 November):14A.

Orlando Sentinel. 1993. "Are Gay Rights a Civil Right?" Editorial, 18 July: 8.

Palm Beach Post. 1994. "Bush Goes to Extremes." Editorial, 18 October: 2A.

Parker, Suzanne. 1992. "Florida: A Polity in Transition." Pp. 106–26 in *Party Realignment and State Politics*, ed. Maureen Moakley. Columbus: Ohio State University Press.

Persinos, John F. 1994. "Has the Christian Right Taken over the Republican Party?" *Campaigns & Elections* (September): 20–24.

Quindlen, Anna. 1994. "Polls, Not Passion." *Baltimore Sun* (10 November): 25A.

Rado, Diane. 1994. "He'll Take Government out of Education." *St. Petersburg Times* (14 November): 1A.

Roberts, Tom. 1994. "Right Takes New Aim at Gays." *National Catholic Reporter* (2 September): 4.

Rose, Allen. 1994. "Just a Few More Words about Election Day." *Orlando Sentinel Tribune* (11 November): 1C.

Scher, Richard K. 1992. *Politics in the New South.* New York: Paragon.

———. 1994. "Administrative Reform and Executive Policy Making in Florida." Pp. 47–51 in *Reinventing Government in Florida,* ed. Jamil Jreisat and Frank P. Sherwood. Tallahassee: Florida Center for Public Management, Florida State University.

Shanahan, Michael. 1994. "Christian Conservatives Fighting for GOP's Soul." *Cleveland Plain Dealer* (6 October): 7A.

States News Service. 1994. "Group Chastises Florida Schools for Banning, Censoring Books." *Orlando Sentinel* (1 September): 10A.

Taylor, John. 1994. "Pat Robertson's God, Inc." *Esquire* (November): 76.

Tomkins, Richard. 1994. "Religious Activists Key Players in U.S. Mid-term Elections." *Deutsche Presse-Agentur* (29 October).

Viguerie, Richard A. 1980. *The New Right: We're Ready to Lead.* Falls Church, Va.: The Viguerie Company.

Weber, Dave. 1994. "Christian Conservative Trio Loses Lake School Races." *Orlando Sentinel* (5 October): 1A.

Willon, Phil. 1994a. "Campaign Strategies on Collision Course." *Tampa Tribune* (5 November): 1.

———. 1994b. "Voters Pick Chiles." *Tampa Tribune* (9 November): 1.

3

Georgia: The Christian Right and Grass Roots Power

Charles S. Bullock III and John Christopher Grant

The Christian Right entered Georgia politics through the 1988 Pat Robertson presidential campaign. Robertson supporters participated in many Republican county organizations and fought traditional Republicans for control of the state convention. During the next several years, peace reigned while religious conservatives developed a grassroots organization.

Through the 1980s, Republicans gained little ground among Georgia officeholders. Despite victories by presidents Ronald Reagan in 1980 and 1984 and George Bush in 1988, Democrats continued to dominate the state. The decade ended much as it had begun, with a single Republican in the congressional delegation, a wholly Democratic roster of statewide officials, and, despite gains, a largely hopeless Republican minority in the general assembly. In 1990 Democrats came within one thousand votes of defeating the state's top GOP officeholder, Congressman Newt Gingrich.

Since 1992, Christian conservatives have been arguably the most significant grassroots force in Georgia politics. Activities by religious conservatives coincided with the emergence of the GOP as a serious competitor.

In 1992 the Christian Right, while often successful in Republican primaries, generally could not elect its preferences. For example, Christian conservatives competed in most congressional districts and won five nominations. Of the three new GOP members of Congress from Georgia, however, only one was closely identified with the Christian Right and he won by fewer than twenty-seven hundred votes over a pro-choice, female Democrat. And while Christian conservative votes were critical in Paul Coverdell's defeat of Senator Wyche Fowler, evangelicals were a major element in a coalition that came within two thousand votes of defeating Coverdell in the GOP runoff primary.

Bill Clinton's narrow victory in Georgia did not discourage religious conservatives, who immediately began planning for the 1994 elections. With the election of record numbers of Georgia Republicans to Congress and the state legislature, the Christian Right recognized that the potential of wresting power from Democrats was not simply a pipe dream. The potential for evangelical votes to be crucial in outcomes was a reality.

Organization

Although the Christian Right is not a single group in Georgia, its most prominent component is the Christian Coalition (CC). Other associated groups include Georgia Right to Life, the Eagle Forum, Concerned Women for America, and Family Concerns. Leaders of these groups meet periodically to discuss common concerns. Informally they work together to combat problems that arise in individual communities such as the opening of a nude dance club. The unifying theme for these groups is the family and family (traditional) values. According to Pat Gartland, head of the Christian Coalition in Georgia, "We're concerned about the family—whatever affects the family" (Gartland 1994).

The CC leader claims at least one chapter in more than half the state's 159 counties and hopes to have an organized presence in 120 to 125 counties by 1996. The Coalition wants to identify five to fifteen people in each of the state's more than 2,500 precincts who support its pro-family agenda. To keep up with current supporters and to help prospect for new members, the Coalition's database includes the voting records of all Georgia voters.

Although the Christian Coalition claims 600 followers in Athens and 700 in the Atlanta suburbs of Gwinnett County, as in a political party, there are far fewer dues-paying members. Executive Director Gartland estimates that the Coalition has 1,000 to 2,000 registered members, "although some don't pay their dues every month" (Gartland 1994). Gartland identifies the objectives of his group as mobilization, education, and training. These goals are promoted, in part, through leadership conferences held around the state. "We teach people how to get involved, how to work for candidates, and how to recruit candidates," explains Gartland. The potential for additional impact at the polls is readily apparent in the estimate that only about one third of the evangelicals vote.

Mobilization

We interviewed a number of public officials, candidates, and party elites for this study, and most of them agreed that the Christian Right's greatest impact comes in mobilizing voters, many of whom had not previously been politically involved. An opponent of the state's sex education curriculum said of the effort, "One of our objectives was to get to the district and get word out to the parents and make the citizens understand that this vote [in a special legislative election] will directly affect your children" (quoted in Pettys 1993). A campaign manager underscored the significance of workers activated by the religious community in general elections by pointing to a small church-related college: "Students from Toccoa Falls College were unstoppable. There was no way [Congressman] Don Johnson would win." Proselytizing by religious evangelicals can win over voters who would otherwise lean Democratic.

A Republican who judged the Christian Right to be "extremely significant" claimed that GOP evangelicals and Democratic evangelicals behave differently when at the polls. "The typical Republican religious voter is more likely to work his way down the ticket. Democratic religious voters are 'one punchers.' When they could not vote a straight ticket with a single punch in 1994, they just voted for [Democratic gubernatorial candidate] Zell [Miller]."

A top Democratic operative who believed the Christian Right to be relatively small acknowledged that its members turn out to vote. A GOP legislator-evangelist agrees, "When other GOP supporters are not going to the polls, you can be sure the Christian supporters go" (Crews 1994). Hot-button issues like abortion get believers to the polls, and use of a litmus test simplifies the decision process.

Recruitment

The Christian Coalition encourages supporters to become politically active, which may include running for office (Strawn 1993). Instances in which ministers run for office are perhaps the clearest examples of attracting candidates, although other legislators point to their fellow worshipers when asked how they mounted their campaigns. The 1992 and

1994 elections added two evangelical preachers each year to the ranks of legislative Republicans.

The growing influence of the Christian Right may impact not just Republican but also Democratic recruitment. A Democratic Party official acknowledged that in some districts it is hard to attract candidates because "it is an additional burden to run if you have to fight the church." To appear to be antichurch would be fatal in much of Georgia.

Voter Information

The Christian Coalition attracts attention and extends its reach beyond its membership through informational activities that include a scorecard of votes on selected issues for state legislators and a voter guide. The 1994 voter guides contained assessments of statewide and congressional candidates as well as state legislators.

Voter Guides

The guides claim to be strictly informational and disavow any attempts at endorsement. Democrats reject this assertion, contending that the publications are thinly veiled pro-GOP propaganda. In support of Democratic suspicions, several GOP campaigners with whom we spoke indicated that they had input into the issues selected for the voter guides.

Information about candidates solicited through questionnaires is an important component of the assessments, but it is augmented by other materials. "If legislators don't answer questions, then we look at public statements, roll calls, newspapers, and press statements," Gartland elaborates. Many Democratic candidates refused to respond to the CC surveys and objected vehemently when policy stands were ascribed to them. Other Democrats charge that the voter guides replaced their responses, which should have given them positive evaluations, with selected roll calls that put them in a negative light with the Christian Right.

Gartland claims to have documentation for all positions attributed in the guides. A Republican campaign manager who has worked with the CC to get favorable treatment for candidates describes the CC as a stickler for documentation. "With the Christian Coalition you need to be exactly true. You have to document down to the T when making a case to the Coalition. If you claim someone is pro-choice, you have to prove it; you have to document it. You may have to get it on videotape."

Critics object that the voter guides, unlike rating schemes of other groups, focus on differences. A Democrat explained that while it would be possible for both candidates to receive the same letter grade from the National Rifle Association (NRA) or other groups if their views are very similar, the Coalition ignores similarities and emphasizes disagreements. A result of this approach is that rather than reporting the stands for all candidates on the same set of issues, different sets of issues are presented for different pairs of candidates. For example, consider the evaluation of the pairs of candidates running for two congressional districts covered in the *Cobb County Voter Guide.* For each contest, candidates were compared on seven issues but only three issues were the same for the two contests—parental choice in education, raising federal income taxes, and a balanced budget amendment. Representative Newt Gingrich (R) and his opponent were compared on additional issues such as abortion on demand, voluntary prayer in school, and taxpayer support for obscene art. The guide compared Representative Buddy Darden (D) and his opponent on items such as congressional term limits and parental notification when a minor seeks an abortion. Since competing pairs of candidates in general elections never agree on the issues included in the voter guides, people unaware of the selection principle might infer that the candidates hold opposing views across an entire spectrum of issues not contained in the guide. Alternatively, one might assume that these are the only issues on which the candidates disagree so that on topics not included, they agree. The voter guides for the primary season differed to the extent that candidates for some offices had no significant differences. For example, coverage of GOP gubernatorial candidates could not focus on the nonexistent policy disagreements. As evidence of the perceived influence of the CC, one Republican gubernatorial candidate circulated a flyer boasting that according to the Christian Coalition, Guy Millner and John Knox agreed on every issue—except taxes. In reality, Knox, who had more support from the Christian Right than did Millner, took a more conservative stand on abortion, limiting it to instances when the mother's life was in danger, whereas Millner accepted the mother's life, rape, and incest as exceptions.

The voter guides have also been criticized for the way issues were framed. For example, the CC characterized a vote to reduce state funding for public television as a vote "to eliminate taxpayer funding for pornography" (Ezzard 1994). Similarly, the CC considered opposition to eliminating state funding for Planned Parenthood to be a pro-abortion vote.

Member dues and donations are used to publish the voter guides, and distribution is done by volunteers. Gartland estimates that between 1.5 and 2 million of the guides were handed out in 1994, with many of them going to churches. Some congregations distributed the guides during Sunday school, while elsewhere stacks of the guides appeared in the vestibule. In some communities, service stations and convenience stores also had guides available. One mall passed out 5,000 copies in a week.

Distribution of the voter guides through churches is seen as very successful because, according to the Democratic son of a Baptist preacher, it "anoints" the message. For some who receive the guides in church the message is underscored with a sermon that stresses the impossibility of being a Christian and a Democrat, or the congregation may be asked to pray for the favored candidate. Said a concerned Democratic Party official, "Distributing the voter guides through churches gives the Christian Coalition an advantage that is almost impossible to fight." A top African American elected official believes that distributing the voter guides at churches is effective, even if not endorsed from the pulpit, since bored parishioners read them during sermons.

Of course, such church-based political activity is not new in Georgia; African American churches have long been important political institutions. In 1994, as in other years, candidates made the rounds of African American congregations. With rare exceptions, the beneficiaries of these Sunday morning appearances were Democrats. The similarities between the role of white evangelical and black churches was such that one campaign manager claimed, "The Christian Coalition has become the black preachers of the Republican Party. There's not a dime's worth of difference between Tyrone Brooks (black activist state legislator) and Pat Gartland."

Legislative Scorecards

Democrats criticize the legislative scorecard on family issues for the choice of roll calls. The scorecard for the 1993–1994 sessions contained nine Senate and seven House roll calls. As with other interest group roll call evaluations, the objective is to mobilize and influence members. The scorecards carry the following message: "It is hoped that if you have a representative who shows strong family values, you will make the decision to help his or her campaign; and if you are one of the many who don't like how your representative stands on the issues, you will work on his opponent's campaign or decide to run yourself."

Most of the issues selected emphasize social conservativism and include positions such as eliminating funding for Planned Parenthood, requiring a period of silent meditation in schools, cutting funding for public television after the showing of *Tales of the City* (a PBS dramatization that included nudity and homosexuality), supporting abstinence-based sex education, and opposing outcomes-based education. Other roll calls, such as support for term limits for legislators, have no obvious link to family values.

While legislators who fared poorly on the scorecard were critical, senators were advantaged by the computational rule used to calculate support scores. Six correct for the nine Senate votes earned a score of 70, whereas three of nine received a 40 percent, rather than 33 percent support. Inflation was not the rule, however, in the House. Five out of seven usually earned a 63 (compared with the conventional 71 percent support), although one Republican got a 75 for this record. Two of seven was depreciated to 25 percent and some House members with four correct were awarded only 50 percent. On the other hand, four correct at times earned the same 63 that went to those with five correct votes. Differences in the support percentages appear to be random and not related to the legislator's party identification.

Democrats charge that the roll calls are selected to make them look bad while enhancing the standing of Republicans with the Christian Coalition and its allies. The inclusion of roll calls dealing with term limits and a Senate vote on lowering the threshold for a general election victory from majority to 45 percent lend credibility to Democratic suspicions that some votes were chosen for their partisan rather than their family component.[1] Further fueling Democratic complaints is that in the Senate no Republican received less than 40 percent and 14 of the 17 had scores of at least 89.[2] In contrast, 50 was the highest score achieved by a Democratic senator while most of them were at 20 or lower. Partisan disparities in the House while great were less pronounced than in the Senate. House Republicans reelected in 1994 achieved a mean score on the CC roll calls of 72.7 compared with a Democratic mean of 20.2.

Even moderate Republicans who score well on CC issues criticize the items chosen to assess legislators' stands. One such Republican characterized the Coalition votes as "off the wall." Another Republican legislator voiced criticism more often heard among Democrats, "it got to the point that if you did not take a stand on certain issues they would portray you as anti-moral."

Is Christian Coalition Information Nonpartisan?

The CC claims that its publications are informational and nonpartisan, and their tax-exempt status depends on the truth of this claim. Gartland claims that his organization supports "a lot of Democrats," an assertion hotly denied by Democratic Party officials. Said one, "It's an almost impossible sell to say that the Christian Coalition is anything but Republican." The view was echoed by a Democratic legislative candidate who believed that "the Christian Coalition supports only Republicans. It is solely a Republican organization. After all it was founded by Pat Robertson and he ran for president as a Republican." A Democratic House leader agreed, "I think their activities thus far indicate they are a Republican organization" (*Marietta Daily Journal* 1995).

During interviews, Democrats invariably cite one or more colleagues who are conservative and strongly committed to the family values that are at the core of the Christian Right yet score poorly on CC roll calls. For example, an ordained minister scored only 25. Another representative, of whom it was said, "He did everything he could for the religious right," fared even worse with a 13. Roy Barnes, the pro-life Democratic gubernatorial candidate in 1990, managed 38, the same score as a Democrat who visits churches speaking about his POW experiences. Complained a Democratic committee chair, "I've been called a non-Christian by these people. I've been an active church member all of my life" (Smith 1994). A Democratic state legislator who lost to a Christian Coalition candidate charged that "there's nothing Christian about them" (quoted in Bennett 1994).

Concern about the CC was such that in early 1995 the House Democratic Caucus met with Gartland. According to those in attendance, Gartland acknowledged problems with the Coalition election publications. In a conciliatory offer, he suggested, "We're still going to do it. But we're going to work with you. You think we picked the wrong bills? You can sit down with us and let's take a look at these bills that are family-friendly" (*Marietta Daily Journal* 1995).

Democrats who feel that they got burned in 1994 CC campaign literature are trying to prevent an encore in 1996. One strategy is to keep Christian Right pet schemes from being put forward as amendments to unrelated pieces of legislation. In this effort the Democratic leadership finds comfort in a ruling by the Republican attorney general holding that attempts to make substantive policy by amending the budget are out of order. A second approach for some legislators is to vote for proposals likely to be included on future CC scorecards.

Democrats' concern is understandable in light of the success of candidates aligned with religious evangelicals in 1994, the topic to which we now turn.

The Christian Right and Election Outcomes

Republicans invariably opined that the Christian Right was most potent in relatively low turnout affairs such as GOP primaries and special elections. Although it is changing, most Georgians still vote in Democratic primaries, making it easier for a cohesive Christian Right to sway a GOP primary. Georgia special elections are nonpartisan and often have large fields of candidates so that, as with Republican primaries, if religious voters weigh in behind one candidate, they may push their choice to victory or at least into a runoff. One GOP campaign manager, whose candidate was not the preferred choice of the Christian Right but was not demonized by these groups either, summed up his approach to this component of the electorate with, "You don't want to piss them off."

An experienced campaigner suggested that the CC is most effective in rapidly growing counties immediately after redistricting. Redrawing district lines may cut neighborhoods and separate voters from their former representatives. Children may be rezoned to different schools to relieve overcrowding. With everything else in flux, the church may be the only unchanged institution. The church, which is already trusted in matters spiritual, may become a beacon in matters political, especially when other cues have been muted.

Primaries

One frequent estimate of the political strength of evangelicals in Republican primaries is about 80,000, based on the vote for John Knox (84,563), the gubernatorial candidate most closely associated with religious conservatives in 1994. GOP campaign managers reject that figure. Said one of the 80,000 figure, "That is too small. Some social conservatives went with Guy Millner because of the winnability factor. Probably about one third of the Christian Coalition backed Millner." Another campaign manager claimed that some of the purist and less pragmatic evangelicals went for Nimrod McNair, who placed fourth with 20,042 votes. A third assessment comes from the campaign of the ultimate GOP gubernatorial nominee Guy Millner (142,263 votes), which compiled a list of 150,000 people. "These were right-to-life people and self-identified born-again Christians who are likely to vote in the Republican primary," a Millner worker reported. A second frequently estimated figure for the numbers of religious voters was about one third of the GOP primary vote. With almost 300,000 votes tallied in the 1994 Republican gubernatorial primary, the one-third estimate would put the Christian Right voting strength at 100,000.

Whether the evangelical vote is 80,000, 100,000, or more, it can be a major factor in GOP primaries. GOP primaries offer limited opportunities, however, since nominations often go uncontested. In 1994 Republican nominations were contested for governor, both Public Service Commission posts, and 5 of 11 congressional districts, but not for 7 other statewide posts. Only 7 of 56 state senate posts and 22 of 180 state house seats had as many as 2 Republican candidates. Overall, fewer than 15 percent of the positions of state legislator or higher had multiple Republican candidates. If one focuses on nominations won by less than 60 percent of the vote or decided in a runoff, then the competitive Republican primaries included governor, both PSC seats, 4 congressional districts, 3 senate elections and 12 house seats.

It is in these hotly contested primaries that the religious vote, if monolithic, can propel a candidate far along the way to a majority. If a third, or even a quarter, of the primary vote is sewed up by a candidate of the Christian Right, it will be challenging for the other Republican candidate to nail down enough of the remaining vote to be nominated. Nonetheless, the candidates more closely identified with the Christian Right did not always win in 1994. Although Millner and his wife were active with prayer groups, he was not the first choice among evangelicals, but as has already been suggested, that vote may have fractured in the primary, although the preferred candidate of the Christian Right was John Knox.[3]

To explore the importance of the Christian Right for Knox, a multivariate model was estimated. The dependent variable is the percentage Knox received of all votes cast in the GOP primary for governor. The independent variable of interest is the percentage of evangelicals, calculated as the number of Southern Baptists and Church of God members divided by the total church membership in the county.[4] Control variables included in the model were 1989 median income, a dichotomous variable indicating whether the county was in a metropolitan statistical area, and a second dummy variable coded one for counties in the northern part of the state. Since Knox had been mayor of a Deep South Georgia city and was the only south Georgian in the primary field, he was expected to run better in the southern half of the state.

As Table 3-1 shows, the Knox vote was strongly related to the percentage of evangelicals in the county. Every four-percentage-point increase in evangelicals added one percentage point to the Knox vote. The former mayor also ran stronger in south Georgia. The other two controls were not related to Knox support.

Table 3-1
Support for John Knox in GOP Gubernatorial Primary

	B	T-test
Constant	.380	
Percentage Evangelical	.253	3.607
North Georgia	−.156	−6.403
Metropolitan Area	.032	.992
Income	−5.79E-06	−.921
R-square	.288	
Adjusted R-square	.270	
F	15.481	
Significance	.0000	

Others who lost nominations despite being preferred by the Christian Right include Ralph Hudgens in the Tenth Congressional District and Seth Harp in Senate District 16. Strong personal organizations and deep roots in the community may explain how Hudgens's and Harp's opponents fashioned narrow victories.

Candidates closely associated with the religious groups who won included Bob Barr in Congressional District 7, Senator Pam Glanton, Reverend J. L. Black in Senate District 53, and Representatives Mitchell Kaye and Jeff Williams. Glanton and Kaye were two darlings of the Christian Right who earned the enmity of the Democratic establishment in the legislature for pushing what members of the majority saw as eccentric or no-win positions.

When asked to assess the significance of the Christian Right in GOP primaries, many Republicans subscribe to the observations of a representative who noted that, "You can't be their nemesis. There is a lot of fear of what they'd do to you if you crossed them. The key is getting them not to work against you." He continued, "Everybody in the party wants to be friends with the Christian Coalition. They provide workers who will do the grunt work. There are some Republicans who play to the Christian Right, supporting their issues but they don't live the Christian life." In GOP primaries and special elections, the Christian Right can make a political novice an instant competitor. A political activist explained a special senate election as follows: "The Christian Right gave McGuire a base where he didn't have the personal ties. He was unknown in the district. He didn't practice law here. Abortion was big in the special election." A Republican legislator who does not fully reciprocate the support that the Christian Coalition gave him cautions that "the Christian Coalition is like the NRA. They want you to believe that their bite is bigger than their bark."

General Elections

In the general election, the religious vote will be a smaller component of the electorate than in the GOP primary. Yet as part of the Republican coalition, Christian conservatives can help push a candidate over the top. After more than a century as an inconsequential minority, in 1994 Republicans were numerous enough to be serious players in statewide and congressional elections and in a growing minority of the legislative posts. Republicans won three statewide positions with no more than 51 percent of the vote and another with less than 55 percent.

The religious vote gets greatest credit in the state school superintendent's election. Opposition to outcomes-based education, support for prayer in school, and concern about sex education and classroom and library materials focused the Christian Right on education leadership. In this low-visibility contest, the incumbent had no inkling he was endangered until a month before the election. Challenger Linda Schrenko made use of the CC grassroots network and campaigned in churches while incumbent Werner Rogers courted school boards and superintendents.

Christian evangelicals also played important roles in behalf of the GOP candidate for lieutenant governor. The Republican nominee, Nancy Schaefer, who polled 42 percent of the vote, is a Christian Right activist, heading a group called Family Concerns. In 1993, as the leading white candidate for mayor of Atlanta, Schaefer attracted attention—if relatively few votes—by opposing a domestic partnership proposal that would have extended health care and other benefits to unmarried family units in the city. Although the beneficiaries of this proposal would not have been exclusively homosexuals, they provided the flash point for opposition.

Polling done for GOP gubernatorial nominee Guy Millner two months before the election shows the link between religious conservativism and party identification. As table 3-2 shows, Republicans are much more likely to have the characteristics of conservative ideology and regular church attendance than are Democrats. Only about one in six white Democrats is a religious conservative, whereas in the GOP more than 40 percent of the strongest partisans are Christian conservatives. Regardless

Table 3-2
Religious Conservatives Share of White Registered Voters,
by Party Identification

Party Identification	Religious Conservatives	N
Strong Republican	44.8%	96
Moderate Republican	32.9%	79
Independent Republican	37.9%	58
Independent	29.6%	81
Independent Democrat	17.1%	35
Moderate Democrat	18.0%	61
Strong Democrat	15.9%	44
Total	30.6%	454

Source: Compiled from data provided by Ayres and Associates. Survey conducted September 6–9, 1994.

of the strength of a Republican's partisan ties, at least one third are religious conservatives. As expected, white religious conservatives strongly supported Republican Millner for governor. Almost two thirds of Christian conservatives expressed support for Millner, compared with only 27 percent who were inclined toward the Democratic incumbent. Among whites who were not Christian conservatives, Miller led by a 47 to 43 percent advantage at Labor Day.

As table 3-3 shows, the religious conservative variable better distin-

Table 3-3
Voter Preferences in Georgia's Gubernatorial Election

	Religious Conservatives (Whites Only)		Abortion Position (All Races)	
	Yes	No	Pro-choice	Pro-life
Zell Miller (D)	27%	47%	57%	39%
Guy Millner (R)	65%	43%	35%	51%
Undecided	9%	10%	9%	10%
N	139	315	260	267

Source: Ayres and Associates. Survey conducted September 6–9, 1994

guished candidate preferences than did a question about abortion. While Millner led among pro-lifers and Miller was the favorite of the pro-choice voters, the margins were narrower than among religious conservatives. One explanation for the muted differences on the abortion question is that all voters are tallied here, whereas only whites are included in the religious conservative category. It should also be noted that the pro-lifers include far more than the Christian Right, with the sample of voters evenly divided between pro-life and pro-choice camps.

To assess the relative impact of evangelical denominations, the measure of percentage evangelical introduced earlier was used in multivariate models for Millner, Schaefer, and Schrenko, three GOP candidates closely associated with religious conservatives. In addition to the controls used in the analysis of the Knox primary vote, the share of the 1992 vote won by U.S. Senator Paul Coverdell in the general election was used as a measure of party strength.[5]

As anticipated, table 3-4 shows counties with concentrations of reli-

Table 3-4
Support for Candidates Associated with the Christian Right in 1994
Georgia General Elections

	Millner	Schaefer	Schrenko
Constant	.133	.044	.130
Percentage Evangelical	.200	.141	.117
	(5.77)	(4.57)	(3.94)
Percentage Coverdell	.429	.584	.500
	(7.05)	(10.73)	(9.57)
Income	8.18E-06	3.90E-06	7.07E-06
	(2.71)	(1.45)	(2.73)
North Georgia	−.047	−.029	−.037
	(−4.28)	(−2.91)	(−3.92)
Metropolitan Area	−.005	.012	.029
	(−.357)	(0.95)	(2.37)
R-square	.559	.670	.664
Adjusted R-square	.544	.659	.653
F	38.496	61.799	60.064
Significance	.0000	.0000	.0000

T-test values in parentheses.

gious evangelicals casting larger shares of their votes for each of the three Republicans. Also as expected, the candidates ran better in the same counties that supported Coverdell. A third feature shared by the candidates was stronger performances in south Georgia once other variables were held constant. The importance of other variables varied across the candidates, with Millner and Schrenko running substantially better in more affluent counties. Schaefer, who had run for mayor of Atlanta and had some name recognition in the Atlanta area prior to her 1994 bid, ran better in urban areas (which are dominated by counties in the Atlanta media market) while for the other two candidates urbanization was not a factor.

Determining precisely how many officeholders owe their elections to religious conservatives or how many candidates favored by evangelicals won is impossible. As mentioned earlier, the CC does not endorse candidates but Republicans usually fare better in the group's publications. Taking the broadest perspective, one might conclude that almost every Republican was favored by Christian conservatives.

A narrower perspective is offered by the state's senior political journalist, who estimates that after the 1994 election, "At least a third of the state's lawmakers owe their allegiances to the Christian Coalition. So do three of the five members of the Public Service Commission and at least four constitutional officers" (Shipp 1994). To these numbers could be added at least three members of Congress and a U.S. senator. In one Atlanta suburban county, the daily newspaper reported that eight of nine local candidates who fit the Christian Coalition profile triumphed in 1994 (Bennett 1994).

Some GOP nominees benefited in the general election by *not* having been the candidate favored by religious conservatives in the primary. In the Eighth and Tenth Congressional Districts, where the 1992 GOP nominees had been closely identified with the Christian Right, the 1994 nominees attracted more independent and Democratic support by appearing more mainstream in comparison with the 1992 nominees and simultaneously retained CC support.

Christian Right Representation in Local and State Legislative Offices

No comprehensive figures are available on the numbers of Christian conservatives holding local office. Republicans close to the scene estimate that in the state's only county having no Democratic officeholder (Gwinnett County in the Atlanta suburbs), all officials are now pro-life. Cobb County, which is the heart of Newt Gingrich's district and the site of the CC headquarters, received national attention when its commission condemned the homosexual lifestyle. This sparked gay and lesbian protests and resulted in the Atlanta Olympics transferring venues of events scheduled for the county. In a bedroom county for Athens, an evangelical school board member has led efforts to remove books from the school libraries that contain profanity or sex scenes. Works by V. C. Andrews, an author writing for junior high readers, have been put on a restricted list (McCarthy 1994).

The Christian Right has attained the kind of position in the state legislature to which interest groups aspire—some of their own serve in the institution. In both chambers a vocal minority espouses concerns embraced by the Christian Right. The house has three Republican fundamentalist ministers and the senate has a Republican pastor from the Three Trinity Holiness Church. These ministers are joined by a number of conservative religious laymen, including a conservative Jew in the house.

Most of the Republicans recently elected to the senate seem to have close ties to evangelicals. Of nine freshmen Republican senators seeking reelection in 1992, all but one scored 100 percent on the Christian Coalition scorecard. In contrast, only three of eight more senior GOP senators always voted the Coalition line. Within the house the most visible junior Republicans are Coalition supporters. Almost all of the incumbent Democrats defeated in 1994 were felled by candidates aligned with Christian evangelicals.

Pragmatists and Purists

Although some see abortion as the defining issue for the CC, Gartland notes that his group's legislative concerns are broader than those of most groups. "Other groups monitor one or two issues. We're concerned about the family—about whatever affects the family," explains Gartland. Showing his pragmatic side, Gartland says, "Hey, I'm just as concerned about a tax increase as I am for the sanctity of life, whether it's for the elderly or the unborn" (Miller 1993). Gartland suggests that abortion may not even be his primary concern: "Pocketbook issues count more right now. Raising taxes is what concerns most people" (Shipp 1993).

Another CC official elaborates on the link between religion and state fiscal policy: "The Bible contains a lot of Scriptures that have to do with money, with taxes, with donating, with good stewardship, with honesty—a lot of things we're talking about" (quoted in Smith 1995). A Democratic campaign manager puts this fiscal conservativism in a different light, saying, "It gives a moral excuse for pocketbook voting. It is just the opposite of a social conscience. It provides a Biblical basis for opposition to social programs."

This focus on issues outside the social agenda is part of a new pragmatic strategy on the part of Christian Right elites. Christian Coalition leader Pat Gartland is among the most pragmatic. One observer explained, "Gartland is not a pure ideologue since he will endorse candidates who he finds acceptable. Some of the other leaders of the Christian Right always go with the more conservative candidate even if that individual has no chance of winning." A GOP campaign manager said of the CC leadership, "It is becoming more reasonable. Their attitude in 1994 was let's win; we don't have to be pure. Go for the good, not the perfect." Such pragmatism is welcomed by party moderates, but the purists in the movement are naturally less favorably inclined. One respondent who believed that candidates got more favorable treatment in the voter guides if they contributed to the expenses of those publications gave the harsh assessment that "the leadership of the Christian Right has become like prostitutes." Even some who are critical of the movement's leadership are careful to distinguish the leaders from the rank and file. "The vast majority of the movement is sincerely concerned about the deteriorating moral fiber of the country," said one of Gartland's detractors. These purists want the Christian Coalition to back only those candidates who take very conservative positions on social issues.

Democrats hope that the Christian Right will focus on those social issues and stake positions that will be repudiated by the electorate. "The GOP is becoming beholden to a group that is not at the political center in Georgia," observed a Democratic leader. This person hopes that his party can get on the right side of voters on issues such as crime and education and convince the electorate that for all its small-government rhetoric, the Christian Right wing of the GOP wants a government that on social issues is too intrusive. A second Democratic leader speculated that "the Christian Coalition may self-destruct. They have to go further to the right to get money." Another Democratic operative believes that the quality of some candidates will weaken the GOP. "The Republicans have so far survived their own wackiness. Some of the new Republicans have no business in the legislature. But it remains to be seen whether Democrats can beat inept legislators," he warns.

Conclusion

Georgia never had a strong labor union movement, and during the long period of Democratic hegemony party organization was equally weak. Republicans, as the minority party, undertook formal organization and embraced modern campaign techniques far more eagerly than Democrats. Mobilizing efforts of the Christian Right now complement party targeting and fund raising. Led by the Christian Coalition, new voters are being brought to the polls while many voters, new and old, are receiving new information. Survey data indicate that religious conservatives have become a major force in the growing ranks of Republican supporters. Candidates favorably reviewed by the CC often run well in GOP primaries but do not invariably win general elections. At times the ideal position for a Republican is to win nomination over an opposing religious conservative. This kind of winner, who already appears relatively moderate, need not rebut Democratic charges of being a religious fanatic, and as the CC becomes more pragmatic, less doctrinaire Republicans can win evangelical support in the general election.

While candidates associated with religious conservatives are growing in number, they remain part of the minority party—at least in terms of state office holding—and as such have had few policy achievements. Republican success at the polls, however, has awakened some Democrats who now hesitate to vote against evangelical policy initiatives. If Christian conservatives experience more success at the polls, they will begin achieving their policy goals as their own ranks expand in the legislature and on school boards and as they gather support from opponents. The CC successes of 1992 and 1994 have increased the pressure on the Democratic Party, already struggling to maintain its disparate coalition. The next couple of elections may determine whether Georgia will have a Republican majority in which religious conservatives are important players or whether the Democratic party can withstand this challenge and emerge as a more organized force.

Notes

We appreciate the many public officials, candidates and party personnel who spoke with us, many under a promise of anonymity.

1. Georgia requires a majority vote both for nomination and for general election.

2. The seventeen are those elected to the senate as Republicans, excluding

Roy Allen, who was elected as a Democrat but switched to the GOP near the end of the 1994 session, thereby becoming the only black Republican legislator in the state.

3. Interestingly, our interviews came across reports of two different candidates who supposedly were the behind-the-scenes preference of Christian Coalition leader Pat Gartland and neither of these was John Knox, who everyone agrees received the largest share of the religious vote.

4. These figures come from Bachtel and Boatright 1993.

5. Georgia does not have partisan registration, so share of the vote is the best measure of partisan strength available.

References

Bachtel, Douglas C., and Susan R. Boatright. 1993. *The Georgia County Guide, 1993.* Athens: University of Georgia.

Bennett, D. L. 1994. "The Christian Wave." *Marietta Daily Journal* (13 November): 1A, 8A.

Crews, Ron. 1994. Interview with Valerie Munguia, 2 November.

Ezzard, Martha. 1994. "Could Christian Coalition be 'Soft on Crime'?" *Atlanta Journal* (17 October): A8.

Gartland, Pat. 1994. Interview by author, 9 February.

Marietta Daily Journal. 1995. "Religious Right Casts Shadow." Editorial, 6 February: 1A, 5A.

McCarthy, Rebecca. 1994. "Book Evaluations Given the Go-Ahead for Oconee Schools." *Atlanta Journal* (19 July): B5.

Miller, Julie K. 1993. "The Pulpit and Politics." *Atlanta Journal* (30 April): E1, E12.

Pettys, Dick. 1993. "Conservative Christians Given Credit for GOP Victories in Senate Elections." *Athens Banner-Herald* (5 July): 1A.

Shipp, Bill. 1993. "Pat Gartland's Mission." *Georgia Trend* (November): 49–51, 69.

———. 1994."Big Winners: Bowers, Perdue." *Georgia Trend* (December): 15.

Smith, Ben, III. 1994. "Evangelicals Undergo Political Baptism of Fire." *Atlanta Constitution* (8 March): E8.

———. 1995. "Robertson's Group Adopts Secular Issues." *Atlanta Journal* (13 February): B1.

Strawn, Keith. 1993. "Georgia Politics' Newest Player." *Marietta Daily Journal* (n.d.): 1A, 7A.

4

Texas: The Emergence of the Christian Right

John M. Bruce

To the casual observer it would appear that politics in Texas operates according to the popular expression "Everything is bigger in Texas." The state's history is full of dramatic, if not exaggerated, political figures. From the days of Ma Ferguson through the time of President Lyndon Johnson, continuing into the recent past with Speaker Jim Wright and others, the state has engaged in politics with a flair.

Over the last decade or so, however, Texas has seen a powerful new voice emerge in state politics. Conservative Christian activists have emerged as a major political force in the state, especially within the Republican Party. Unlike the colorful figures that have existed throughout Texas political history, those associated with this movement seek to avoid attention. What the movement lacks in colorful leaders, however, it more than makes up for in passion and influence.

The mobilization of the Christian Right in Texas was several years in the making. This chapter will first attempt to place the Christian Right into historical context. Did the emergence of the Christian Right reverse an existing trend, clarify an uncertain pattern, or reinforce a trend already in motion? Next the chapter will focus on the 1994 elections, which represent the high-water mark to date for the Christian Right in the state. Just how powerful was the Christian Right, and how did it seek to influence the elections? Finally, the fate of the Republican Party in the face of this mobilization is considered. What is the relationship between the Christian Right and the Republican Party? What has happened to the party in the last few years, and what seems most likely to happen next?

The Historical Political Context

The historical pattern of Texas politics resembles that of other southern states following Reconstruction. The Democratic Party was, in reality, the only party, so politics within the state took the form of intra-party conflict. In the thirty-one presidential elections since 1872, Texas voted for the Democratic candidate in all but eight. The state did not elect a Republican for governor from the end of Reconstruction until 1978. Similar dominance by the Democratic Party was visible in the state legislature: Republicans were absent or, at best, extraordinarily scarce during this period.

Time was not kind to the Democratic Party in the decades following the New Deal realignment. Texas represented an environment where the Democratic Party was most likely to crack over the social issues that emerged in state and national politics during the 1960s and beyond. Indeed, as figure 4-1 shows, the first real gains made by the Republicans came during the administration of John F. Kennedy. The lines in the figure represent the increasing percentage of the state house and senate chambers held by Republican members, as well as the percentage of the vote received by Republican gubernatorial candidates. As is clear from the pattern, the early gains represented the start of a long-term, steady growth of political power for the Republicans in the state.

The slow transition from a one-party state to a more competitive system took serious hold when the national Democratic Party began to

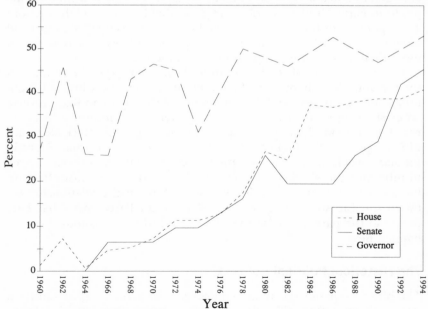

Figure 4-1. Republican Success in Texas Indicators of Electoral Strength

pursue an agenda involving various social concerns. As the national party pulled to the left, conservative Texas Democrats became increasingly uncomfortable, and this produced a fertile environment for Republican growth. For almost two decades, this growth did not threaten Democratic control of the state. By the end of the 1970s, however, the first critical point had been reached. A Republican was elected to the governor's mansion in 1978, and two years later the state went for Ronald Reagan by a sizable margin. Although the two parties have alternated control of the governorship ever since then, the state has supported Republican presidential candidates in all subsequent elections. Republican numbers in both chambers of the state legislature have doubled since 1980, and continued Democratic control of each of the chambers is in doubt.

When conservative Christians were energized by the Reagan presidency during the early 1980s and mobilized by Reagan's reelection campaign in 1984 and Pat Roberston's campaign in 1988, Texas was receptive. A young and growing Republican Party was gaining on the once-monolithic Democratic Party. The population of the state was as open to the message of the Republicans as it was repelled by the Great Society programs associated with the Democrats. As is often true in states with long domination by one party, the Democratic Party was neither strong in organization nor unified in message. Thus, all the pieces were in place that would allow a committed and organized group to enter the political arena and exert a significant influence.

Background: Texas and the Christian Right

Religion in Texas has always been visible and influential. The strength of the Catholic Church in the Hispanic community, the state-wide presence of the United Methodist Church, and the sizable numbers of Southern Baptists have all helped to make religious institutions important. In this environment politics and religion coexisted, but the relationship was more symbolic than meaningful. The mobilization of conservative Christians by the Christian Right has changed that, for these new activists believe that they must act to stop the serious moral decay in government caused by declining religious faith. Government policies over the last twenty years are seen as taking apart the moral fiber of the nation and state.

Perhaps the central issue on the Christian Right agenda is abortion. The national headquarters of Operation Rescue has recently moved to the state that was the source of *Roe v. Wade*. There is a Texas Right to Life Committee and an affiliated political action committee (PAC), as well as numerous local pro-life organizations. Clinic protests are frequent, as are attempts to induce the legislature to pass restrictive laws on abortion.

A second concern among the conservative Christians is education. Christian Right activists believe that the public school system encourages immoral behavior and has created an environment in which religion is not tolerated. They lament the absence of school prayer and the teaching of evolution instead of creationism in biology classes. Moreover, they believe that the curriculum encourages immoral behavior by providing information on contraception, homosexuality, AIDS, and basic human reproduction, and they strongly oppose programs that distribute condoms or other birth control devices in the schools. The Texas Home School Coalition represents parents who have removed their children from public schools, and the Committee on Educational Excellence advocates conservative reforms in the school system.

A number of multi-issue organizations are active, including the Associated Conservatives of Texas (PAC), the Texas American Family Action Committee (PAC), the Texas Eagle Forum (PAC),[1] Concerned Texans, and the Texas chapter of the Christian Coalition. Many of these groups have existed in the state for some time and pursued their own diverse agendas with little coordination, but the Christian Right had no real statewide presence until just before the 1992 presidential election.[2] What happened to transform this collection of similarly focused groups with little political visibility into a significant force in the state? While many forces were pulling in the same direction, one element stands out: in 1991 Dick Weinhold took over as chairman of the Texas Christian Coalition.

The Christian Coalition, formed by Pat Robertson following his failed presidential bid in 1988, has several aims: to represent Christians before various government bodies, to train Christians for effective political action, to disseminate information on key issues, and to defend religious rights under the law. There was a Texas chapter prior to 1991 but it was not well run, and when Weinhold took over as chairman there were fewer than nine thousand members. The state organization was largely inactive and ineffective. As the new chairman, Weinhold brought a significant background of experience to the task. He had spent almost a decade as a national fund-raiser for Campus Crusade for Christ, and he served as national finance director for Robertson's presidential bid. In this capacity he oversaw the finances of a campaign that raised more money than any other Republican candidate, including George Bush. After the election, Weinhold became a member of the national board of directors for the Christian Coalition.

Like many Christian Coalition leaders, Weinhold uses moderate rhetoric and works closely with political leaders and the media. Even those who disagree with his views are likely to acknowledge the reasonable manner with which he engages people. Former state Republican chair Fred Meyer said, "I think Dick's a good man. He's a very effective and responsible leader. It is not an ego trip for Dick. He uses persuasion, not intimidation" (*Fort Worth Star Telegram*, 10 June 1994). Thus, Weinhold brought a rather unique and powerful collection of resources and connections to his new task.

Regardless of how well qualified an individual is, no one person can make huge political changes alone. Weinhold recognized this and did two things as a result, one internal to the Texas Christian Coalition and one external, reaching out to the other conservative Christian groups. One of the early steps taken by the new chair was to hire Alice Patterson as the state field director for the Christian Coalition. Patterson was a veteran political activist, with a significant history of work for the Republican Party, and a former president of one of the state's chapters of the Eagle Forum, providing a nice link to another group. One of her strengths was the ability to organize local chapters of the Christian Coalition and assist in the development of the existing chapters. Her work has produced significant results. There are now chapters in roughly half the counties in the state, and membership has grown from under nine thousand in 1991 to just under seventy thousand at the start of 1995. Obviously, internal organization brought its own rewards.

The second critical action taken was external and involved an attempt to link the various groups together. The leaders of various pro-family groups in the state get together on a monthly basis to coordinate and share information. This meeting, which is open only to invited guests, is sometimes referred to as "The Gathering." While it is not clear whether this meeting was entirely Weinhold's idea, he did describe it as one of the ways in which the Christian Coalition has attempted to coordinate with others in the state (Weinhold 1995). He described the existing groups as working with the right ideas, but with limited impact because of a lack of effective coordination. Sharing information and resources and mounting joint efforts where possible produced greater coordination and greater political strength for all groups.

Although the Texas Christian Coalition is but one of a collection of groups that have been described as the Christian Right, it is clearly the most active in terms of mobilizing activists. Although many political scientists have suggested that the target audience of the Christian Coalition is comprised primarily of evangelical Christians and a few conservative Catholics, Weinhold indicated that the group represents "families with children." Obviously, the latter represents a much larger potential group of backers, but also a more diverse group, many of whom may find certain portions of the Christian Coalition's message problematic. No clear demographic data on the state membership are available, but it is safe to assume that the membership more closely resembles the first definition of target population.

Weinhold stressed repeatedly that the Coalition wanted to train members how to participate in the process. Indeed, the newsletter from the state chapter devotes an entire page to the rules on how to take part in the precinct convention and how to select delegates to the district (*Christian American* 1994). The state chapter has gone beyond just advising how to participate in precinct conventions, however. It has held training seminars in cities throughout the state, recruiting and training activists. Many of those attending these workshops are aiming at running for precinct chair.[3] The theme of the message is a broad one of involvement at all levels and in all capacities.[4]

The focus of the activities of the Christian Coalition in Texas has reflected the collection of interests represented by the various conservative Christian bodies active in the state. Social and moral policies have been the most visible, with abortion, sex education, and prayer in school comprising the lion's share of the discussion. Recently, in conjunction with a shift in emphasis at the national level, the Coalition appears to be reducing the prominence of the social agenda. The national group organized against the Clinton health care plan, spending almost $1.5 million along the way. Leaders of the Coalition are also speaking out on term limits, the balanced budget amendment, and other issues not usually associated with the conservative Christian movement. Guy Rodgers, a former national field director, advised members to "drop redemptive language" when talking about politics. One of the aims of the change in emphasis was to reduce the number of divisive issues. However, internal publications continue to stress social issues: analysis of four issues of the *Christian American* in 1994 revealed five times as many articles about social issues (abortion, education, and homosexuality) than about the economy and health care.[5]

As a nonprofit group, the Christian Coalition cannot endorse candidates, but it does otherwise work to influence candidates and officeholders.[6] The Coalition participates in national events, such as the postcard campaign against health care reform, and state-level events, such as education reform. Both the Coalition's literature and Weinhold note that they are a nonpartisan group. The director of training in the state chapter is a Democrat, and one of the regional directors had been active in the Ann Richards gubernatorial campaign of 1990. Additionally, some county chairs are Democrats. However, most state members are Republicans.[7]

One of the principal activities of the Coalition is the development and distribution of a voter guide, expressing the views of the candidates on issues important to the Christian Coalition. These guides have themselves become controversial, for the Coalition sometimes fills in material when a candidate does not respond to the survey. Some have argued that these "inferences" are biased. Similarly, some argue that the whole nonpartisan nature of the guide is false, and it is in fact an endorsement of Coalition-backed candidates. Weinhold noted that the guide has been used to reach into minority communities, even containing Spanish translations.[8]

The Christian Coalition, while perhaps the dominant organization among the conservative Christian movement, is but one part of this larger political force. In Texas as elsewhere, a multitude of local groups have formed to influence politics. Perhaps the best examples of this activity are the various state and local races for school board during the period prior to 1994.

Across the country, the Christian Right has mobilized to elect candidates to school boards in an effort to influence curriculum and the content of school libraries. A key force behind this mobilization has been the Citizens for Excellence in Education, associated with Robert Simonds's National Association of Christian Educators. Simonds noted that an "active Christian parents' committee" in every district would allow complete control of all school boards. In a pamphlet called "How to Elect Christians to Public Office," Simonds stated: "We need strong school board members who know right from wrong. The Bible, being the only true source on right and wrong, should be the guide of board members. Only Godly Christians can truly qualify for this critically important position, although many conservative non-Christians are trying to hold up most of our Christian agenda. Spiritual discernment is needed in every decision." [9]

In Texas this activity took place at the local level prior to 1994. Numerous school board elections have been contested by members of the Christian Coalition as well as by various other conservative Christians. Indeed, Robertson's 1988 state campaign manager ran unsuccessfully for a north Texas district board in 1993. During his campaign he suggested that Coalition members on the board would be able to screen potential administrators for "correct moral attitudes as opposed to Northeast liberal ones."[10] The themes of other races in the 1992–93 period tended to center on concerns about sex education, discussion of homosexuality, prayer in school, and secular teachings.

In some cases, candidates from the Christian Right ran as slates. This was the case in Pasadena Independent School District, where a three-person slate lost after campaigning on the need for Biblical principles in the schools. More often candidates run without being slated, as happened in Klein in 1993.[11] The Klein races are interesting because of a countermobilization that developed. The two conservative Christian candidates forced two incumbents into a runoff. The Texas State Teachers Association mobilized, and the passionate campaign resulted in high turnout and a sound defeat of the two challengers.[12]

In the city of Round Rock, the Christian Right gained control of the seven-member school board in 1993 and promptly bought out the remaining years on the superintendent's contract. Although his tenure had seen increased test scores and national recognition of several of the district's schools, he had discontinued public prayer before football games.[13]

Christian Right activity in school board elections serves two purposes. First, it allows the Christian Right to address the perceived shortcomings of the public education system. Second, it provides a training ground for conservative Christian candidates who may aspire to higher office.[14] In some sense, then, the period of buildup from the mid-1980s to 1993 represented a period of groundwork for the 1994 elections. We now look at the role of the conservative Christians in 1994.

The 1994 Elections and the Christian Right

The midterm elections of 1994 offered a chance for the conservative Christians in the state to flex their muscles. All the environmental factors were right: a sitting president who generated passionate opposition but only tepid support, a midterm election that traditionally generated low turnout, a pool of experienced candidates and campaign workers, and a variety of statewide Christian Right organizations which were more coordinated than ever.

The most important race in Texas in 1994 was that for governor. The incumbent, Ann Richards, had high approval ratings but was quite unpopular among those generally associated with the Christian Right. She was challenged by George W. Bush, son of former president Bush, who had carried Texas in the 1988 and 1992 elections. Although Richards maintained her high approval ratings up to and even after the fall contest, Bush won by an unexpectedly large margin. The other high-profile race in the state was for the U.S. Senate seat vacated by Lloyd Bentsen in 1993. Republican Kay Bailey Hutchison had won the special election to fill the seat for the remainder of the term, and in the general election for a full term she soundly defeated Richard Fisher.

In other races, the entire delegation to the U.S. House of Representatives was up for reelection, as was the entire state house and half of the state senate. Also up were seven of the fifteen seats on the state board of education. The level and nature of competition varied across all of these races, ranging from an unopposed incumbent in the U.S. Congress (Republican Bill Archer) to wildly unexpected upsets (the defeat of Democrat Jack Brooks).

The involvement of the Christian Right varied across these contests. In the two salient statewide races, Christian conservatives were unhappy with the moderate positions that Bush and especially Hutchison took on abortion. Indeed, in some lower-level Republican conventions, Christian Right activists refused to vote for a resolution of support for Hutchison. Yet no Christian Right candidate challenged Bush or Hutchison in the primary, because both were seen as sure winners. After their primary victories, Christian Right groups backed both candidates.

Democrats remain the majority in both the state house and state senate, although the size of those majorities has been eroded. A subset of candidates received financial support and campaign volunteers from the Christian Right. At least ten winning candidates for the U.S. Congress were aligned with or supported by the Christian Right in some way. In the state senate, at least ten of the fifteen races involved candidates aligned with the Christian Right, and in half of these the Christian Right candidate won. In the state house, at least thirteen of the races involved at least one candidate aligned with the Christian Right, and in some cases both the Democrat and Republican candidates were associated with the Christian Right. Of the thirteen races noted, nine were won by candidates aligned with the Christian Right. At the level of the state school board, there were seven seats up in 1994, and a group called Citizens for Responsible Education (CARE) slated seven conservative candidates for those slots. Of those, four won. CARE spent at least $300,000 in support of their slate.[15]

The Christian Right mobilized their resources in many of these races.

One of the most visible efforts was the Christian Coalition's statewide distribution of almost three million voter guides prior to the general election, more than were passed out during the 1992 presidential election.[16] In an effort to reach out to the Hispanic community, the 1994 general election guides were printed in both English and Spanish. Distributed through bookstores, churches, and mailing lists, the guides represented the most visible activity of the Christian Coalition in the state, reaching far more voters than anything else done by any other conservative Christian organization.

Another effort of the conservative Christians in the state was a preelection radio show that was broadcast statewide. This special production was aimed at conveying information about the various candidates and their stands with respect to the issues. The show, which was heard on Christian radio stations around the state, was unlikely to reach audiences beyond the target constituency, but it is likely that it stimulated interest and turnout in the election among conservative Christians in the state.

Although these activities influenced the 1994 elections, the Christian Right had its greatest long-term impact through the mobilization and politicalization of a new set of local-level activists. Before the May primary the Christian Coalition ran a series of local seminars on how to be active in the process. The long-term effect of this mobilization is being felt in a variety of ways. First, by mobilizing activists in the primary, the Christian Right is able to exert significant influence in the selection of the Republican nominees, resulting in candidates whose positions are more sympathetic toward Christian Right concerns. In the general election, as Republican fortunes continue to rise in the state, the conservative Christians are likely to see their candidates swept into office. And once elected, the new Republican officeholders must be aware of the demands of the conservative Christians, for the mechanics of the party nomination process are under the control of the Christian Right.[17]

The Mitovsky International exit poll showed that 33 percent of state voters were white born-again or evangelical, groups that constitute the main constituency of the Christian Right. Other reports suggest that the proportion of the state population that thinks of themselves as born again is in the 20 to 25 percent range. White evangelicals constituted a greater percentage of the electorate than of the general public, suggesting that the Christian Right was successful in mobilizing their target constituency to the polls.

Those individuals that would be identified as likely supporters of the Christian Right are different from the rest of the state in a number of ways. White evangelicals were more likely than other Texans to be members of the National Rifle Association (NRA), to believe that their economic situation had grown worse in the last four years, and to report having a "great deal of interest" in politics.

In addition, they were much more likely to disapprove of Richards's performance: 62 percent of white born-again Texans indicated disapproval, compared with only 38 percent of other state residents. They also are more likely to disapprove of Clinton's performance as president. This is not surprising, because white evangelicals in Texas tend to be Republicans. Fully 55 percent of white born-again or evangelical Christians in the Mitovsky exit poll called themselves Republicans, compared with only 31 percent of other voters. Half reported having voted for Republican candidate Clayton Williams in 1990, compared with only 36 percent for Richards,[18] and over half indicated that they had voted for Bush in 1992, with an additional 15 percent voting for Perot.

In 1994, white evangelicals voted overwhelmingly for George W. Bush for governor, giving him 62 percent of the vote in the gubernatorial election. Richards won among other voters with 58 percent. The Republican tilt among evangelicals was even larger in the U.S. Senate race: 75 percent backed Hutchison, whereas only 52 percent of other Texas voters voted for her.

When asked the reasons for their votes, white evangelicals were more likely than other Texas voters to mention the issue stands of the candidate as a reason for supporting their gubernatorial choice, but they were actually *less* likely to cite most of the issues in the survey, including crime, unemployment, and the importance of electing women, and the experience of the candidate. Surprisingly, few evangelicals or other voters cited family values as important in their vote decision, perhaps because Bush did not stress the social agenda. Evangelicals were only slightly more likely than other voters to indicate that their vote was for change.

Thus in 1994 white evangelicals and the Christian Right gave strong support to two Republican candidates at the top of the ticket who took moderate positions on social issues. Although this might seem like a Pyrrhic victory, in other ways 1994 was a good year for the Christian Right. In a number of nomination contests they succeeded in winning nomination for their favored candidates, and their efforts on behalf of these candidates helped elect some of them.[19] Their influence on the party platform made it a very conservative one. Thus, the total effect of the activities of conservative Christians in Texas in 1994 is quite impressive. Following the election, the movement finds itself in de facto control of the Republican Party, which raises serious questions about what the religious right can and may do, as well as how more moderate Republicans in the state may react to this situation.

The Future of the Republican Party in Texas

The emergence of a well-organized and strongly mobilized conservative Christian force in the state of Texas has significant implications for the future of the Republican Party in the state. While the organizations of the Christian Right are theoretically nonpartisan, the Republican Party is the arena where they are most active, for that is where their conservative agenda is most likely to prevail. This is true even in states such as Texas, where the Democratic Party has historically been rather conservative. Thus Christian activists have concentrated their energies within the Republican Party.[20]

This activity could show up in two ways. First, the formal structure of the party might be influenced or even taken over by the new conservative voice in the party. Second, the composition of the party activist core may change, having real implications in the nomination process and the general election.

The formal structure of the Texas Republican Party is now controlled by the Christian Right. At the state convention in June 1994, thousands of members of the Christian Right worked to elect a state Republican chair who clearly and publicly supports their agenda.

Heading into the convention, there were three nominees for the office of chair.[21] Congressman Joe Barton had been elected to the House in 1984, where he had clearly established himself as a backer of the new conservative agenda. During his time in Congress, he had gone to significant lengths to build a strong conservative organization in his district. Moreover, Barton was the choice of the outgoing state chair and received the endorsement of both Senators Gramm and Hutchison.[22] The second candidate was Tom Pauken, a lawyer from Dallas who had served in the first Reagan administration as the head of the ACTION agency. Pauken was clearly in solid support of the goals of the Christian Right. The third candidate was Dolly Madison McKenna. A businesswoman from Houston, she expressed support for reproductive freedom as well as concern about the increasingly conservative agenda of the Republican Party. After she warned delegates that some members of the party were trying to turn the party into a church, she was soundly booed at the convention. Given the strength of the conservatives in the party, it is realistic to describe the race as a two-way race between Pauken and Barton, with McKenna's candidacy reduced to a largely symbolic effort.

A race such as the one that developed for the state chair was, to many conservative Christians, a wonderful thing. The incumbent chair, Meyer, was considered too moderate by many Republicans. Bill Price, head of Texans United for Life, said that with Meyer's withdrawal "the major victory has already been won" (*Dallas Morning News*, 22 May 1994). With McKenna's marginal status in the race, many perceived the Barton–Pauken race as a win-win situation. Among the conservatives there was little concern about the possibility of sounding too conservative. Indeed, Cathie Adams, president of the Texas Eagle Forum, announced that "moderation equals loss at the polls" (*USA Today*, 13 May 1994). The Christian Coalition entered the convention saying that either of the two leading candidates would be acceptable to them. However, before a vote could be taken at the convention, Weinhold released a letter endorsing Pauken as chair. Addressing his letter to "pro-family delegates," Weinhold said he was backing Pauken because of Pauken's commitment to the "grass roots."

The race for chair came to a quiet end, never being put to a floor vote. After straw polls showed Pauken leading the race, both Barton and McKenna withdrew from the race. Pauken was elected in an uncontested vote.[23] This successful bid represented the culmination of a long-term plan of action by conservative Christians. About six months before the state convention, Pat Robertson sent a letter to his supporters in the state, attempting to raise both money and interest in the upcoming political campaign. Spearheading what he called "Operation Precinct," Roberston warned that "if we don't get involved now, the same old radicals will fill the gaps, and Texas will be run by those people who want to ban people of faith from participating" (*Dallas Morning News*, 22 May 1994).

How was this "capture" of the party possible? Robertson's letter represented the first shot in the campaign, but it was but one effort in the midst of many. The Christian Right built an informed base of activists through newsletters, seminars, and other means. The value of the training and information provided by the religious right in the state was especially important because of the nature of the party's political system.

The parties in Texas use primaries to select nominees, but party business—including the selection of delegates to higher-level conventions and the consideration of resolutions—is conducted at a precinct convention at the end of voting on the day of the primary. Historically, turnout at these affairs has been extraordinarily low: sometimes there are more delegate slots to fill than participants. Delegates selected at the precinct conventions go next to the state senate district convention, where the process is repeated for the state convention.

The most important contribution of Christian Right groups was information on the importance of these conventions and step-by-step rules on how to run a precinct-level convention.[24] In 1994, a mobilized and informed group of Christian Right activists overwhelmed the more moderate, traditional body of activists in the state. While the conservative Christians as a mobilized political force are not a numerical majority in the party or the state, they do outnumber the smaller body of activists that control the state party, develop the party platform, and select state party officials. Moreover, once in control of the party structure, they can adjust the rules to make the playing field a bit more favorable.

The selection of Pauken represents one measure of the success of this approach. However, other available indicators suggest more clearly how effective the conservative Christians were in the mobilization of their membership into party politics. When the 1994 Republican Party convention was called to order in Fort Worth, there were six thousand delegates with an equal number of alternates present. Of those twelve thousand activists who had been selected at party conventions held in state senate districts, 60 to 65 percent of them were evangelical Christians, many of whom belonged to the Christian Coalition or home schooling, pro-life, or other groups sympathetic to the Christian Right agenda. Many of these newly mobilized Christian activists were new to Texas Republican politics: over half of all delegates to the state convention had never before attended a state convention.

The precinct, district, and state conventions all passed very conservative resolutions that reflected the social agenda of the new activists.[25] For example, one district convention adopted a resolution suggesting that people with AIDS should be quarantined, while another passed one stating that abortion should be "regarded as the shedding of innocent blood which will surely bring God's judgement upon our nation" (*Dallas Morning News*, 22 May 1994). At the state convention, the platform was described by party leaders as strongly "pro-life and pro-family." The platform opposed abortion except to save the mother's life and called for reduced welfare benefits and stricter rules on immigration. The preamble to the document states that the ideas in the platform stand in "stark contrast to the liberal, socially destructive agenda of the Democratic Party" (*Dallas Morning News*, 12 June 1994). A proposed resolution by party moderates to adopt a statement that acknowledged that Republicans have a range of views on any given issues was soundly defeated.

There is little doubt, then, that conservative Christians dominated the party convention. One key question for the future of the party is whether these new conservatives can work with the older, more moderate Republicans. In the language of the late Lee Atwater, would the party be a "big tent"? At this point, the answer appears to be no. One delegate, not an advocate of a "big tent" approach, described the situation this way: "There's just a few big tent people around. Reagan may have talked about the big tent, but he didn't believe in it." Another said, "Right now, the majority of the party is pro-life. And if people can't live within the Republican Party as it is, then they should move" (*New York Times*, 12 June 1994). Other social conservatives felt it was payback time after years of being excluded by the moderates in the state. Moderates, such as McKenna, felt that their party had been hijacked for religious purposes. Long-term activists were pushed aside by new activists drawn from the ranks of the conservative Christian movement. The whole shift created stress within the party. One Republican consultant said, "There is a whole lot of grumbling from the party establishment, but [the religious right] out-organized, out-worked, and out-hustled the current party leadership" (*Dallas Morning News*, 22 May 1994).

Harris County: A Struggle for the Soul of the Local Party

Harris County, encompassing the fourth largest metropolitan area in the nation—Houston, was the scene of one of the more interesting battles between the two wings of the party. In the end, as in many military conflicts, declaring a winner is a very difficult task.

In Harris County, the Christian Right and moderate factions fought to elect the county chair of the party. In March 1992, Betsy Lake was elected county chair, replacing Sherry Johnson.[26] Although Johnson had been willing to accommodate the religious right in the county, Lake was a pro-choice Republican, unacceptable to the more conservative voices in the county and unwilling to see the party lurch to the right on social issues. As county chair, Lake headed the county executive committee, which was comprised of the precinct chairs in the county. Many of these precinct chairs were Christian conservatives, therefore setting the stage for conflict to come.

In May 1992, at her first meeting as chair of the county, Lake was asked by the social conservatives to resign. She declined. Later in the meeting, having failed to convince her to resign, the executive committee passed a rules change that limited the powers of the county chair.

Although this had some impact, the duties of the county chair are not defined by the executive committee and a chair cannot be reined in by the committee.[27]

Leading the charge against Lake from the time of her election through the period of the split in the party was Dr. Stephen Hotze, who represented the extreme of the Texas Christian Right. His activities in the city dated back to at least 1985, when he helped to organize a set of city council candidates, called "Straight Slate," who unsuccessfully ran on the platform of opposition to civil rights for homosexuals. Hotze's ideas reflect a strong religious tone as applied to politics. For example, he is quoted as defining liberty as "the freedom to do what is biblically right." He made reference to "God's Law-Word," to which both church and state should conform. In an essay in one of the Houston newspapers, Hotze wrote that "every civilization has a religious foundation that defines its people's code of conduct. A nation's laws simply enact that code."[28] Hotze opposed abortion under any circumstances, denounced the Supreme Court decisions limiting worship in public schools, and wanted to eliminate the welfare system, the Internal Revenue Service, and the Federal Reserve.[29] As a measure of Hotze's local strength, he claimed to have a mailing list of over thirty-five thousand names.

The squabble in Harris County was noteworthy for political reasons because not only was this the county that President Bush claimed as his home residence, it was also to be the host county for the national Republican convention that summer. Significant pressure was put on Lake to smooth over the differences in the lead-up to the general election that year, lest the controversy hurt Bush's chances for reelection.

After the November election and the defeat of Bush, Lake concluded that she could not work with the elements of the religious right that had emerged in the county. As a result, she announced that she was, in essence, splitting the local party. She would remain chair of the Harris County Republican Party, but she was also creating a separate group called the Republican Federation of Harris County.[30] Lake described the new group as an "association of mainstream conservative Republicans" who recognized that the party cannot "survive as an exclusive, restrictive organization" (*Houston Chronicle*, 18 November 1992).

In December 1992, the executive committee of the county party met to address the issue of the split and to select a new leader for the party apparatus. Although Lake remained the elected county chair of the party, the executive committee decided to create an advisory board that would assume some of the duties abandoned by Lake. Hotze defeated Johnson (the county chair that Lake had defeated in 1992) and assumed many of the duties formerly held by Lake.[31] In a letter to precinct chairmen asking for their support, Hotze said that "Harris County can lead the way to restoring our nation to its Christian heritage."

Hotze's ascent to official party power was short-lived, however. Before the 1994 election of county chair, Hotze's organization had been locked out of their building for nonpayment of rent. He publicly stated that he was closing the office due to lack of funds. In March 1994, Betsy Lake was reelected as party chair in Harris County in an unopposed race.[32] Hotze's position of influence in the party continued even as his official position disappeared, however. In October 1994 (some seven months after Lake's uncontested reelection), Senator Phil Gramm held a fund-raiser for Hotze. He has also been able to raise significant contributions from other sources, including at least one $50,000 donation. Hotze's efforts are clearly aimed at expanding his power statewide, as he is developing small pockets of support around the state.

Lake was quick to point out that the Christian Coalition is "not like Hotze," and it is clear that he is far more extreme than the leaders of that organization. Yet the passionate and organized interests that Hotze brought to the political table do greatly resemble the characteristics of the membership of the Coalition or any of the other conservative Christian organizations in the state. Members of the Texas Right to Life group are likely to be just as inflexible in their feelings about Lake as Hotze. Those of the Christian Coalition are just as likely as Hotze to oppose the inclusion of homosexuals in the party. So, although the style of conflict may be different, the effect of the participation is not.

Has the presence of the religious right peaked in Harris County? The answer is almost certainly no. Lake acknowledges as much when asked about why she was unopposed in 1994, saying of Hotze and company, "I guess they realized that they didn't need the chair to do what they want." In the scheme of things, Lake's observation is correct. The agenda of the conservative Christians can be fully pursued without assuming the responsibilities of county-level chairs. The new conservatives have strong ties to state-level officials now, as well as the attention of elected officials. This, combined with a ready force of activists, makes the movement a difficult thing to counter.

Strategic Considerations

What sort of response might the moderates of the party be able to use to counteract the Christian Right in the state? Dolly Madison McKenna argued that there was no longer a moderate wing in the party, because all of them have been driven from their posts by activists from the religious right. Nevertheless, there are some options open to those seeking to keep the party from going any further to the right, especially on social issues.

Although once party moderates might have tried to change party rules to retain control of the party apparatus, this is no longer an option. In fact, the moderates may find themselves in a position of defending the current rules, for several changes have been proposed that would make it more difficult to replicate what the Christian Right did within the party in 1994.

The second option is to borrow a page from the play book used by the Christian Right in their successful bid to pursue their agenda—that is, pursue a course of countermobilization. The strength of the Christian Coalition was in the ability to train and turn out thousands of faithful around the state. Some moderates are banking on the same philosophy to take back the party. Lake, describing her actions in Harris County, said she is reaching out to younger women and minorities. She acknowledges that both groups represent a difficult sell, given the present message of the party. The hard-line pro-life stand of the party hurts with young women, while the crusade against affirmative action doesn't win friends in the minority community. McKenna suggests a similar strategy. Following her loss in the race for state chair, she has developed a nonprofit group aimed at generating turnout across the board, but focusing especially on conveying information (via public service announcements, for example) on how to participate in the precinct conventions held during the nomination period. McKenna argues that by emphasizing the inherent value of participation, those who have not been participating will be more likely to do so.

The principal problem with a strategy of countermobilization is that it depends on the moderates having a level of commitment as high as that of the Christian conservatives. Given the evangelical nature of the religious right's foray into politics, this seems unlikely to happen. The alternative is to mobilize a much larger group of activists, using sheer numbers to compensate for the lack of commitment. McKenna argued that if you can mobilize a force that is ten times as large as the religious right (which should not be impossible in a precinct), that force can be one tenth as active. This way, even with weak commitment and attrition at each meeting, the moderates should be able to stand up to the religious right. This might work in theory, but the actual success of such a process is far from certain. Still, given the position the moderates found themselves in following the 1994 election, this strategy does offer some possibility of victory.

The last available option for the moderates is the use of information. The key to this approach is to expose linkages between candidates and the Christian Right and to detail the full social and economic agenda of the religious right. This strategy was used successfully by opponents of the Christian Right candidates in a school board race in Klein, and across the country. In the Klein race, representatives from the Texas State Teachers Association got involved in the school board race, working to focus media attention on the beliefs of the religious right candidates. The result was a solid trouncing of those candidates in the runoff election. The strategists of the religious right are aware of this weakness, as they advise candidates to downplay strong religious language and not to feature their religious background or perspectives prominently in the campaign.[33]

This strategy also has problems, however. Dolly McKenna, in a Republican primary race for Congress against a conservative Christian candidate, was unable to get the press to focus on the religious elements of her opponent's agenda. She summed up the situation by noting, "The press simply will not cover these things."[34] While McKenna is correct in noting that the press, for a variety of reasons, is ill-equipped to deal with the Christian Right, the strategy of pursuing full press coverage is probably one that is more likely to be successful than the countermobilization strategy discussed earlier.

The Republican Party in Texas is now firmly under the influence of the religious right. The principal means of this takeover was through an invasion of the pool of activists by newly mobilized conservative Christians. Moderates in the party, caught unprepared, are now in the position of having to struggle to be heard in party discussions. In order to regain control, or even a strong voice, the moderates face a very difficult task. The best guess is that the state party will remain under the strong influence of social conservatives for at least the next decade.

Conclusion

Conservative Christians in Texas have made significant progress in advancing their agenda at the state and local levels. They have also positioned the state to be a valuable resource for national candidates. The principal vehicle for their progress has been the Republican Party. By organizing and training at the local level, the Christian Right has been able, as a numerical minority, to seize control of the party apparatus. This has given it the ability to vigorously seek changes in the party agenda, as well as in the nature of the party's activists. It has also done some damage to the party, but that damage may not be visible for some time.

While the Christian Coalition and their allies may be able to control the party and strongly influence the range of choices available to voters, they are not in a spot to dictate to the state population as a whole. While a majority in the state think of themselves as conservative Christians, the support for a strongly conservative social agenda is not present. Should the Republican Party nominate social conservatives that please the Christian Right, they are nearly certain to face defeat in the general election. The challenge, then, that faces the GOP is to hold together two factions that do not like each other. Pauken, the new state chair, knows this. He acknowledges that without the economic conservatives the party is a minority party, just as it was without the social conservatives. The rabbit that Pauken must pull from his hat is a plan that allows Weinhold and his backers, who cannot compromise on the social agenda, to work with people like Betsy Lake, Dolly McKenna, and even Senator Hutchison, who do not want to see the party bound too tightly to that conservative social agenda. If he fails, Pauken will be identified with the party's missed opportunity, and he will have to take difficult steps to rebuild the party. Should he succeed, he will probably be at the helm of the party as Texas becomes a Republican state for the first time since Reconstruction.

Notes

I would like to thank Mae Bruce, Betsy Lake, Dolly McKenna, Galen Nelson, Dick Weinhold, and Clyde Wilcox for sharing their information and insight with me. Any mistakes in the resulting interpretation are the product of the author.

   1. Although the Eagle Forum started largely as a single-issue group (opposition to the ERA), it has expanded in focus to address a broader range of concerns. Also, the Eagle Forum has PACs at the state and local levels.
   2. This is not to say there was no local-level activity. Indeed, there was. However, it was uncoordinated as a rule, and lacked impact farther up the ballot.
   3. In Texas, the precinct chairs sit on the county executive committee of the party.
   4. Convincing the membership to work in some of the less visible ways is not always easy. One of Alice Patterson's columns in the newsletter addresses the feelings of those "called by God to run for public office." The theme of her

message was that "before we rule, we must learn to serve," and she cautioned members to not seek a spot on the ballot without first learning how to work within the system ("From the Field," supplement to *Christian American*, February 1994).

5. This information is taken from *The Two Faces of the Christian Coalition* (Washington, D.C.: People for the American Way [n.d.]).

6. Technically, the Coalition is classified as a 501(c)4 nonprofit.

7. A survey of state members reported in the February supplement to the *Christian American* indicates that 85 percent of the respondents intended to vote in the 1994 Republican primary (n = 1,034). These results should be treated cautiously, as no information is available on the methods used in the survey.

8. It is interesting to note that Weinhold said a few members objected to the inclusion of Spanish on the guide, arguing that English is the language of choice in the United States. The potential gain in the highly Catholic Hispanic community far outweighs the possible loss of a few disgruntled members, a fact of which Weinhold is very aware.

9. Quoted in *The Religious Right and School Boards: 1992 and 1993* (Washington, D.C.: People for the American Way, 1993).

10. Quoted in *The Religious Right and School Boards*.

11. The September/October 1992 newsletter of the Committee for Excellence in Education (CEE) published tips on how to win school board elections. One of these tips was to not run as a slate, but rather to "campaign individually, and meet privately on a regular basis."

12. One of the defeated candidates described the TSTA as an "anti-parent organization with a socialist agenda" (*Austin American-Statesman*, 22 March 1993).

13. While observers agreed the decision about pregame prayer was the critical issue, the board simply cited the desire to have a superintendent with a different leadership style.

14. This is the exact sentiment expressed by Alice Patterson in her column in the supplement to the *Christian American*, as well as that expressed by Weinhold and other leaders.

15. These data are drawn from a state-by-state postelection report prepared by the People for the American Way.

16. According to Weinhold, the Christian Coalition distributed over two million guides in the primaries in May. The Coalition summarized candidates on both the Democratic and Republican sides, maintaining a nonpartisan appearance.

17. One example of this is Senator Hutchison. Although she was not the first choice of the religious right, since taking office she has worked to befriend that element of the constituency. At one point she acknowledged that the support of the conservative Christians had been a critical part of her reelection campaign.

18. Fourteen percent reported that they did not vote in 1990.

19. In the press accounts after the election, activists from the religious right

(including Ralph Reed) claimed that their activities has made critical differences in a number of races, including David Stockman's defeat of Jack Brooks. One of Bush's advisors gave significant credit to the mobilization of the religious right as key to Bush's victory.

20. There has been some activity on the Democratic side. In at least one U.S. House race, Christian Right support went to both a Republican and a Democratic candidate during the primaries. In addition, some moderate local activists report Christian Right activity in the Democratic Party.

21. The incumbent, Fred Meyer, stepped down rather than face a bruising fight with the religious right. He argued that he would win such a fight, but that it was in the interest of the party to avoid such a showdown.

22. Interestingly, being endorsed by an established figure may have hurt Barton, as many of those voting at the state convention were rebelling against the government in Washington and the status quo. As a member of Congress and pick of the establishment, Barton may have suffered somewhat.

23. While Pauken was the choice of many conservatives in the party, some were moderates concerned about the effect of such a conservative choice. One party worker was quoted as responding to the election with "Welcome to Armageddon" (*Dallas Morning News*, 12 June 1994). Conservative control of the administrative structure of the party was consolidated in the months after the election. Pauken replaced nearly every staffer at the state party headquarters, selecting new workers who reflected a commitment to a more conservative agenda.

24. See the Texas supplement to the February 1994 issue of the *Christian American* (note 4, above) for an example of this type of information.

25. The conservative nature of the delegates was also evident in their words and actions not passed. Several districts, upset at Hutchison's moderate views on abortion, refused to pass pro forma resolutions honoring her. In San Antonio, delegates chanted antiabortion slogans at the senator. She was also the subject of some comment for her vote to force Admiral Kelso to retire from the Navy at the two-star rank following the Tailhook scandal.

26. Lake said that she received "high profile encouragement" from Republicans to run for county chair. This quote, and much of the information below, came from a telephone interview with Betsy Lake, 13 February 1995.

27. Lake was stripped of some organizational powers, including a restriction on her ability to appoint committee members. She was also censured for encouraging homosexual Republican partisans to be active in the party.

28. *Houston Chronicle,* quoted in *Church & State,* February 1993.

29. Hotze was identified with the Christian Reconstructionist movement, being active in the Coalition on Revival. The general thrust of the Reconstructionists' argument is that the law should be based on the Bible (including the Old Testament). While it is not clear how strongly Hotze endorsed this view, many Reconstructionist leaders call for the death penalty for those who violate Biblical law, including adulterers, homosexuals, blasphemers, and incorrigible

children. Hotze described his ideas of proper government as limited to "its God-ordained role of providing justice based upon God's law, restraining wickedness, punishing evildoers and protecting the life, liberty and property of law-abiding citizens." See Joseph L. Conn, "Trouble in Texas," *Church & State* (February 1993); and *The Religious Right in the Republican Party* (Washington, D.C.: People for the American Way, 1994).

30. A similar split by a GOP leader had been discussed in Oregon.

31. Press accounts of the meeting suggest a bit of a rowdy atmosphere, with a sermon being shouted outside as Lake, Hotze, and Johnson all debated inside. Hotze also had the whole affair videotaped, saying he wanted to make it available to other conservatives who wished to get involved in precinct politics.

32. It is not exactly clear where this leaves Lake's federation of moderate Republicans and the legal party structure.

33. Recall the statement by Ralph Reed that praised the "stealth strategy" as an approach to winning elections.

34. This quote is from a telephone interview with Dolly McKenna, 20 February 1995. The religious right candidate, who lost in the general election, did receive some coverage of his religious views in the general election. In this case, his views represented good copy for the papers. The candidate, Eugene Fontenot, had been quoted as saying that "the Lord God would put it into our hearts to buy certain pieces of furniture" for his new home (*Baltimore Sun*, 3 November 1994).

References

Committee for Excellence in Education newsletter (September–October 1992).

Conn, Joseph L. 1993. "Trouble in Texas." *Church and State* (February).

Lake, Betsy. Author interview by telephone (13 February 1995).

McKenna, Dolly. Author interview by telephone (20 February 1995).

Patterson, Alice. 1994. "From the Field." *Christian American* (February).

People for the American Way. 1993. "The Religious Right and School Boards: 1992 and 1993." Washington, D.C.: People for the American Way.

———. 1994. "The Religious Right and the Republican Party." Washington, D.C.: People for the American Way.

———. n.d. "The Two Faces of the Christian Coalition." Washington, D.C.: People for the American Way.

Weinhold, Dick. Author interview by telephone (14 February 1995).

5

Oklahoma: The Christian Right and Republican Realignment

Nancy L. Bednar and Allen D. Hertzke

On November 8, 1994, Oklahoma Democrats were stunned by an unprecedented GOP tide in the midterm elections. Just two years before, the Democrats had still looked like the majority party: they held the governor's office, a 5–3 majority in the congressional delegation, and huge majorities in the state legislature. On Wednesday morning they woke up to a new reality. Republicans swept the offices of governor and lieutenant governor, picked up seats in the state legislature, and seized a remarkable 7–1 majority in the congressional delegation. Not since the 1920s had the Republicans sent a majority to Washington, and never by such a margin.

Of equal significance is the nature of that congressional delegation. All five of the victorious Republican House members and both of the senators have ties to the Christian Right and received strong backing from conservative evangelical voters. The lone surviving Democrat is conservative representative Bill Brewster. From the standpoint of the Christian Right, therefore, the elections were a smashing success; Oklahoma's delegation to Washington will be highly sympathetic to their policy goals.

What produced this outcome was a fortuitous blend of discontent, resources, and opportunity. Successful social movements need resources to channel discontent and favorable opportunities to exploit. All those came together in Oklahoma. Discontent with the drift of secular society, accentuated by deep displeasure with President Clinton (who embodied the "counterculture" in the White House), galvanized conservative evangelicals. In turn, this discontent was channeled by sophisticated Christian Right leaders and fueled by expanding resources (money, media outlets, and a volunteer corps). Finally, Christian Right activism rode the crest of a huge Republican tide. Clinton's approval ratings were low, antagonism toward the federal government was waxing hot, and such potent issues as gun control slashed at traditional Democratic loyalties.

Oklahoma indeed may offer the ideal environment for Christian Right mobilization. A conservative Bible Belt state, it gave Pat Robertson his largest primary vote (21 percent) in 1988. In addition, the 1992 presidential election results gave 43 percent of the Oklahoma vote to George Bush, not to Bill Clinton as did the rest of the nation. Oklahoma still has a huge Democratic edge in voter registration, but many are religious traditionalists and social conservatives. Christian Right mobilization, therefore, had the potential to cut deeply into traditionally Democratic voting habits, which is precisely what occurred. To the extent that such underlying forces move down the ticket, as we think they may, then further Democratic erosion will follow. Thus religious dynamics have helped to solidify a Republican realignment that appears to be occurring in the state.

The Christian Right as a Social Movement

The Christian Right can accurately be described as a social movement engaging in electoral politics. To better understand the dynamics of this effort, it is helpful to draw upon scholarship in the field of social movements. The dominant stream of research is resource mobilization theory (McCarthy and Zald 1973, 1977). The most recent advance and refinement of this theory is that of Doug McAdam (1982), whose political process model argues that anything that members of a social movement wish to accomplish must occur within the framework of the political process. McAdam argues that social movements develop in response to political opportunities and decline when circumstances are less favorable to their development.

What made the outcome of the 1994 congressional elections particularly significant is that the Christian Right had been presumed dead. The misunderstanding of the development and decline of social movements led observers to bury something not yet dead. Many scholars argued that after the 1988 elections the Christian Right was in decline (Bruce 1988; Wilcox 1992). Hurt by the televangelist scandals and the failed presidential candidacy of Pat Robertson, divided when Jerry Falwell endorsed George Bush over his ministerial colleague Robertson, it looked as though the Christian Right was in retreat. The 1992 elections made things look even worse for the Christian Right. Accused of fostering the divisive atmosphere at the Republican Convention, the Christian Right was blamed for Bush's defeat. Bill Clinton's campaign rhetoric indicated that he was a more centrist Democrat, and Clinton's membership in a Southern Baptist Convention church amplified the centrist image the Clinton campaign wanted to display. Also, Clinton's campaign focus of "It's the Economy, Stupid!" and the success of this approach seemed to indicate that the troublesome social issues raised by the Christian Right were no longer as salient as they had been during the 1980s.

What made such a difference between 1992 and 1994? One reason is that the demise of the Christian Right was prematurely declared. Wilcox (1992) noted that the issues that mobilized the Christian Right remained salient to those involved in the movement. Also, Kellstedt, Green, Guth, and Smidt (1994) contend that Clinton got it wrong and "It's the Culture, Stupid!" Kellstedt et al. argue that "cultural affinities constitute the long-term basis of electoral alignments, introducing fundamental values into politics and structuring the debate over them, while economic forces generate temporary disruptions of these culturally defined alignments" (28). Using this argument, Clinton's victory was the result of a temporary economic disruption and not due to the demise of the Christian Right.

In addition, in the period from 1988 to 1994 Christian Right leaders began to realize the importance of Congress to their policy goals. They did not have the sympathetic presence of Ronald Reagan in the White House. Moreover, members of Congress were generally unresponsive to their agenda. Dobson and Bauer (1990) relate how members of Congress could be inundated by telephone calls and letters from conservative Christians on a particular issue and then vote against the conservative Christians. Hertzke (1988) and Moen (1989) also relate the problems that conservative Christian lobbyists had when dealing with hostile members of Congress. The problem was lack of access. Dobson and Bauer argued that this was because Christians were not holding members of Congress accountable, and they began to urge conservative Christians to get rid of members of Congress who did not support their agenda.

This realization was coupled with increasing sophistication of the Christian Right social movement organizations. Pat Robertson, using the newly mobilized troops from his unsuccessful presidential campaign, founded the Christian Coalition to give the Christian Right a vehicle to interact with the political process. Ralph Reed, the Coalition's executive director, began organizing chapters in the fifty states, as well as a lobbying office in Washington D.C. James Dobson is the director of Focus on the Family, the most prominent parachurch organization within conservative Christianity. Gary Bauer, a former Reagan appointee, is head of the Family Research Council, a conservative Christian lobbying and research organization.

The aforementioned organizations, particularly Focus on the Family, provide the indigenous organization strength that McAdam (1982) argues is necessary for successful social movement insurgency. McAdam argues that some of the necessary components of organizational strength are leaders, members, and a communications network. Dobson is widely respected by all segments of the Christian Right. Moen (1992) argues that if one wanted to name a nationwide leader for the Christian Right, Dobson would be the best candidate for the job. Moen also states that Dobson is wary of accepting such a role. Dobson is the host of a successful radio program, "Focus on the Family," that airs several times a day on Christian radio stations throughout the nation. In addition, Focus publishes a monthly magazine, also called *Focus on the Family*, which it distributes to anyone who wishes to receive it, free of charge. Focus also publishes magazines for children and teens, teachers, doctors, pastors, and most recently, single parents. The ministry of Focus has become more politically involved as time has passed. In 1986 Focus added an additional magazine to its publication list. This magazine, available for a twenty-dollar subscription fee, is called *Focus on the Family Citizen*. *Citizen* concentrates most of its attention on the Washington scene, discussing issues, legislation, and members of Congress. In addition, Dobson produces a monthly church bulletin insert that talks about marriage, child rearing, and other family issues. The bottom of the insert contains a two- to three-sentence political alert concerning family issues. These inserts are distributed to evangelical, fundamentalist, charismatic, and pentecostal churches throughout the nation. The radio program and publications of Focus provide an excellent communications network that allows the dissemination of information to members of the Christian Right.

Other social movement organizations that help to mobilize the Christian Right include the Christian Coalition and Concerned Women for America. The Christian Coalition, because of its affiliation with Robertson, has access to his "700 Club" television show that airs on the Family Channel and Christian television stations across the nation. The 700 Club has recently expanded its programming to include thirty minutes of news at the beginning of every program. The 700 Club news devotes at least half of its air time to Washington. Conservative members of Congress are featured on the program. The 700 Club news is not done in the soundbite fashion made famous by the major networks and CNN, but spends several minutes developing each story. Robertson often puts his own spin on the stories that are reported. Concerned Women for America is the ministry of Beverly LaHaye. Her hourlong radio program, carried on Christian radio throughout the country, discusses issues of importance to Christian families. Concerned Women for America is also an organization with chapters in churches throughout the nation.

When the communications networks of Focus, 700 Club, and Concerned Women for America are taken in total, they provide a powerful means of disseminating information to conservative Christians throughout the country. In addition, they perform the function that McAdam calls cognitive liberation. In the work of Piven and Cloward (1979) cognitive liberation is described as a three-stage process. The first stage is that the system loses legitimacy because the system is perceived to be wrong. The second stage is a change from a fatalistic attitude to one of asserting one's rights as a citizen. The last stage is a sense of efficacy, a perception that it is possible for members of the group to change their position. One of the primary functions of these social movement organizations has been to convince conservative Christians to become engaged in the political process. After the first manifestation of Christian Right activities in the 1920s, fundamentalists determined that withdrawal from the political world to focus on the spiritual world was the appropriate response for Christians (Wilcox 1992). The process of cognitive liberation is necessary to reengage these people with the political process. The rhetoric of these groups is designed to convince Christians that it is God's will for them to become involved in the political process.

Predicting Congressional Elections

Most literature on congressional elections points to the importance of local and candidate factors in the midterm, with at best modest influence from national forces (Tufte 1975; Ragsdale 1980; Fiorina 1981; Jacobson and Kernell 1983; Jacobson 1990; Herrnson 1995). Models based on these and other factors have generally predicted pretty well the loss of seats to the president's party in the midterm. However, as Jacobson (1994) noted, these models predicted a twelve- to twenty-seat pickup for the Republicans rather than the fifty-two seats they actually won. How could they have been so wrong? Jacobson suggests that the reason had to do with how successful the Republicans were in nationalizing the elections.

Our analysis of the Oklahoma case suggests that the Christian Right played an important role in nationalizing these campaigns. For some time scholars in religion and politics have argued that political scientists need to include religious factors when exploring American politics (Leege and Kellstedt 1993). If the political scientists modeling the congressional elections had included Christian Right mobilization as a variable in their equations, they would have generated a prediction that would have conformed more closely to the reality of the results. Indeed, Christian Right social movement organizations have been working to nationalize congressional elections since the late 1980s, using national Christian media to highlight their message. The election of Clinton and his subsequent actions gave the Christian Right the tools to nationalize the 1994 elections. It is impossible to overstate how abhorrent Bill Clinton is to the Christian Right. Appointments of Lani Guinier, Roberta Achenberg, and Joycelyn Elders; executive orders on abortion, fetal tissue research, and testing of RU-486; and the gays-in-the-military fiasco graphically demonstrated how far Clinton's values are from the values of the Christian Right. The debate on national health care, with the inclusion of abortion as a part of reproductive services in the Clinton plan, looked to conservative Christians like they would be forced to subsidize medical procedures with which they did not agree. As Kellstedt et al. (1994) argue, this is a cultural divide between people with radically different values. The necessity of stopping Clinton's policy proposals turned the spotlight on the other policy-making branch of government, the Congress.

In addition, Christian Right social movement leaders talked a lot about representative democracy, with a special emphasis on the notion of representation. Christian Right leaders were easily able to present Clinton as unable to represent conservative Christians, and when Congress went along with Clinton's proposals, these leaders were able to argue that Congress did not represent them either. Christian Right leaders then encouraged their supporters to find candidates who could descriptively stand for them and to work to get them elected. Since this was happening on national Christian media, the right candidate, in any of the congressional or senatorial seats being contested nationwide, was an individual who was either a conservative Christian or could speak to Christian Right concerns, as we see in the case studies below.

The Oklahoma Prelude: 1993 Special Election

In early 1993, longtime Democratic incumbent Glenn English resigned his House seat representing the sprawling, rural Sixth District in western Oklahoma. After a primary and runoff election to determine the nominees, the special election for the open seat pitted Democrat Dan Webber, a staffer for Senator David Boren in Washington, against Republican Frank Lucas, a member of the Oklahoma House of Representatives and a rancher. The campaign was hard fought. Senator Boren provided assistance to his protege with a personal endorsement, several commercials, funding, and campaign appearances. The national Republicans, sensing the possibility of another congressional victory in response to the growing unpopularity of President Bill Clinton, provided assistance. Several Republican members of Congress came to Oklahoma to campaign on Lucas's behalf.

An experienced vote-getter, Frank Lucas was also very conservative and appealed to evangelicals. Thus the campaign provided an excellent test of the Christian Right's electoral aspirations. Though the Oklahoma Christian Coalition was then still in its infancy, the national organization prepared voter guides for it to distribute. While these Christian Coalition voter guides are ostensibly nonpartisan, the issues selected push obvious hot buttons for conservative evangelicals and make the "right" choice obvious. Crude, oversimplified, but devastatingly effective, these guides also illustrate the role of strategic choices in the selection of issues (for example, gun control was one of the issues included on voter guides in 1993 and throughout Oklahoma in 1994). The Christian Coalition claims to have distributed over 100,000 guides during the special election, and also to have participated in some telephone banks and other get-out-the-vote activities. Lucas won the election, and the 5–3 Democratic delegation was even at 4–4.

During the Webber–Lucas contest in the Sixth District, rumors began to swirl that the state's senior senator, David Boren, was tired of the Washington rat race and was interested in the presidency of the University of Oklahoma. Boren's subsequent resignation set a chain of events in motion. Two veteran members of Congress, Republican James Inhofe and Democrat Dave McCurdy, gave up their seats to run for the Senate. This opened up two new seats, creating fresh opportunities for the Christian Right.

The Primaries

Two primaries stand out for their significance. With Inhofe vacating his position in the First District, the open seat attracted a wealth of contenders that looked like a who's who of Tulsa Republicans. The list included a former state party chair, a state house member, a former mayor, a county treasurer, and another well-known activist. All of these people were strategic politicians (Jacobson and Kernell 1983) waiting for the right shot at an open seat. But the person with the greatest name recognition was Steve Largent, former Tulsa University and Seattle Seahawk all-star wide receiver. Largent, in Canon's (1993) classification, is an ambitious amateur who ran when the chance to win looked good. With deep roots in the evangelical world, including youth evangelization through the Fellowship of Christian Athletes, Largent is well connected to the Christian Right. He has appeared on James Dobson's "Focus on the Family" radio show and Pat Robertson's "700 Club." Largent's church, a nondenominational fundamentalist fellowship, is centered in the top five Republican precincts in the district. In addition, Largent was a formidable candidate—telegenic, a dynamic speaker, and an energetic campaigner. Some were concerned that his extreme position on abortion, which he believes should only be allowed to save the life of the mother, might hurt him. Yet he won the primary outright, gaining over 50 percent of the vote in a field of six quality challengers.

Largent's methods were the perfect combination of money, expertise, technology, and an army of volunteers. Largent's campaign manager, formerly affiliated with a conservative family policy council, used a high-tech approach to the primary. Using data from previous elections they identified Republicans most likely to vote and contacted them. They organized 80 of the top 100 Republican precincts and worked them systematically. Each precinct captain organized a phone bank that polled the precinct, using blind identification to see who the voter favored. Every undecided was visited door to door, with Largent personally walking the ten most Republican precincts. In addition, every undecided was contacted by phone before the primary in a get-out-the-vote effort. The marriage of high-tech expertise and volunteer activity enabled Largent to avoid a runoff.

Meanwhile, in the Second District the Christian Right backed a Democratic challenger to liberal eight-term representative Mike Synar. In 1992 Synar had been wounded in a bitter primary challenge. In 1994 he found himself again in a runoff, this time against Virgil Cooper, a retired school principal, Baptist lay leader, and political neophyte. Cooper campaigned by driving his pickup truck around the district and sticking business cards on the windshields of cars. Cooper, who had no full-time campaign staff and personally spent just under $17,000 in the race, defeated Synar, who had spent hundreds of thousands of dollars in his effort to keep his seat.

Cooper became something of a folk hero in his quixotic challenge to the incumbent, and he received national media attention. Not so well appreciated was the role of the Christian Right. Not only did Cooper fill out the Christian Coalition survey, but sources at the Christian Coalition also state that he wrote on the top of it, "Check me out, I'm what you're looking for." The Christian Coalition claims to have distributed 110,000 voter guides the week before the election with results that were devastating to Synar. The issues selected were hot-button issues for the district, including tax increases, school prayer, abortion, teaching homosexuality as acceptable, homosexuals in the military, and gun control. There was nothing subtle in how the Coalition presented the candidates; on every issue, Cooper and Synar were polar opposites. The Christian Coalition voter guide reinforced the notion that Synar was out of touch with his district. Notably, the primary also demonstrated the possibility of a Christian Right Democrat, at least in Oklahoma.

The General Election

By the time of the general election the Republican congressional lineup was solidly affiliated with the Christian Right. In the First District was Steve Largent. In the Second District was Tom Coburn, a well-known Muskogee physician and Baptist Sunday school teacher. The Third District was the only one with no credible Republican candidate. In the Fourth District was J. C. Watts, an African American conservative Republican and youth pastor at a local Southern Baptist church. In the Fifth District was Ernest Istook, a conservative Mormon with strong Christian Right backing, who won without a Democratic opponent. In the Sixth District was Frank Lucas, who posted an easy win against a weak Democratic opponent six months after his special election victory.

In the First District Largent had no trouble disposing of Stuart Price, the Democratic nominee. Price's campaign acknowledged the role of the Christian Right and conceded that segment of the vote to Largent. Price's volunteer coordinator demonstrated a lack of knowledge of the district when he assumed that the conservative Christian vote could be easily dismissed. The first district of Oklahoma, encompassing Tulsa and the surrounding suburban areas, is home to several large charismatic Christian ministries. Notable among these are Oral Roberts University, Kenneth Hagin's Rhema Church and Bible Training Center, and Willie George's Church on the Move and related children's ministries, including the "Gospel Bill" television program. Largent's volunteer coordinator stated that eight to nine hundred people had performed volunteer work for the candidate. In addition to volunteers from Largent's church, a huge corps of students from Oral Roberts University, working to fulfill an American Government class requirement, aided in the effort. An intriguing consequence was that a sizable number of African American students worked in Largent's campaign. So plentiful were Largent's volunteers that some went to help with Inhofe's Senate campaign, with the blessing of Largent.

Largent's campaign also indicates how the movement's growing sophistication overcame what Wilcox (1992) identified as doctrinal antipathies between fundamentalists and charismatic/pentecostals that in the past undermined cooperative efforts. The fundamentalist members of Largent's church had no difficulty working with the charismatic students from Oral Roberts University. Additional evidence comes from the J. C. Watts campaign. Watts, a Southern Baptist youth minister, was the guest speaker at the Sunday night service at a nondenominational pentecostal church. The pentecostal pastor included Watts in all aspects of the service. One of the members of the pentecostal church was a staffer for Watts's campaign, and the pastor spoke of the role the young man was filling for Watts with approval. One of the indications of the maturing of the Christian Right as a social movement is the evidence of the ability to check doctrinal differences at the door and work in political campaigns together.

The races in the Second and Fourth Districts were the pivotal races that changed the partisan makeup of the House delegation. Dr. Tom Coburn, the Republican nominee, emerged from a primary among three candidates equally acceptable to the Christian Right. The Coburn campaign operated from the beginning under the assumption that Synar was the true opponent. Cooper's victory in the runoff completely blew their strategy and left them with a dilemma. How could they say negative things about a nice, 71-year-old fellow Christian? Cooper's inexperience ultimately caught up with him, and he made several mistakes that made it easier for the Coburn campaign to question his competence. The most notable mistake Cooper made was to announce to the press that Coburn was going to Washington to sign the Contract With America, and that the Contract was terrible for the Second District. Tom

Cole, the political consultant working with the Coburn campaign, correctly noted that signing the Contract would be disastrous in the heavily Democratic Second, and told Coburn not to do it. Coburn was able to announce that he had no intention of signing the Contract, but that he was creating a special contract between him and the Second District. Cooper appeared to be uninformed and looked like he was making false charges against Coburn. This was the closest congressional race in the state, and Coburn won, 52 percent to 48 percent.

The race in the Fourth District also pitted an underfunded Democrat, David Perryman, against a well-funded and well-organized Watts. The Christian Coalition targeted this district as one of the most competitive. They distributed voter guides, and Watts campaigned in evangelical circles. When attacked during the campaign for financial irregularities, Watts had the pastor of his church make a commercial for him attesting to his good character. When questioned about his conservative views, Watts's response was that he is not a conservative because he is a Republican, he is a conservative because he is a Christian. Watts had several national Republican leaders, including George Bush, appear on his behalf. What made this campaign so unusual is that the Democrat, Perryman, attempted to interject race into the campaign. He aired a television spot that featured a picture of a young Watts sporting a large Afro haircut, which drew heavy criticism by Democratic African American leaders. Watts handled the ad with the quip that he worked hard for his Afro and that at the time he was leader of the Fellowship of Christian Athletes. He prevailed, and the delegation count was 6–1 Republican.

The Senate race pitted Fourth District Democratic Representative Dave McCurdy against Republican representative Jim Inhofe. McCurdy was the darling of the Fourth District, pictured as the ideal representative (Copeland 1994). However, McCurdy had never faced difficult electoral challenges while running for reelection. Inhofe, on the other hand, had never had an easy election in his twenty years in politics. Inhofe's sister, Joanne Johnson of Tulsa, is identified by knowledgeable Republicans as one of the most important Christian Right activists in the state, and Inhofe had the support of the Christian Right. Christian Coalition voter guides painted a stark contrast between the two candidates, and one that depicted McCurdy as far more liberal than he actually is. Aiding Inhofe's campaign was a vigorous National Rifle Association barrage against McCurdy that included a vicious television spot by Charlton Heston. Here we see how other issues dovetailed with Christian Right mobilization. In an exit poll of the Fourth District some 40 percent of the voters said they were gun owners, and of those two thirds voted for Inhofe. The fact that the Christian Coalition chose as one of its issues "banning ownership of legal firearms" suggests a strategic marriage of disparate elements of opposition to McCurdy. Inhofe defeated McCurdy by fifteen points, and McCurdy was unable to carry the Fourth District, which had sent him to the House for seven terms. The transformation was complete: the delegation was 7–1 Republican.

All told the Christian Coalition distributed over half a million voter guides that aided the GOP cause. The Christian Coalition distributes questionnaires covering forty to fifty topics and creates its voter guides from this information. The issues included on the voter guides are tailored to the individual state, selecting issues that are salient in that location. The issues included were abortion, gun control, federal tax relief for families, and special rights for homosexuals. In addition, the Resource Institute of Oklahoma, affiliated with Dobson's Focus on the Family, produced voter guides distributed through inserts in the two major newspapers in the state. Like the Christian Coalition materials, the Resource Institute guides were blunt instruments designed to paint a stark contrast between liberal and conservative candidates.

The Merging of Social Movement and Political Party

The surge in Christian Right mobilization was an important factor in Republican successes. But it is necessary to note that this surge was effective only because of the growing organizational sophistication of the Oklahoma Republican Party. Thus the merging of these two forces produced the rather dramatic outcome.

There has been a debate in the political science world concerning the condition of political parties. For example, Wattenberg (1986) argues that American political parties have declined in the period from 1952 to 1984, while Sabato (1988) argues that parties will remain a viable force in politics. Gibson, Cotter, Bibby, and Huckshorn (1983, 1985) argue that even though party influence in the electorate has weakened over the last thirty years, party organizational strength has increased. They present various measures of organizational strength, including a full-time headquarters, full-time paid state party chair, and paid staff. Sabato (1988) concedes that one current weakness of political parties is a lack of volunteers to accomplish the tasks of the party. Members of the Christian Right, as church members, have a strong volunteer ethic, because that is how most church work is accomplished, and members of the Christian Right carry that ethic to the party when they become involved. Salmore and Salmore (1989) note that Republicans often pay for tasks that Democrats have volunteers perform. The infusion of members of the Christian Right into Republican Party politics provides the volunteers needed to make the organization run. The infusion of members of the Christian Right into the Republican Party may equalize the lack of volunteers that Salmore and Salmore (1989) note. In addition, volunteers allow precious campaign funds to be used more effectively. Hershey (1993) argues that group involvement is not necessarily detrimental to political parties, and can be beneficial, especially in terms of fundraising. Members of the Christian Right, as church members, have the habit of contributing to causes in which they believe, and this habit also moves into the party with Christian Right activism.

While the Christian Right provided an infusion of volunteers, the Republican Party provided the expertise necessary to effectively use the volunteers. Clinton Key, chair of the Oklahoma Republican Party, and Tom Cole, a Republican political consultant, former chair of the Oklahoma Republican Party, and former executive director of the National Republican Congressional Committee, are credited with reinvigorating the Republican Party. The Oklahoma Republican Party has the paid staff and stable headquarters that Gibson, Cotter, Bibby, and Huckshorn (1983, 1985) argue are necessary for a party that is organizationally strong. Since becoming chair in 1989, Key worked to recruit and train Republican challengers for various positions. With the exception of the Third District, there was a quality candidate running in each of the other congressional districts. Cole, a savvy political operative who knows Oklahoma politics, consulted on the campaigns of Largent, Coburn in the Second, Watts in the Fourth, and Lucas in the Sixth, in addition to the governor's race. In addition, the three open seat candidates hired political professionals to run their campaigns, contrary to earlier findings that more "Democratic than Republican campaigns are managed professionally" (Herrnson 1995, 64). The work of these paid professionals demonstrates the importance of having figures who facilitate party building and weave together Christian conservative concerns with a broader Republican agenda.

A third key figure, whom Cole calls "the heart and soul of the Republican Party in Oklahoma," is Senator Don Nickles. Since his first election in 1980, Nickles has been identified as a national Christian Right leader, yet he can move within all of the components of the Oklahoma Republican Party and be accepted. Most important, Nickles has worked to invigorate the Republican Party, lending the expertise of his staff to other Republican campaigns and campaigning himself for all the Republican challengers who requested his help.

How "Christian Right" Were These Candidates?

While strategic Republican players assisted the candidates in Oklahoma, this does not diminish the importance of the religious identity of these new members of Congress. All of the Republican congressional victors took conservative stands on social and economic issues. All present themselves as pro-family and pro-life. All share the basic critique of the culture one finds in conservative Christian publications.

Two vignettes give an added flavor of the evangelical dimension in the election. The first was not an electoral event, but a celebration of the twenty-fifth anniversary of a prominent pastor in a large pentecostal church in Oklahoma City. With some five thousand in attendance, the special guests included Roman Catholic Senator Don Nickles, Mormon Representative Ernest Istook, and other members of the Oklahoma state legislature. In a display of coalition building, Istook was introduced as one who "shares the values we hold dear." This is remarkable when considering the view of many evangelicals that the Mormon Church is a cult. When Senator Nickles was introduced as the soon-to-be senior senator of Oklahoma, he received a standing ovation. Such a display of affection by pentecostals for a Catholic would have been inconceivable a generation ago. The next vignette occurred at the University of Oklahoma's Lloyd Noble Center, where a youth evangelism crusade was conducted by rising evangelistic star Steve Russo. Watts, Largent, and Nickles all spoke to an enthusiastic crowd, and all emphasized for the youth the necessity of carrying your faith into all aspects of your life, including politics.

There was also a decided religious style to these campaigns. In these very competitive races none of the main Republican congressional candidates campaigned on Sunday. The schedulers for Coburn, Largent, and Watts stated that they scheduled nothing on Sunday, because it was a day for worship and family, and Cooper, the Christian Right Democrat, did not campaign on Sunday either. In addition, many of the watch parties served no alcohol. Even though there were candidates from the state house and other races sharing in the Watts celebration, the party was still dry. One campaign manager from another campaign went to the bar and brought in a beer in a paper cup, and was worried that someone would discover what was in the cup. And at Watts's party, his pastor gave an invocation after the victory was announced.

Finally, exit polls found evidence for a continuing realignment of evangelicals to the Republican Party, if not in registration, certainly in voting. In the Fourth District, for example, 76 percent of the born-again sample voted for Watts, and 74 percent for Inhofe. While many evangelicals remain registered Democrats, they have been voting for Republican presidential candidates for some time. What we now see is this pattern moving down the ticket. Campbell (1992) argues that during the Reagan years, Reagan's coattails were wasted because there were no candidates available to take advantage of them. The 1994 elections in Oklahoma demonstrated that if there were quality Republican candidates who run savvy campaigns, those Reagan Democrats could be persuaded to vote Republican for congressional and statewide candidates. Clinton Key, the Republican Party chair, reported that more people came to him during this election cycle and told him they had changed their registration to Republican than ever before.

The election of 1996 will determine whether a Republican realignment is indeed occurring. If Republicans consolidate these gains and extend them to the state legislative level, realignment will have occurred in Oklahoma. While religious forces are but one of several factors in that potential realignment, and they certainly have the potential to cut both ways, in Oklahoma in 1994 they were powerful forces indeed.

References

Bond, Jon R., Cary Covington, and Richard Fleisher. 1985. "Explaining Challenger Quality in Congressional Elections." *Journal of Politics* 47: 510–29.

Bruce, Steve. 1988. *The Rise and Fall of the New Christian Right.* New York: Oxford University Press.

Campbell, James E. 1992. "The Presidential Pulse of Congressional Elections, 1868–1988." Pp. 49–72 in *The Atomistic Congress: An Interpretation of Congressional Change,* ed. Allen D. Hertzke and Ronald M. Peters, Jr. Armonk, N.Y.: M. E. Sharpe, Inc.

Canon, David T. 1993. "Sacrificial Lambs or Strategic Politicians? Political Amateurs in U.S. House Elections." *American Journal of Political Science* 37: 1119–41.

Copeland, Gary W. 1994. "The Closing of Political Minds: Noncandidates in the 4th District of Oklahoma." Pp. 136–49 in *Who Runs for Congress: Ambition, Context, and Candidate Emergence,* ed. Thomas A. Kazee. Washington D.C.: CQ Press.

Dobson, James, and Gary L. Bauer. 1990. *Children at Risk: The Battle for the Hearts and Minds of Our Kids.* Dallas: Word Publishing.

Fiorina, Morris P. 1981. *Retrospective Voting in American National Elections.* New Haven: Yale University Press.

Gibson, James L., Cornelius P. Cotter, John F. Bibby, and Robert J. Huckshorn. 1983. "Assessing Party Organizational Strength." *American Journal of Political Science* 27: 193–222.

————. 1985. "Whither the Local Parties? A Cross-Sectional and Longitudinal Analysis of the Strength of Party Organizations." *American Journal of Political Science* 29: 13–60.

Herrnson, Paul S. 1995. *Congressional Elections: Campaigning at Home and in Washington.* Washington D.C.: CQ Press.

Hershey, Marjorie Randon. 1993. "Citizen's Groups and Political Parties in the United States." *Annals of the American Academy of Political and Social Sciences* 528 (July): 142–56.

Hertzke, Allen D. 1988. *Representing God in Washington: The Role of Religious Lobbies in the American Polity.* Knoxville: University of Tennessee Press.

Jacobson, Gary C. 1990. *The Electoral Origins of Divided Government: Competition in the U.S. House Elections, 1946–1988.* Boulder, Colo.: Westview Press.

————. 1994. "The 1994 Midterm: Why the Models Missed It." Extension of Remarks, *Legislative Studies Group Newsletter* (December): University of Colorado-Boulder.

Jacobson, Gary C., and Samuel Kernell. 1983. *Strategy and Choice in Congressional Elections,* 2nd edition. New Haven: Yale University Press.

Kellstedt, Lyman A., John C. Green, James L. Guth, Corwin E. Smidt. 1994. "It's the Culture, Stupid! 1992 and Our Political Future," *First Things* 42: 28–33.

Koopman, Douglass L. 1994. "The 1994 House Election: A Republican View." Extension of Remarks, *Legislative Studies Group Newletter* (December): University of Colorado-Boulder.

Leege, David C., and Lyman A. Kellstedt. 1993. *Rediscovering the Religious Factor in American Politics.* Armonk, N.Y.: M. E. Sharpe.

McAdam, Doug. 1982. *Political Process and the Development of Black Insurgency.* Chicago: University of Chicago Press.

McCarthy, John D., and Mayer N. Zald. 1973. *The Trend of Social Movements in America: Professionalization and Resource Mobilization.* Morristown, N.J.: General Learning Press.

————. 1977. "Resource Mobilization and Social Movements: A Partial Theory." *American Journal of Sociology* 82 (no. 6): 1212–41.

Moen, Matthew C. 1989. *The Christian Right and Congress.* Tuscaloosa: University of Alabama Press.

————. 1992. *The Transformation of the Christian Right.* Tuscaloosa: University of Alabama Press.

Piven, Frances Fox, and Richard A. Cloward. 1979. *Poor People's Movements.* New York: Vintage Books.

Pitkin, Hanna Fenichel. 1967. *The Concept of Representation.* Berkeley: The University of California Press.

Ragsdale, Lyn. 1980. "The Fiction of Congressional Elections as Presidential Events." *American Politics Quarterly* 8: 375–98.

Sabato, Larry J. 1988. *The Party's Just Begun: Shaping Political Parties for America's Future.* Glenview, Ill.: Scott, Foresman/Little, Brown College Division.

Salmore, Barbara G., and Stephen A. Salmore. 1989. *Candidates, Parties and Campaigns: Electoral Politics in America,* 2nd edition. Washington D.C.: CQ Press.

Tufte, Edward R. 1975. "Determinants of the Outcomes of Midterm Congressional Elections." *American Political Science Review* 69: 812–26.

Wattenberg, Martin P. 1986. *The Decline of American Political Parties, 1952–1984.* Cambridge, Mass.: Harvard University Press.

Wilcox, Clyde. 1992. *God's Warriors: The Christian Right in Twentieth-Century America.* Baltimore: Johns Hopkins University Press.

6

Virginia: God, Guns, and Oliver North

Mark J. Rozell and Clyde Wilcox

In early 1994, Virginia Senator Chuck Robb appeared to be the most vulnerable Democratic incumbent to seek reelection. Once touted as a potential Democratic presidential candidate, Robb spent much of his first term defending himself against charges that he had attended parties where drugs were used, had engaged in extramarital affairs, and had known that his aides had possessed illegally taped cellular telephone conversations of longtime rival Governor Douglas Wilder. *Playboy* magazine had featured an account of his alleged affair with Tai Collins, replete with pictorial. Robb's own account of their encounter—that they had disrobed, drank a bottle of champagne, and then stopped at a backrub—struck most Virginians as unlikely.

Robb's difficulties were even more evident when he launched his campaign in March 1994. He issued a letter to Virginia Democratic leaders and activists in which he admitted to having had extramarital sex, although he denied on other occasions that this contact had ever included intercourse. This fine distinction made him no friends among moral conservatives, who disapproved of any extramarital sexual contact, or among liberals, who found his behavior sexist and his account implausible.

Yet on election night, Robb survived a nationwide Republican tidal wave to win a surprisingly easy victory over Republican candidate Oliver North. North spent approximately $20 million, more than four times Robb's total, and had a huge volunteer army that covered the state with placards. He had the strong endorsements of Reverend Jerry Falwell and Reverend Pat Robertson and could count on the organizational efforts of the Christian Coalition, the Family Foundation, and the National Rifle Association. In the home state of the former Moral Majority and the Christian Coalition, however, North failed to carry Lynchburg (home of Falwell and the former Moral Majority) or Chesapeake, and only narrowly carried Virginia Beach (home of Robertson and the Christian Coalition). He lost the populous suburbs surrounding Washington, D.C., by a substantial margin.

How Virginia Republicans came to nominate perhaps the only person in Virginia who could not beat Chuck Robb is a story of political institutions and Christian Right mobilization. The consequence of this mobilization is a split party that may lose the other Senate seat in 1996, as conservative Christians back a challenger to incumbent John Warner.

The Context

In his seminal *Southern Politics in State and Nation* in 1949, V. O. Key, Jr., described Virginia as a "political museum piece." He wrote that "of all the American states, Virginia can lay claim to the most thorough control by an oligarchy" (Key 1949, 19). At the time, Virginia politics was dominated by the Democratic political machine of Harry F. Byrd, who headed but did not rule it. Byrd served as governor of Virginia from 1926 to 1930, and as U.S. senator from 1933 until he retired in 1965. He assembled his machine from the county courthouse organizations of the landed gentry, who preferred stability over economic growth and were fiercely committed to racial segregation (Barone and Ujifusa 1993).

The Byrd machine succeeded by restricting participation. Long after the demise of the organization, the state holds its gubernatorial and other statewide elections in odd-numbered years. This has long meant that organized interests can exert disproportionate influence in the general election.

Republicans nominate their candidates in large, statewide conventions that allow almost any citizen to participate who is willing to pledge to support the party nominees and pay a registration fee. These conventions select the candidates and pass the planks of the party platform. As the Republican Party has grown, attendance at these conventions has grown. In 1994, more than fourteen thousand Virginians descended on Richmond to select the party nominee for U.S. Senate.

These party nominating conventions also favor candidates backed by organized interests, and in the past fifteen years this has meant the Christian Right and the pro-life movement. Ralph Reed, head of the Christian Coalition, told us that "the caucus-convention nominating process in the [Virginia] Republican Party is unusual in that it does tend to give [our] grassroots activists a greater voice than they have in primaries" (Reed interview).

Although the Christian Right has great influence on Republican nomination politics, this has frequently led to the defeat of Republican candidates. The urban corridor that includes the D.C. suburbs has a majority of the state's population, and the northern Virginia suburbs are distinctive in their affluence, their relatively low levels of religious involvement, their social liberalism, and in their many Republican voters. Many of these Republican voters are unwilling to vote for candidates backed by the Christian Right, and have defected in large numbers to moderate Democrats in the past several elections.

Virginia is a heavily Protestant state, full of Baptist and Methodist churches. Surveys show that nearly half of the state's residents profess an affiliation with an evangelical denomination and that more than 10 percent identify as fundamentalists. More than 40 percent of likely voters indicate that they believe that the Bible is literally true. The northern Virginia area has sizable numbers of Catholics, and even non-Judeo-Christian immigrants. John Green notes that "Virginia is one of the most cosmopolitan and diverse of the southern states, which are the most religious overall" (Green interview, 17 January 1995).

During the late 1970s and early 1980s, Virginia was home to the Moral Majority, a Christian Right organization based in the Baptist Bible Fellowship that was centered mainly in the fundamentalist right. Reverend Jerry Falwell, former head of the Moral Majority, lives in Lynchburg, and his huge congregation is a major institution in that region of the state. In the 1990s, Virginia is head to the Christian Coalition, an organization which grew out of Marion (Pat) Robertson's failed presidential campaign. Although Robertson's campaign appealed mainly to charismatics and pentecostals, the Christian Coalition has sought to build bridges to other religious groups.

Not surprisingly, then, the Christian Right has long exerted influence in Virginia politics. In 1978, conservative Christians attended the Democratic Convention to back G. Conoly Phillips, a Virginia Beach car dealer who said that God had called him to seek the Democratic nomination for the U.S. Senate. Phillips professed surprise that the call had specified the Democratic Party, but his campaign mentor Pat Robertson may have urged that choice based on his father's many years as Democratic senator from Virginia. Phillips lost the nomination, although his strong showing surprised many observers. A few Christian conservatives participated in the Republican nominating convention, backing the eventual nominee, former state GOP chair Richard Obenshain. Obenshain was

killed in a plane crash soon after the convention, and the party committee eventually selected John Warner as the nominee.[1]

The Republican realignment took on metaphysical overtones in the
1980s, as the Christian Right moved into the Republican Party. In 1981
the Moral Majority was credited with sending some seven hundred delegates to the Republican nominating convention, primarily to support
lieutenant governor candidate Guy Farley, a former Byrd Democrat
turned born-again Republican. Farley lost the nomination, but Falwell
later endorsed the Republican ticket led by Attorney General Marshall
Coleman. Yet Falwell is not popular in Virginia, and in 1981 as in all
elections since, Democrats ran ads linking the Republican candidate to
Falwell and the Christian Right. Democrat Chuck Robb won the governorship easily, and the rest of the Democratic ticket triumphed as well.

In 1985, Christian conservatives mobilized behind the candidacy of
Wyatt B. Durrette. Durrette took a strong pro-life stand, opposing abortions even in cases of rape and incest and supporting a Constitutional
amendment to ban abortions. He also advocated organized nondenominational prayer recited aloud in schools, and a constitutional amendment to permit those prayers (Cox 1985). Once again Falwell endorsed
the Republican ticket, and again a moderate Democrat, Gerald Baliles,
won by portraying the gubernatorial candidate as a pawn of the Christian Right.

In 1988, Pat Robertson's presidential campaign did poorly in the state
primary but quite well in the local and congressional caucuses that selected delegates to the national convention. Because the state party central committee is selected out of those caucuses and the resultant state
convention, Christian conservatives gained a strong foothold in the
party apparatus.

In 1989, the Republicans experimented with a party primary, but Marshall Coleman won in a close three-candidate race by abandoning his
moderate stance on abortion and opposing abortion in almost all circumstances. The *Webster* decision was handed down after the nomination and left Coleman scrambling toward the middle on abortion in an
election that centered on the issue (Cook, Jelen, and Wilcox 1994).
Large numbers of moderate Republicans defected to support Lieutenant Governor Douglas Wilder, who became the nation's first black
elected governor.

By 1993 Christian conservatives had a strong foothold in the party.
The party chair, Patrick McSweeney, had won office by appealing to the
Christian Right, and approximately a third of the state central commit-
tee were strong supporters of Christian Right organizations and issues. A

number of organizations, including the Christian Coalition, Concerned Women for America, and the Family Foundation (associated with Focus on the Family) were active in Virginia politics, and their members were primarily Republicans. But in 1993 it was the Christian home-schoolers who dominated Republican politics.

The 1993 convention nominated Michael Farris as the Republican candidate for lieutenant governor. Farris was a former Washington state Moral Majority executive director, a former attorney for Concerned Women for America, and currently is the head of a legal defense organization for home-school parents. Farris's supporters were new to Republican politics, but they flooded the nominating convention. Farris won nomination easily at a convention marred by rude and occasionally violent rhetoric and actions.

At the top of the ticket was former U.S. Representative George Allen, who appealed to Christian activists with promises to push hard for parental notification on abortion, support for charter schools, and roll-backs in the state's Family Life Education program. Yet unlike Republican nominees in previous contests, Allen did not stake a strong pro-life position on abortion or focus his campaign on other Christian Right issues. Instead his campaign emphasized promises to cut taxes and to abolish parole. Although Allen initially trailed badly, his Democratic opponent Mary Sue Terry ran a spectacularly bad campaign and Allen eventually won in a landslide, as did Republican attorney general candidate James Gilmore.

Farris, however, lost. Don Beyer, his Democratic opponent, characterized Farris as a Christian Right extremist who would ban books such as the *Wizard of Oz* and whose ideas were dangerously out of the mainstream.[2] Farris was a prolific author, and a number of passages from his books gave Beyer ample ammunition.

Although Robertson and the Christian Coalition were actually more supportive of Allen and Gilmore than Farris, Terry had no success in linking the likable Allen to the Christian Right. It is likely that Allen benefited from the comparison to Farris. Voters could compare Allen to Farris and conclude that Allen was far more moderate.

Warner refused to endorse Farris, although he did campaign on behalf of the rest of the Republican ticket in 1993. When North won the nomination for the U.S. Senate in 1994, Warner publicly stated that the Iran-Contra figure was not fit to serve in the Senate, and encouraged Marshall Coleman to run as an independent. Christian conservatives largely blame Warner and Coleman for North's defeat. The factional battle between party moderates (led by Warner) and Christian conservatives (led by Farris and North) is likely to influence the 1996 Senate contest as well.

The 1994 Republican Nomination

North won the Republican nomination at Virginia's Republican state convention, where fourteen thousand state residents who affirmed that they would support the party nominee and who paid the $45 registration fee attended. His opponent was Jim Miller, a former Reagan administration director of the Office of Management and Budget. North had considerable personal liabilities. He was a former Marine Corps lieutenant colonel who achieved notoriety during his televised testimony in the Iran-Contra hearings. North's performance at the hearings earned him the support of many on the right, but other Americans were troubled by his admission that he had lied to Congress. North was later convicted of three felony counts, including illegally accepting a security fence paid for with Iran-Contra funds, and perjury, but the verdict was overturned on a technicality relating to the immunity that was granted him for his congressional testimony. North's veracity was also questioned by those who alleged that he diverted funds intended for the Contras to his personal use, and that he frequently lied about his personal interactions with Reagan and other administration officials and about his personal heroism in various covert operations. *Readers' Digest* published an article in 1993 detailing occasions of North's alleged dishonesty, entitled "Does Oliver North Tell the Truth?"

It is likely that North would have lost to Miller in a party primary, but Christian Right and pro-gun activists dominated the party nominating convention. North had spent several years campaigning for the U.S. Senate, speaking at prayer breakfasts on behalf of state and local Republican candidates across the state. He had won early commitments from Christian social conservatives, including Pat Robertson and Ralph Reed, and from gun groups such as the NRA and Gun Owners of America.

Initially almost no one had given Miller any chance of defeating North. But Miller ran a surprisingly credible campaign and lost to North in the delegate count by only 55 to 45 percent.[3] Miller's campaign was aided by the endorsements of numerous prominent Republicans, including several Reagan administration cabinet members. Former president Reagan even denounced North during the GOP contest, giving a boost to Miller's campaign.

Miller's strategy consisted of two tactics. First, he argued that he was the most electable candidate. He pointed to a March 18–20 Mason-

Dixon poll that showed that in trial heats North trailed Robb by 17 percent, whereas Miller was tied with Robb. North's negative rating statewide stood at 50 percent.[4] Yet North's supporters were unmoved by Miller's arguments about electability. Many believed that once North began to campaign and voters heard his message unfiltered through the "liberal" media, Virginia voters would respond. Others viewed North as a genuine hero, and were determined to support him regardless of the likely outcome in November.

Second, he took very conservative positions on social issues, including abortion. Indeed, Miller ran to the right of North on abortion, although he had earlier taken a moderate position on the issue. Miller counted on support from party moderates, who would oppose North in any event, and sought to win votes from Christian conservatives. Yet ultimately he failed to attract many pro-life voters, who saw his late conversion on the issue as evidence of political opportunism.

North's convention nomination speech featured anti-Clinton and antiestablishment themes. He told the cheering delegates: "Today we send the Clintons and their cronies a simple but unmistakable message. This is our government. You stole it, and we are going to take it back." North expressed his strongest disdain for the institution in which he wanted to serve.

> Virginians are sick and tired of a Congress run by back-slapping good old boys, and a White House governed by a bunch of twenty something kids with an earring and an ax to grind. . . . [In Congress] they want a senator who'll join their club, pay the dues of compromise and take the perks of privilege. Well, I've got news for them. They will never see Ollie North crawling up the steps of Capitol Hill to kiss their big fat rings.[5]

After North received the nomination and after all of the hoopla and celebration, the GOP convention still had some unfinished business to complete: to adopt the report of the resolutions committee. Most of the delegates had gone home, and of the fourteen thousand convention participants, only about one thousand remained to vote on the resolutions.

Among the resolutions that passed were ones supporting voluntary prayer in public schools and a constitutional amendment to prohibit abortions and one stating that the state's Family Life [Sex] Education curriculum encourages students to "engage in sexual immorality." One resolution called on the state to "interpose" itself between the citizenry and the federal government to prevent "further federal government depredations." Another said that the GOP is "rightly and forever proud of the Commonwealth's Colonial, Confederate and American heritage." One resolution favored legislation "to ensure that military firearms suitable for militia be readily available to the 20th century militia of Virginia" and that "semi-automatic rifles (assault weapons) are 20th century militia firearms." As the voting on the resolutions took place, several persons carried "Farris" posters with the words "YES" and "NO" inscribed on the back to instruct delegates on how to vote.[6]

Party centrists left the convention in dismay, and many announced their support for the independent candidacy of Marshall Coleman. Farris angrily attacked these party defectors: "I think what it really says is the 'big-tent' theorists really don't believe their own theory" (Schapiro, 1994b). Farris maintained that a double standard existed: when the GOP nominates centrists, Christian conservatives are told to "stay loyal" and not express any objections. But when a Christian conservative achieves the nomination—Farris in 1993 and North in 1994—the centrists encourage dissent and disloyalty within the party (Farris interview).

North and Miller Delegates

Our survey of the 1994 convention delegates shows that despite Miller's conservative positions on social issues, the contest was one between the Christian Right and moderate party factions.[7] Large religious differences between the two sets of delegates are shown in table 6–1. Delegates who supported Miller were more likely to belong to mainline Protestant churches, whereas North's were more likely to belong to evangelical, fundamentalist, or pentecostal denominations. These denominational differences were mirrored in differences in religious identity: nearly two thirds of Miller's delegates identified as mainline Christians, while North's delegates were comparatively more likely to adopt orthodox identifications such as evangelical, fundamentalist, charismatic, or pentecostal. More than 40 percent of North's delegates indicated that they were born-again Christians, compared with only 10 percent of those who backed Miller. North's delegates were more likely than those who backed Miller to believe that the Bible was literally true, to attend church more than weekly, and to watch religious television at least occasionally.

Although there were large religious differences between these two sets of delegates, the stereotypes attributed to each party faction are clearly exaggerations. Miller's delegates were also religious: nearly half attended church at least once a week, and an additional quarter attended

Table 6-1
Religious Differences: North and Miller Delegates, 1994

	North (percent)	Miller (percent)	
Denomination			
Mainline Protestant	29	54	**
Evangelical Protestant	19	7	
Fundamentalist Protestant	7	2	**
Pentecostal Protestant	10	1	**
Catholic	21	18	
Religious Identity			
Mainline Christian	35	62	**
Evangelical	29	8	**
Fundamentalist	20	4	**
Charismatic	16	1	**
Pentecostal	7	1	**
Born-again	42	10	**
Agnostic	0	1	
Bible Interpretation			
Literally True	36	7	
Inerrant	31	30	
Inspired , with errors	33	51	
Not God's word	0	12	**
Attend Church			
More than weekly	31	11	
Weekly	37	32	
Monthly +	17	23	
Few times a year	12	22	
Never	3	12	**
Watch Religious TV			
Daily	2	0	
Frequently/ occasionally	49	21	
Seldom/never	49	79	*
Asked to Attend Convention by Someone in Church	4	1	

Percentage of each candidate's supporters who fall into each cell.
* = p≤.05   ** = p≤.01

church almost every week. And North's supporters did not receive their political insights from a steady diet of religious television: only 2 percent of North's supporters watched religious television daily, and only 4 percent had been asked to attend the convention at their church.

Despite Miller's efforts to position himself as the more conservative candidate, his delegates were more moderate than those who backed North on every issue except free trade. Table 6–2 shows the policy positions of the delegates who supported each candidate, and the correlation between candidate choice and each five-point item. The divisions were most evident on issues that resonate with Christian Right activists: the gold standard, capitalism and Christianity, the death penalty, pornography, abortion, gender roles, AIDS, homosexuality, and education issues.

Not surprisingly, the delegates also differed substantially in their evaluations of leading GOP personalities, which are shown in table 6–3. Christian conservatives rated Farris and North very favorably, whereas the moderates rated them quite coolly. The moderates were warm toward Senator Warner, while the Christian conservatives were hostile. Three prominent Virginia Republicans fared well with both groups: Governor George Allen received very favorable marks from both factions. Jim Miller and attorney general Jim Gilmore received positive marks from both groups, too, but not nearly as strong as Allen.

Although many of North's delegates were Christian Right activists, others were mobilized by his opposition to gun control. Our survey data showed that among those delegates newly mobilized by North (who were attending their first Republican convention), two distinctive groups were evident. The larger group were Christian Right supporters and members, who took conservative positions on most issues but were not especially warm toward the NRA. The second group were libertarian gun enthusiasts who wanted government to stay out of all kinds of private decisions, including whether to buy an AK-47 or whether to have an abortion.

The Four-Way Race

Soon after the Republican nomination, Senator Warner persuaded former Republican attorney general Marshall Coleman to run as an independent candidate. Coleman lacked the personal scandals of Robb and North, but was vulnerable to the charge of political opportunism. In 1989, as a GOP gubernatorial candidate, Coleman had praised North's actions in Iran-Contra. As a 1994 U.S. Senate candidate, Coleman, like

Table 6-2
Policy Differences: North and Miller Delegates, 1994
(Percent Taking Conservative Positions on Each Issue)

	North	Miller	Correlation
Economic Issues			
Cut taxes even if deficit rises	39	33	.14
Return to gold standard	42	23	.24**
Free trade is important	46	73	−.24**
Capitalism only economic system consistent with Christianity	57	30	.39**
Government not provide health care to poor	79	66	.10
More environmental protection not needed	68	67	.11
Government not provide minimum payment to poor families	50	43	.09
Country gone too far in helping minorities	64	56	.09
Foreign Policy			
Defense spending not reduced	86	70	.16
Russia can't be trusted	62	51	.16
Crime			
Death penalty mandatory for murder	67	48	.19**
Abolish parole and build more prisons	61	51	.12
Not stop crime by improving neighborhoods and jobs	39	20	.21*
Free Expression/Censorship			
Government should regulate pornography	38	12	.32**
Government should reduce TV violence	62	55	.08
Social/Moral Issues			
Ban abortion	57	21	.41**
Parental notification	89	79	.21**
No Equal Rights Amendment	78	78	.03
Men are better suited to politics	19	12	.29**
Working mothers cannot have as warm a relationship with kids	44	31	.21*
AIDS is God's punishment to gays	30	7	.30**
Known homosexuals should be jailed	26	4	.40**
Education Issues			
Mandatory school prayer	30	13	.33**
Mandatory teaching of creationism	61	24	.39**
Ban gay teachers	75	53	.27**
Encourage home schooling	60	30	.30**

Percentage of each candidate's supporters who fall into each cell.
* = p≤.05   ** = p≤.01

Table 6-3
**Differences in Evaluations of Groups and Political Figures:
North and Miller Delegates, 1994**

	North	Miller	
Groups			
Christian Coalition	71	38	**
Moral Majority	64	30	**
Operation Rescue	57	27	**
Concerned Women for America	72	44	**
NRA	72	44	**
Chamber of Commerce	64	65	
Fundamentalists	62	35	**
Charismatics	57	28	**
Pentecostals	60	38	**
Catholics	64	59	
Jews	69_	60	
People for the American Way	24	24	
ACLU	16	23	
Sierra Club	29	32	
NOW	12	18	
Feminists	20	25	
NAACP	27	35	
AFL–CIO	28	22	
Political Figures			
Farris	82	45	**
Kilberg	31	53	**
Beyer	23	33	**
North	93	38	**
Miller	65	86	**
Allen	90	83	
Gilmore	81	73	
Reagan	87	84	
Robertson	68	33	**
Falwell	56	26	**
Graham	80	69	**

Average evaluation of each group or figure by Farris and Kilberg
delegates.　　** = p≤.01

Warner, lambasted North as unfit for public service. When asked about his changed view of North, Coleman replied, "I used to think O. J. Simpson was a great guy too" (Whitley 1994b). In 1989, in an effort to court the Christian Right, Coleman had taken a strong pro-life position which may have cost him the election, but in 1994 he ran as a moderate on the issue.

Coleman initially was optimistic about his prospects. The early opinion polls showed that he was competitive and that he had the fewest negatives of the candidates. Warner pledged to help Coleman raise funds and some prominent Republicans continued to express reservations about North. Coleman's centrist conservatism gave him potentially strong appeal among suburban voters. Unlike Robb and North, Coleman had a clean reputation in both public and private life. Yet Coleman lacked a natural constituency. His appeal to suburban moderates was undermined by his abortion stance in his earlier campaign for governor.

The former Democratic governor, Douglas Wilder, also announced an independent candidacy, setting up a four-way contest. Wilder proclaimed that the two major party nominations had made Virginia a national "laughingstock." Wilder too had good reason to feel encouraged about an independent bid. He could claim strong support in the black community, which comprises 17 percent of the populace in Virginia—a potentially very strong base in a four-person campaign. Furthermore, Wilder had received widespread, if sometimes grudging, respect for his fiscal management of the state during a recession. Nonetheless, Wilder's gubernatorial agenda resulted in many unpopular cutbacks in government spending. His ill-fated presidential campaign in 1992 and penchant for engaging in personal rivalries made him very unpopular in Virginia by the time he had left office.[8]

The *Washington Post* handicapped the four-person race on 16 June 1994: "For each of the four candidates . . . it may boil down to the 30 percent solution: Start with some original base of support, and figure that 30 percent of the November votes could be enough to win."

North benefited most from a multicandidate field. He could count on a committed base of Christian social conservatives and gun enthusiasts who were certain to turn out on election day. North's senior campaign adviser Mark Goodin acknowledged that fact: "Put six or seven or eight candidates in the race and that would help Ollie even more. The more people that are in, the more it becomes a contest of the 'base vote' that is going to support you no matter what" (Jenkins, 1994a).

Both Coleman and Wilder faced many of the problems that traditionally plague independent candidacies. Both candidates needed to raise money under the rules that govern campaign financing of national campaigns, which are far more stringent than those that apply to state elections in Virginia. Both major parties mobilized their financial constituents on behalf of their candidates and tried to shut off financing for the independent candidates, and potential contributors to Coleman and Wilder were deterred by a second strategic problem—the self-fulfilling prophecy that independent candidates seldom win.

In September, after a number of prominent black politicians and preachers endorsed Robb, and following a private meeting with President Clinton and continued weak showings in the polls, Wilder withdrew from the race. Wilder's departure from the race and later endorsement of Robb helped revive the Democratic campaign. Wilder made numerous campaign appearances on Robb's behalf in the last two weeks of the election. He appeared with Robb before several black churches to help shore up the Democratic campaign's base. These attempts to mobilize black voters for Robb were aided by GOP state chairman Patrick McSweeney, who implied that it was a waste of time and effort for Republicans to reach out to black voters: "It doesn't make sense from a cost-effectiveness standpoint. . . . In the short-run, what sense does it make to go trying to butt your head against a wall" (Jenkins, 1994b).

North's enormous advantage in spending allowed him to lead in the polls until late in the campaign, but Coleman's supporters were sufficiently numerous to affect the outcome. In polls taken in mid-October, Coleman was drawing 17 percent of likely voters, a figure that was almost certain to drop by election day. The final outcome would depend on whether these voters returned to the Republican Party, sat at home, or voted for Robb.

North's chances to pick up wavering Coleman supporters and undecided Republicans were dashed by Nancy Reagan. During a televised talk show appearance in New York City on October 27, Mrs. Reagan denounced North as a liar who "has a great deal of trouble separating fact from fantasy" (Hardin, 1994). According to a Virginia Commonwealth University poll, Mrs. Reagan's statement effected a sharp decline in the percentage of voters who considered North trustworthy.[9]

God, Guns, and Republican Politics

North benefited from the strong support of Christian Right and gun groups. Although Michael Farris in 1993 had downplayed his Christian Right connections and focused his campaign on economics and other issues, North's campaign emphasized his religious convictions and experiences. North made numerous appearances throughout the campaign before evangelical church congregations. In one such appearance, before the Annandale Capital Baptist Church on September 18, North delivered a half-hour sermon on how he became a born-again Christian. North told the story of the most important day of his life: when faith healed his ailing back. North said that in 1977 a born-again Christian, Lieutenant Colonel John Grinolds, "closed his eyes, reached out and touched me and said, 'Lord Jesus Christ . . . heal this man' and the pain went out of my back and the feeling came back in my legs." In the sermon, North also compared members of the Iran-Contra committee to "Roman emperors" who persecuted Jesus (Resnick, 1994).

North spoke on religion in politics to a large audience on October 18 at Chancellor High School at an event sponsored by the Christian Leadership Forum. North brought two props for the speech—the Bible and the U. S. Constitution. To cheers of "Amen," North declared every word of the Bible literally true. In the speech, North gave his constitutional arguments for some of his policy views, including his pro-life stand and defense of gun owners' rights. The pro-North crowd cheered enthusiastically when he gave one of his favorite campaign lines: that he would prove the critics wrong and show that a man who spoke openly about his Christian faith could be elected to public office (Toler 1994). North also frequently told crowds that the Bible was the only book he had ever read more than once.

Although North had his strongest ties to charismatic Christianity, he received strong support from fundamentalists like Farris. The Christian Right in Virginia has gone far in overcoming the limits of religious particularism, and fundamentalists, charismatics, evangelicals, mainline Protestants, Catholics, and even Mormons now work together in organizations and on campaigns. Our analysis shows that North drew support from all kinds of conservative Christians.

Critics of North's candidacy frequently asked how Christians who professed to value honesty could support a man who admitted that he had lied to Congress and who many other Republicans believed had lied on other occasions. The *Washington Post* ran a Herblock cartoon showing North at a podium holding forth a Bible and declaring that every word in it was literally true. The finger of God was pointing from the clouds to North, and a box showed a series of Biblical passages condemning lying.[10]

Many Christian conservatives were troubled by the fact that North lied to Congress, but Christian conservative activists and leaders inevitably told us that they had "come to terms with" the honesty question, and supported North. Some argued that North would vote their interests in the Senate and Robb and Coleman would not. More important, North was a professed born-again Christian who attended a charismatic church and was unapologetic about openly expressing his faith. On the Sunday before the election, Christian Right groups, including the Christian Coalition, passed out over a million voter guides in churches throughout the state.

North's campaign was also backed by groups representing gun enthusiasts. North regularly proclaimed at campaign stops in the southern part of the state that deer were "rats with antlers," and that the Constitution protected the rights of citizens to own all kinds of guns. Although the media focused principally on North's Christian Right constituency, his support among gun groups was ultimately even more important.

The General Election

In the final weeks of the campaign, Coleman supporters began to switch to Robb. Coleman ultimately received 11 percent of the vote, although polls indicated that he would have done much better had he been seen as viable. Robb ultimately beat North by 46 percent to 43 percent, and polls indicate that had Coleman dropped out of the race, his victory margin would have been even greater.

White evangelicals and gun enthusiasts turned out in large numbers to support North. One exit poll found that white fundamentalists constituted 15 percent of the electorate and that 14 percent of voters were whites who indicated that they supported the Christian Right. North won more than 80 percent of the votes of both groups. Gun enthusiasts constituted a much larger portion of the population and provided a much larger percentage of his final vote.

A different exit poll by Mitovsky International found that 17 percent of the electorate were white born-again Christians who attended church weekly and that 38 percent were supporters of the NRA. North received approximately 60 percent of the votes of those who fell into one or the other category and fully 81 percent of the votes of those who were born-again, churchgoing gun enthusiasts. But these two groups combined to form a minority of the electorate. Among the 57 percent of the electorate who fell into neither category, Robb won 65 percent of the vote.

Despite his promises, North never proved that those unnamed critics who charged that he was unelectable were wrong. His candidacy prompted a countermobilization by moderate and liberal voters that more than matched his appeal in the Christian conservative community.

Turnout in Virginia set a record for a midterm election in 1994, and voting was heavy in the Washington, D.C., suburbs. A majority of those who voted for Robb and an overwhelming majority of those who voted for Coleman indicated that they had cast a negative vote.

Exit polls showed that North lost primarily because voters perceived that he was dishonest. A majority of voters in one exit poll indicated that they thought that North did the morally wrong thing in Iran Contra, including a surprising 16 percent of his own voters. So North's defeat was not primarily due to his association with the Christian Right but rather with his personal liabilities, which more than matched those of Robb (Rozell and Wilcox 1994). North's visible association with the Christian Right was also part of the countermobilization, however. A survey by Frank Luntz conducted for the Christian Coalition after the election found that only 8 percent of voters listed North's ties with the Christian Right as the reason for their vote. Yet Robb won by only 3 percent, so it is quite possible that mobilization against the Christian Right provided the margin.

A statewide survey by Mason-Dixon Political Media/Research in July 1994 showed that only 15 percent of state voters indicated that an endorsement by the Christian Coalition would make them slightly more likely to support a candidate. On balance men and women alike indicated that an endorsement by the Christian Coalition, Falwell, or Robertson would make them *less* likely to vote for a candidate. Evaluations of Robertson and Falwell were far more negative than positive—in the case of Falwell, 10 percent of the state residents held favorable opinions, and 52 percent were unfavorable. Robb capitalized on the unpopularity of Falwell and Robertson, and ran ads linking North to the two men.

Thus, in both 1993 and 1994, Christian Right activists helped nominate a candidate for statewide office with strong ties to the movement. These candidates had not previously held elective office, and they lost close elections in years of Republican landslides. In each election, the Democratic candidate successfully made an issue of ties between the Republican candidate and the Christian Right. In both elections, a different Republican candidate would almost surely have won. Yet in 1993 both factions united behind the candidacy of George Allen.

The Christian Right and George Allen

The Allen campaign is a pivotal case. Christian Right activists point to their support for Allen as evidence of a growing "maturation" of the

Christian Right, and of their pragmatic willingness to support candidates who offer only half a loaf (and a few stray fishes) but do not fully endorse the Christian Right agenda. Only time will tell whether this interpretation is correct, but there are reasons to be skeptical. First, Allen was the most conservative candidate running in 1993, and so Christian conservatives had the choice of backing him or backing no one. Second, in 1994, only one year later, the Christian Right chose to back the unelectable Oliver North instead of equally conservative Jim Miller, who might have won the general election.

Allen's performance while in office suggests that the Christian Right in Virginia might do well to adopt such a pragmatic strategy, however. Allen has made numerous overtures to the Christian Right in his appointments and his policies. In the personnel area, Christian conservatives have been delighted with the governor's actions. The state's leading pro-life activist and former lobbyist for the Family Foundation, Anne Kincaid, is the governor's director of constituent services. The director of the transition team was Michael E. Thomas, a former executive director of the Virginia Society for Human Life. Thomas now serves as the governor's secretary of administration. Pro-life activist Kay Coles James is the state's secretary of health and human services. James formerly served as public affairs director for the National Right to Life Committee. Her husband, Charles Everett James, former co-chair of the Bush-Quayle '92 Family Coalition, serves as director of personnel and training. Allen's secretary of education, Beverly H. Sgro, is an opponent of the Family Life [sex] Education program and an advocate of private school vouchers. The superintendent of public instruction, William C. Bosher, Jr., also opposes the Family Life Education program and is an advocate of student-initiated prayer.

Allen's policies, too, have pleased Christian conservatives. In his first legislative assembly session, Allen signed into law a bill permitting student-initiated prayer in public schools. He pushed a tough parental notification requirement for teenaged girls seeking abortions. When the state legislature passed a compromise bill that was less stringent than that favored by Christian conservatives, Allen vetoed the measure and promised to push the issue again at a later time, although in 1995 such a bill did not pass the assembly. Allen has also tried to promote the "Champion Schools" concept that is favored by the Christian Right.[11] He quashed a state college initiative to grant medical benefits to the partners of homosexual faculty. Allen also stopped an effort by the state housing authority to provide loans to unmarried couples.

Thus in 1981, 1985, and 1989, Christian Right activists pushed the Republican ticket to the right and Virginia voters chose moderate Democrats. In 1993, the Christian Right backed a candidate who did not fully endorse their agenda, and this has resulted in the election of a governor who made appointments and pushed policies that are clearly preferred by Christian conservatives over those of previous Democratic administrations.

Marriage Made in Heaven or Holy War? The Christian Right versus the Centrists

In the aftermath of the 1994 elections, the Republican Party is at once stronger than ever and deeply divided. Governor Allen and John Warner are the two most popular figures in the state, and the party is still favored to gain control of the state legislature for the first time since Reconstruction, although once this seemed certain but now appears only probable. Yet the division between Christian social conservatives and centrists runs deep.

Our surveys of party delegates to the 1993 and 1994 conventions, of members of the state central committee, and of members of the Fairfax County Republican Committee show that all three groups of Republicans are roughly equally divided between a Christian Right and a moderate faction. Our data confirm some of the conventional wisdom concerning the Christian Right mobilization within the Republican Party. Christian Right supporters are more likely to be recent party activists: a substantial majority had been active in party politics for less than three years, whereas an overwhelming majority of party centrists had been active for a longer period. Christian Right supporters are more likely than party moderates to be motivated by purposive goals, to oppose compromise, and to believe that there is a single Christian answer to most policy questions.

There are small differences between these two groups in their demographic profiles, with centrists somewhat better educated and more affluent, but nearly 70 percent of Christian Right delegates have a college degree. The differences are larger on religious attributes: half of Christian Right activists hold that the Bible is literally true (rather than merely inerrant); nearly half attend church more than once a week; a substantial majority call themselves born-again Christians; and about a third identify as fundamentalists, pentecostals, evangelicals, and/or charismatics. Centrists mostly practice a different kind of Christianity: a majority attend church at least monthly, but they attend mainline Protestant (especially Episcopalian) churches, while the Christian Right Republicans are more likely to attend Baptist or Assembly of God churches.

The two groups agree on some issues: a majority favor tax cuts, parental notification on abortion, increased defense spending, free trade, and the death penalty. Enthusiasm for these positions varies across groups, but these are consensus issues for the Virginia GOP. They are deeply divided, however, on social issues, especially those relating to government policy regarding sexual behavior and roles and toward education. The most divisive issues are abortion, government regulation of "pornographic" material, home schooling, and teaching of creation in the classroom.

The party factions are deeply divided in their evaluations of party figures, and Farris and Warner are especially polarizing symbols. On a 100-point scale, Christian conservatives rate Farris at 90 and Warner at 31. The centrists, by contrast, rate Farris at 32 and Warner at 66. Some respondents penciled in scores of − 10,000 for Warner, while others did the same for Farris. Other respondents compared the leader of the other faction to warm buckets of various noxious emissions of whales.

Warner's refusal to endorse Farris and his active campaigning against North are widely perceived in GOP circles to have cost both men victory, although our analysis suggests that this vastly oversimplifies reality. State Republican chair Patrick McSweeney threatened soon after the election that Warner would be "dealt with" in 1996. In fact, it seemed the chairman couldn't wait even that long. Soon after North's defeat, McSweeney spoke of going to Capitol Hill to convince GOP leaders to deny Warner the chairmanship of the Senate Rules Committee. As of July 1995, both Jim Miller and McSweeney are considering a challenge to Warner for the party nomination, and they will compete for the support of the Christian Right faction of the party.

There is currently some legal question as to whether the party will choose its 1996 Senate nominee by convention or by primary. In our survey we asked delegates to choose among Farris, Miller, and Warner. Farris came in first, with Warner last. If Warner lost the Republican nomination at a convention he might run as an independent, marking two consecutive elections in which the Republicans would have fielded two candidates. It appears likely, therefore, that the Republicans will again wage a holy war amongst themselves in the 1996 Senate race.

Conclusion: The Christian Right and the Virginia GOP

The Virginia elections of 1993 and 1994 lend credibility to the thesis that voters distinguish between candidates who are from the Christian

Right and those who are merely supported by the movement. In the cases of North and Farris, close associations with movement groups and leaders made it easier for Democratic opponents to characterize the GOP candidates as outside the political mainstream.

Perhaps the lesson of the Christian Right for these elections is that it is more profitable to back GOP candidates such as Governor Allen, who have broad-based appeal and who support much but not all of the Christian Right agenda, than to seek to nominate a candidate who most likely cannot win a general election. To be sure, many Christian conservatives worry that a GOP candidate not from the movement will make gestures toward the Christian Right merely to get the political support of that group and then govern as a moderate. That concern has been strongly voiced in Virginia where, for example, in 1989 Marshall Coleman adopted a strongly pro-life plank to get the GOP gubernatorial nomination and then softened his position during the general election. Yet Allen's appointments and policies are surely closer to those preferred by the Christian Right than any Democratic candidate, and unlike those with close ties to the movement, Allen won.

Although Christian Right elites maintain that they have become more politically pragmatic in recent years and are willing to support for public office a candidate such as Allen who is not openly pro-life, the evidence from 1994 in Virginia shows that they do not always act pragmatically. The leading Christian Right figures in Virginia in 1994 either backed Oliver North against Jim Miller or stayed neutral in the GOP contest. They did so even though Miller was unarguably the much stronger general election candidate and Robb most likely would have lost to any credible Republican. Once North had lost the race, the Christian Coalition quickly publicized the result of its exit poll, with the headline "Virginia Poll Shows North Unable to Overcome Iran-Contra."

North's fate echoed those of several GOP House challengers in Virginia in 1994. In four congressional districts that should have been competitive—Second, Fourth, Fifth, and Ninth—GOP challengers lost by sizable margins. In all four cases the GOP nominated strong conservatives with ties to the Christian Right. In at least one race, the Democratic incumbent attacked his challenger by airing an ad in which his opponent was "morphed" into Oliver North.

The one exception was the Eleventh Congressional District of northern Virginia in which moderate Republican Thomas M. Davis III, chairman of the Fairfax County Board of Supervisors, defeated first-term incumbent Democrat Leslie Byrne. Davis was the only GOP challenger in Virginia to distance himself from North. On election day, over forty thousand voters in the district split their ballots by voting for Davis and against North. The House of Representatives election results in Virginia in 1994 lend further credibility to the view that the Christian Right fares best when it backs GOP candidates with broad-based electoral appeal.

The 1994 elections in Virginia show that the Christian Right is not nearly as politically pragmatic as many of its leaders now claim. Although the elites undoubtedly have learned to play the political game much better than ever, the activists who now participate in state- and local-level GOP contests continue to show a strong preference for candidates either from the Christian Right or at least closely aligned with the movement. And they continue to do so in the face of considerable evidence that their interests are best represented by a more pragmatic approach to GOP politics.

Notes

1. It is a testimony to the tenacity of the Christian Right that they persisted after 1978. Those who worked in the Phillips campaign were confident that God would give them the victory, and those who worked hard for Obershain must have been shocked when he died in an event that is sometimes called an act of God.

2. Actually, the charge that Farris had sought to ban *The Wizard of Oz* in his legal suit was not true, although he had sought to ban other books from the public school curriculum in the past.

3. Official Republican Party of Virginia figures.

4. The Mason-Dixon Political Media/Research poll of 837 registered/likely voters had a margin of error of 3.5 percent. See Gomlak, 1994.

5. Republican Party of Virginia Convention (Richmond, Va.), June 3–4, 1994, attended by author. Excerpts from speech in accounts by the *Richmond Times-Dispatch* and the *Washington Post.*

6. Resolutions meeting attended by author. See Whitley 1994a; Schapiro 1994a.

7. We mailed 1,000 surveys to delegates to the 1993 and 1994 conventions, and received more than 440 responses in a single mailing. In this analysis, we include only those who attended the 1994 convention, and we have weighted the data to account for the unequal probability of selection of those who attended both.

8. The final Mason-Dixon Political Media/Research poll on Wilder's governorship evidenced this unpopularity, with only 39 percent of Virginians rating his tenure favorably. That contrasted sharply with the final tallies for his predecessors Gerald Baliles (63 percent) and Robb (73 percent). Mason-Dixon poll, January 27–29, 1994, 807 registered voters, 3.5 percent margin of error.

9. Scott Keeter, "If Truth Be Told," *The Polling Report*, November 21, 1994, pp. 1, 4.

10. *The Washington Post,* October 9, 1994: C6.

11. The House of Delegates Education Subcommittee blocked the advancement of Allen's charter school initiative in the 1995 session. (See Intress 1995.)

References

Barone, Michael and Grant Ujifusa, 1993. "Virginia." Pp. 1301–1306 in *The Almanac of American Politics 1994.* Washington, D.C.: The National Journal.

Cook, Elizabeth Adell, Ted G. Jelen, and Clyde Wilcox. 1994. "Issue Voting in Gubernatorial Elections: Abortion in Post-*Webster* Politics." *Journal of Politics* 56: 187–99.

Cox, Charles. 1985. "Baliles, Durrette Dramatize Differences." *Richmond Times-Dispatch* (3 November): C2, C6.

Farris, Michael P. 1994. Author interview, Purcellville, Va., 12 August.

Gomlak, Norman. 1994. "Support for North Heads South." *Fairfax Journal* (23 March): A1, 9.

Green, John C. 1995. Author interview by telephone, 17 January.

Hardin, Peter. 1994. "North Lied, Former First Lady Says." *Richmond Times-Dispatch* (28 October): A1.

Intress, Ruth S. 1995. "Charter Schools Shelved." *Richmond Times-Dispatch* (28 January): A1.

Jenkins, Kent, Jr. 1994a. "Coleman Emerges as Strong Force in Senate Race." *Washington Post* (2 June): B3.

———. 1994b. "North Gives Nancy Reagan No Back Talk." *Washington Post* (28 October): A14.

Key, V. O., Jr. 1949. *Southern Politics in State and Nation.* New York: Knopf.

Reed, Ralph. 1994. Author interview, Washington, D.C., 29 September.

Resnick, Amy. 1994. "North Preaches to Baptists in Annandale." *Fairfax Journal* (19 September): A1, 7.

Rozell, Mark J., and Clyde Wilcox. 1994. "Robertson Not to Blame for Ollie North's Defeat." *Richmond Times-Dispatch* (19 November): A17.

Schapiro, Jeff E. 1994a. "Spotlighting Sidelights on State Government at the GOP Convention." *Richmond Times-Dispatch* (12 June): F2.

———. 1994b. "Virginia Politics: Is the Party Over?" *Richmond Times-Dispatch* (6 June): A12.

Toler, Jim. 1994. "North Exhorts His True Believers." *Fredericksburg Free Lance-Star* (19 October): B1, 2.

Whitley, Tyler. 1994a. "Allen Appears at Unity Fest After All." *Richmond Times-Dispatch* (6 June): B1, 3

———. 1994b. "North Not Fit, Coleman Says." *Richmond Times-Dispatch* (12 July): B5.

7

South Carolina: The Christian Right Wins One

James L. Guth

Early in the 1994 campaign, South Carolina Democratic humorists quipped that only two skills were required to win a Republican gubernatorial nomination: speaking in tongues and handling snakes (Carney 1994). The reference, of course, was to the expanding role of conservative Protestants in the state's Republican Party. Ironically, the winning Republican candidate for governor was a Southern Baptist who neither practiced glossolalia nor played with reptiles.

Unfortunately, Democratic strategists understood the dynamics of conservative Protestantism no better in South Carolina than elsewhere, and on November 8 the joke was on them. David Beasley, a born-again Southern Baptist (but converted in an independent fundamentalist church), received strong backing from pentecostal and charismatic activists and votes from conservative Protestants of all stripes in first winning the GOP gubernatorial nomination and then defeating a popular Democratic lieutenant governor for the state's top post. Beasley's success proves that identification with a Christian Right movement organization is not always an insuperable barrier to political success, but his victory also brings into focus the broader role of conservative Protestants in South Carolina's continuing development into one of the nation's most Republican states. At the same time, the race demonstrates the complexities of Christian Right politics, highlighting the religious heterogeneity of the movement and the difficulties of managing that diversity.

The Prologue

South Carolina has long been one of the "buckles" on the Bible Belt, dominated primarily by conservative Protestants, especially Southern

133

Baptists, who alone constituted over 40 percent of the church members in the state in 1990. The state also has a large number of adherents to mainline Protestant churches, such as the United Methodist Church (14 percent), the Presbyterian Church in the U.S.A. (4 percent), and the Episcopal and Evangelical Lutheran denominations (2 and 3 percent, respectively). There are also numerous but largely uncounted independent fundamentalist churches, usually Baptist congregations. The African American community is dominated by various black Baptist groups (16 percent of the state's population) and many other historically black churches such as the African Methodist Episcopal Church Zion (Bradley et al. 1992, 31).

Given the historic predominance of conservative Protestants in the state, religion has seldom played a clear role in party or factional politics. During most of this century, the centrality of the racial issue prevented the development of two-party politics, so there was little opportunity for religious groups to become attached to competing parties, as occurred earlier in the Northeast and Midwest (Kleppner 1970). True, churches would occasionally align themselves behind one of their own seeking statewide or local office, but their only major political role was generally confined to issues related to the regulation of liquor and gambling. Although many analysts claimed that the conservative churches served elite purposes as instruments of social control (Key 1949, 137–43; Pope 1942), the fluid multifactional character of South Carolina politics prevented any long-term religious structuring of electoral politics. With economic development and increased population movement, however, religious diversity increased, raising the potential for religious conflict and for the first appearance of religious politics in the Palmetto State.

Although often neglected by analysts preoccupied with the politics of race and class, conservative Protestantism has played a considerable role in the appearance of a two-party system in South Carolina. The nascent GOP of the 1950s and 1960s reflected the religious background of the new urban (and often "immigrant") business interests that constituted the driving force in the party's reemergence (Black and Black 1987). Thus, the GOP religious tone was set by traditional upper- and middle-status mainline Protestants' such as Episcopalians, Presbyterians, Methodists, and a leavening of better-off Southern Baptists. As the party and its candidates emerged as a viable option for conservative voters, however, other religious interests began to demand a role in party affairs.

In 1976, a network of fundamentalist activists centered at Bob Jones University in Greenville moved into the party in force, hoping to turn the state GOP away from President Gerald Ford and toward challenger

Ronald Reagan. Although some BJU activists had participated in GOP politics at least as early as the 1964 Goldwater crusade, they now demanded a direct voice in party affairs and captured the Greenville county organization, situated in the center of one of the state's emerging metropolitan Republican strongholds. Although there was much initial conflict between the insurgents and party regulars—who withdrew for a brief time into their own business-oriented "Piedmont Republican Club"—the electoral disasters endured by the GOP in 1976 soon forced the two sides together.

Within a few years the BJU activists were largely assimilated into the GOP organization by the efforts of party leaders such as Fourth District Congressman Carroll Campbell and Governor James Edwards, becoming almost indistinguishable from other conservative Republican activists and officeholders. As Terry Haskins, an influential member of the BJU contingent, told journalist Alan Ehrenhalt, the fundamentalists and the traditional Republicans soon "agreed on everything except where to go to church" (Ehrenhalt 1991, 98). Ultimately, the BJU activists' strict religious separatism prevented them from forming a distinct conservative Christian political movement or from joining one formed by other religious groups or leaders. Their theology precluded organizational cooperation with those not sharing their religious views, leading to vigorous verbal battles with, among others, Jerry Falwell, whose Moral Majority was willing to accept Catholics, Mormons, Jews, or mainline Protestants who agreed with Falwell's political views. Rather than joining with "apostate" religious forces, then, BJU's stance encouraged followers to involve themselves directly as individuals in Republican affairs. During the late 1970s and early 1980s, BJU fundamentalists played a role all out of proportion to their numbers in GOP politics in the upstate and, to a lesser extent, in other parts of South Carolina, supplying a large cadre of skilled activists who usually supported the most conservative (and religiously compatible) candidate available in primaries, but invariably behaved as pragmatic tacticians, supporting the ultimate Republican candidate in the general election (Smith 1994, 1995).

A decade later, however, a new and more challenging religious insurgency confronted the GOP, as the charismatic and pentecostal forces of religious broadcaster Marion G. "Pat" Robertson infiltrated 1987 Republican precinct meetings and almost captured the state convention, repelled by GOP regulars (with the help of many BJU allies) only through astute legal maneuvering before friendly judges. Robertson's organizational victories were not repeated in the state's 1988 presidential primary, however; he finished a poor third, getting only 21 percent of the vote, far behind winner George Bush. Robertson failed to expand his base much beyond his original pentecostal and charismatic constituency, numerically small in South Carolina. BJU activists split among the GOP choices, but most favored the feeble candidacy of Jack Kemp, while Bush captured the state's dominant Southern Baptists and other mainline Protestants, all traditionally suspicious of pentecostals (Wilcox 1992). Party leaders recognized that the Robertson forces were much more interested in controlling the state GOP organization than the BJU fundamentalists had ever been. Nevertheless, Governor Campbell's mediating efforts on behalf of the Bush campaign gave the invaders some party offices and influence, including a large number of actual delegates to the 1988 and 1992 national GOP conventions.

Temporarily inactive in 1989–90, the Robertson forces were reorganized as the South Carolina Christian Coalition in 1991, led by chairwoman Roberta Combs (Hoover 1994g). This development reflected, of course, the national revival of the Robertson campaign forces under a young but savvy political operative, Ralph Reed. The Coalition's major activity during the 1992 campaign was distribution of hundreds of thousands of "voter guides" which informed potential supporters of candidates' positions on issues of importance to conservative Christians, such as abortion, gay rights, and school prayer. Coalition activists helped George Bush carry the state handily in the 1992 presidential race and assisted challenger Bob Inglis in his stunning defeat of incumbent Fourth District congresswoman Liz Patterson, a Methodist. Although some observers (and the defeated candidate) emphasized the Coalition's role, it was not the only religious force involved in Patterson's upset: Inglis's large grassroots campaign organization was filled by activists from his own conservative denomination, the burgeoning Presbyterian Church in America, and he had rock-solid support from the large BJU constituency in the Fourth District. Nevertheless, the Coalition was pleased to take credit for the results, at least until the Federal Election Commission launched an investigation of its involvement and that of member pastors in the campaign. Still, buoyed by such victories, by continued organizing in the state's three major metropolitan areas, and by some success in recruiting Southern Baptists and other conservative Protestants (especially from South Carolina antiabortion groups), the Christian Coalition flooded the 1993 GOP precinct meetings, narrowly controlled the state Republican convention, and elected Henry McMaster as state GOP chairman over Greenville Republican Knox White, a moderate conservative who had nevertheless built strong ties with the BJU Republicans (Graham, Moore, and Petrusak 1994). Although Mc-

Master added Coalition activists to the state party staff, he proved rather independent, staving off Coalition efforts to gain operational control of the state GOP executive committee. He also worked hard to keep disgruntled regulars, led by his predecessor, Barry Wynn, from setting up an alternative organization, with considerable success.

The 1994 Primary Campaign

In any event, the Coalition's GOP convention victory paved the way for its gubernatorial favorite, David Beasley. Born to a wealthy and politically influential banking family, Beasley was elected to the state legislature at the age of twenty-one and rose quickly to become Democratic majority leader in the South Carolina House of Representatives. Brought up as a "Methodist-Presbyterian," he exhibited few religious interests until he underwent a religious conversion in 1985. Soon Beasley found that his inherited Democratic identity clashed with his new "born-again" conservative convictions on both social and economic issues. He became an outspoken advocate for antiabortion legislation and in 1991 he crossed over to the GOP side of the aisle (Bursey 1994). During the next three years Beasley ran a quiet "two-tiered" campaign for governor. First, he traveled to a myriad of conservative churches to recount his religious conversion, in a stump speech that was distributed via audiotape and religious TV stations all over the state. Although he spoke frequently in pentecostal and charismatic churches, he also cultivated the BJU crowd and certainly was one of the few speakers welcomed in both venues. But his main focus was on congregations and pastors of his own new denomination, the South Carolina Baptist Convention (SCBC). Perhaps because of his favored status with Pat Robertson's forces, many South Carolinians assumed that Beasley himself was a part of the Christian Coalition's religious constituency. Recognizing the importance of the Southern Baptist vote, Beasley worked hard at getting the word of his own membership out among Baptist churches. As he told political scientist Oran Smith, this meant bypassing SCBC bureaucrats, many of whom were closet political moderates and even Democrats, and appealing to the more conservative elected leaders and Baptist laity who had come to dominate the state Convention's recent proceedings. All these efforts, in Beasley's judgment, had considerable effect (Smith 1995).

At the same time, Beasley did not neglect traditional Republican constituencies, cultivating business groups, fellow GOP state legislators and, most important, Governor Campbell's formidable electoral machine, which had carried the state for George Bush in two presidential primaries and two general elections. He won the endorsement of a large majority of state GOP legislators, thereby countering the claim that he was an outsider. And Beasley won assistance from the incumbent chief executive as well. His campaign organization was run by Campbell loyalists and the governor's preference for Beasley was no secret, although he remained formally neutral in the GOP primaries.

Thus, as the 1994 campaign started Beasley was both the candidate of religious insurgency and of much but not all of the GOP establishment. In the first Republican primary he garnered 47 percent of the vote in a three-way race with Charleston congressman Arthur Ravenel (32 percent) and former congressman Tommy Hartnett (21 percent). Like Beasley, both Ravenel and Hartnett were Democratic converts and had benefited from Christian Right support in earlier campaigns, but in this race religion became a major dividing line within the GOP primary constituency. During the first primary the folksy Ravenel, of aristocratic French Huguenot heritage, clearly positioned himself as the anti–Christian Right candidate; meanwhile, Hartnett complained that his Roman Catholic faith was turning out to be a major electoral disadvantage. Both aggregate voting and poll data demonstrate the importance of religious factors in the primary results. Beasley's vote was highest in counties with the largest population of Southern Baptists and pentecostals, while Ravenel did better in areas where these groups were less numerous. Some proprietary poll results confirm the nature of the religious divide: First Impressions Research found that Beasley won 66 percent of the (largely Southern) Baptist vote, with Ravenel getting most of the rest. Among mainline Protestants, Beasley carried a narrow majority of Methodists and a plurality of Presbyterians, but Ravenel took majorities among Episcopalians, Lutherans, and other mainliners, while he and Hartnett split the state's small Catholic population. Church attendance data enriched this picture: Beasley won 61 percent of Republican voters who attended church every week, slipping to a 43 percent plurality among those who attended most weeks. Ravenel, on the other hand, was the overwhelming favorite of less frequent attendees and those who seldom or never darkened a church door. The results by voters' religious self-identification were in the same vein: Beasley captured 75 percent of those claiming to be "charismatic," 67 percent of "evangelicals," 66 percent of "fundamentalists," but only 43 percent of "mainline" Christians, slightly fewer than Ravenel (Smith 1995).

In the runoff primary, Ravenel desperately appealed to "regular" Republicans by vigorously attacking his rival's Christian Coalition ties: "Mainstream Republicans know that the only way we can keep one of Bill Clinton's hand-picked candidates from taking the governorship is by keeping Pat Robertson's hand-picked candidate from taking our nomination" (Hoover 1994a). His charge was echoed by the third-place finisher, Tommy Hartnett, who asserted that a Christian Coalition candidate like Beasley could not win in November and endorsed Ravenel. Ravenel himself persisted with this theme throughout the run-off; indeed, at times it seemed to be his only weapon in a very desultory campaign. For his part, Beasley retorted that the strategy amounted to no more than "Christian bashing" (Hoover 1994b). In any event, Ravenel's efforts were to no avail as Beasley won 58 percent of the vote. Aggregate data analysis again shows that Beasley's totals were highest in strong Southern Baptist and pentecostal counties, while Ravenel retained his mainline Protestant constituency from the first primary. Although we do not have poll data for the runoff comparable to that for the first primary, no doubt the same patterns obtained, with Beasley capturing the conservative Protestant, church-going vote. Indeed, given the religious composition of South Carolina, Ravenel's strategy of attacking the Christian Coalition seemed doomed from the outset. After the primary, Ravenel explained that his verbal assaults were "just campaign rhetoric" and, with Hartnett, endorsed Beasley for the general election (Hoover 1994e).

Even without help from the candidates, the Christian Coalition was quite visible during both primaries, sending out 100,000 voting guides by mail and distributing 400,000 more through friendly conservative churches. Although evidence suggests that only about a third of evangelical churches cooperated to some degree (Hoover 1994c), even this level of involvement is a striking departure from their traditional apolitical stance. Despite the impressive mobilization, however, the victory of the Coalition's gubernatorial favorite was tarnished by the demise of other Christian Right candidates. Dr. Henry Jordan, a longtime religious activist, failed to win the GOP nomination for lieutenant governor; Gerald Stiles, an administrator at a fundamentalist Bible college, came in a distant second to the incumbent Republican superintendent of education, Barbara Nielsen; and Van Hipp, a former state party chairman and favorite of the right, lost a closer runoff fight for the nomination to Ravenel's vacated First District seat. Although the first two candidacies evoked much controversy about the role of the Christian Right, both were easily turned back by regular Republicans. The vote totals in these and other races suggested that the Christian Coalition and other conservative religious groups could muster only 35 to 40 percent of Republican primary voters when "pure" Christian Right types ran up against GOP regulars. When a conservative Christian candidate had other political credentials as well, such as Hipp or Third Congressional District winner Lindsey Graham, the result was usually much closer. Whatever the result, the political maturation of the Christian Right groups was demonstrated by the subsequent willingness of their losing candidates to fall in behind the GOP regulars for the general election, even backing a noted moderate such as Superintendent Nielsen (Hammond 1994). And the primary campaign efforts of the Christian Right and the religious squabbling among candidates no doubt contributed to high turnout: for the first time, a state GOP primary matched the level of participation in the Democratic primary, a fact that did not augur well for statewide Democratic candidates in the fall.

The General Election

In the November general election, Beasley faced a formidable Democratic figure, Lieutenant Governor Nick Theodore of Greenville. An amiable political veteran, Theodore began with substantial "friends and neighbors" loyalty in his native upstate area, otherwise a Republican and Christian Right stronghold, but was hurt by a nasty Democratic runoff with Charleston mayor Joseph Riley, Jr., which seriously divided Democratic activists. During the fall campaign, both Beasley and Theodore stressed economic development (Hoover 1994f), but from that point they diverged: Beasley emphasized family values and crime, advocated tax cuts, opposed a state lottery (a hot-button issue for religious conservatives), and suggested consideration of educational vouchers, while Theodore endorsed a state lottery to increase education funding (for public schools only), took a strong pro-choice stance on abortion (Beasley tried to downplay the issue), and constantly attacked Beasley's connection to the "extremist" Coalition. Thus, most of the issues that dominated the campaign had strong religious or moral overtones.

During the fall campaign, the Christian Coalition was again much in evidence, distributing guides and contacting friendly voters through phone banks. But there was also a broader Christian Right effort that received much less coverage in the press: the BJU crowd turned out an overwhelming vote for Beasley, and the Palmetto Family Council (associated with James Dobson's Focus on the Family), the American Family Association of South Carolina, and a growing number of local religious groups also issued voter guides and worked in races for state, county, and school board offices (Belli 1994). Indeed, the strength of the movement was such that several mainline Protestant and Catholic leaders issued strong warnings on the danger of identifying the Christian faith with partisan (i.e., Republican) agendas.

On November 8, Beasley won the governorship with 51 percent of the vote to Theodore's 48 percent. The closeness of the race complicates explanations of its meaning, of course. Finances were not a factor in the outcome, as Theodore outspent Beasley throughout the campaign (Fox 1995). Many observers blamed the Democrats' loss to an "unpopular" and "extremist" Republican candidate on the failure of reconciliation between the Theodore and Riley camps, on the lackluster Theodore campaign, on low African American voter turnout, and on the great unpopularity of Bill Clinton among South Carolinians.

Nevertheless, the results suggest that Beasley also benefited from a united Christian conservative effort. Although the BJU fundamentalists, the Christian Coalition, and Southern Baptists might not worship together, they certainly combined behind the Republican ticket. The Christian Right clearly mobilized a new, hard-core Republican constituency: of the 20 percent of white voters who said they were part of the "religious right" in the Voter News Service exit poll, 80 percent voted for Beasley (and for other Republican candidates). He won equally strong support from those who said family values were an important issue or that religion influenced their vote (Hoover 1994h). Overall, Beasley won 70 percent among white born-again Christians, who constitute a majority of the state's population. Although he did less well among white mainline Protestants, he still drew considerable statewide support from establishment Republicans. Aggregate voting analysis shows that, like other recent successful Republican candidates, Beasley did well in the high-income counties of the Greenville-Spartanburg, Columbia, and Charleston metroplexes. But even controlling for the "economic vote," Beasley attracted the most voters in counties with large Southern Baptist and pentecostal populations. Evidently Beasley's open and prominent identification with the Christian Coalition did not turn away most mainstream Republicans, although he did trail slightly behind the other Republican winners in a virtual sweep of constitutional offices, most of whom attracted 53 to 63 percent of the vote. It is important to note, however, that almost all of these candidates also had quiet Christian Coalition backing and help from other conservative Protestant activists, but outpolled Beasley in some traditional GOP strongholds such as the Charleston area, noted for its more "liberal" social values.

Conclusions

All in all, events in South Carolina require some carefully nuanced conclusions on the Christian Right's role. The outcome suggests that most observers have focused too exclusively on Pat Robertson's Christian Coalition (Bandy 1993; Hoover 1994d). Although the limitations of exit poll data unfortunately preclude detailed analysis of religious voting, Beasley and other GOP candidates clearly attracted support from a wide range of religious conservatives, not just the Coalition. Many of Beasley's born-again ballots no doubt came from his fellow Southern Baptists, the state's dominant church, increasingly Republican and conservative but still organizationally aloof from the Coalition. Indeed, Governor-elect Beasley's first major postelection appearance was not on the "700 Club," but rather a surprise visit to the South Carolina Baptist Convention's annual meeting, where he received a wild (for Southern Baptists) standing ovation. Beasley thanked his fellow Baptists for their votes and asked them "not to slow down your prayers but, in a fervor that you've never known before, to pray for your country and to pray for me as governor" (Barnett 1994). Thus, after twenty years of religious reshuffling, the GOP has become the party of united conservative Protestantism, attracting fundamentalists, charismatics, pentecostals, and conservative Southern Baptists in a powerful alignment, adding these elements to its traditional mainline Protestant base.

With or without the Christian Coalition, then, conservative Protestant politics would be leaving its mark on South Carolina. As conservative white Protestants move in force into the GOP, they are often followed by their legislators: after the election Democratic defections gave the GOP control of the state house of representatives for the first time since Reconstruction. Given the predominance of the broad evangelical constituency in South Carolina, the Democrats are left with a truncated religious coalition of African American Protestants, Catholics, liberal Protestants, other religious minorities, and secular voters—hardly the stuff of a majority party in a Southern state. In a larger sense, the GOP's religious strategy has broken up the alliance between working-class whites and African Americans which kept the Democratic party dominant—or at least competitive—in South Carolina during the 1970s and 1980s (cf. Lamis 1984).

Whether this pattern persists will depend in part, of course, on a variety of forces external to South Carolina, from the national economy to world events. But Beasley's own performance will matter as well. Will he be able to accommodate both traditional economic Republicans and the Christian Right by simultaneously producing on economic development and on social issues such as abortion, school prayer, gambling, and "family values"? If so, the new Republican coalition may be as formidable in governing as it has been in electing. The GOP starts with two initial advantages: First, "economic" and "moral" conservatives are not really very different in the South Carolina GOP, at least as compared with their counterparts elsewhere, disagreeing primarily in the degree of their conservatism and the priorities put on economic and social issues. Second, ancient racial divisions and issues still serve at times to unite most white Protestants of all religious stripes (cf. Baker, Steed, and Moreland 1991; Graham, Moore, and Petrusak 1994).

Beasley's initial actions as governor suggest that he is aware of the need to cultivate both parts of his constituency. He told the GOP governors' conference soon after election day that the Republican Party ought to embrace both school prayer and fiscal issues, arguing that the GOP's mandate was "broad enough for both" (Hoover 1994i). On inauguration day, the new chief executive put the religious and spiritual themes to the fore: he spoke at a prayer breakfast at Columbia's strongly conservative First Baptist Church and emphasized these themes directly in his inaugural address. "While we reaffirm religious liberty for all, historical truth teaches the Judeo-Christian ethic as the guiding light that made America great and can make America great once again." South Carolinians, he went on, had "declared independence from a morally neutral society." He promised that government would be reexamined with emphasis on two questions: "Is every program and policy pro-family and pro-business?"

Whatever the rhetorical commitment, the new governor's behavior did not seem markedly different from that of his Republican predecessor, Carroll Campbell. Beasley's cabinet was a deft mixture of holdovers from the Campbell regime and new appointees, most of whom followed conventional form as conservative, business-oriented, if predominantly youthful, Republicans (Hammond 1995). The first weeks of the new administration were characterized by proposals for property tax relief, limiting the terms of elected officials, welfare reform, and tougher criminal penalties on repeat offenders, rather than direct action on the social issue agenda of the Christian Right.

Unless Beasley fails completely in his two-pronged endeavor, the new Republican religious coalition in South Carolina will provide a high baseline for future Republican electoral campaigns and, given the numerical predominance of conservative Protestants in the state, may even insulate the party from national electoral disasters, such as that endured by the Bush campaign in 1992. If the greatest problem for the southern GOP has always been building a grassroots organizational base, the activities of Christian Right groups may well have provided something of a surrogate. The party's internal divisions are evident, but they may not be fatal: only time and political negotiation will determine whether the commercial right and the Christian Right can continue to do business together.

Note

I wish to thank a number of people for their contributions to this article. I have benefited from many conversations with former students active in several of the campaigns described in this chapter and have often depended on their reporting. Robert Furr, Walter Whetsell, Dan Herrin, and Michael Greer were especially helpful. In addition, Dan Hoover of the *Greenville News* and Lee Bandy of *The State* (Columbia, S.C.) are indispensable sources for reporting and analysis of South Carolina politics.

References

Baker, Tod A., Robert P. Steed, and Laurence W. Moreland. 1991. "Preachers and Politics: Jesse Jackson, Pat Robertson, and the 1988 Presidential Nomination Campaign in South Carolina." Pp. 94–112 in *The Bible and the Ballot Box: Religion and Politics in the 1988 Election*, ed. James L. Guth and John C. Green. Boulder, Colo.: Westview.

Bandy, Lee. 1993. "There is No One Christian Right." *The State* (14 June): 1A.

Barnett, Ron. 1994. "Beasley Pays Surprise Visit to Convention." *Greenville News* (17 October): 1C.

Belli, Steve. 1994. "Church Groups Distribute Voter Guides." *Greenville News* (27 October): 1C.

Black, Earl, and Merle Black. 1987. *Politics and Society in the South*. Cambridge: Harvard University Press.

Bradley, Martin, Norman M. Green, Jr., Dale E. Jones, Mac Lynn, and Lou McNeil. 1992. *Churches and Church Membership in the United States, 1990*. Atlanta, Ga.: Glenmary Research Center.

Bursey, Brett. 1994. "David Beasley." *Point* (4–6 October): 19.

Carney, Elizabeth Newlin. 1994. "On Nov. 8 A Nice Guy May Finish Second." *National Journal* 26: 2467.

Ehrenhalt, Alan. 1991. *The United States of Ambition*. New York: Random House.

Fox, William. 1995. "1994 Governor's Race Was Costliest." *Greenville News* (11 January): 2C

Graham, Cole Blease, Jr., William V. Moore, and Frank T. Petrusak. 1994. "Praise the Lord and Join the Republicans: The Christian Coalition and the Republican Party in South Carolina." Presented at the annual meeting of the Western Political Science Association, Albuquerque, N.M., 10–12 March.

Hammond, James T. 1994. "GOP Conservatives Back Nielsen." *Greenville News* (9 September): 2C.

——. 1995. "Beasley Assembles Young, Conservative Team." *Greenville News* (8 January): 1A.

Hoover, Dan. 1994a. "Ravenel Hopes to Cut Gap With Beasley." *Greenville News* (11 August): 1A.

——. 1994b. "Christian Coalition Role Shapes GOP Debate." *Greenville News* (16 August): 1A

——. 1994c. "Little Political Activity in Churches." *Greenville News* (22 August): 1A

——. 1994d. "Christian Coalition Seen As Force—But Image May Be Overblown." *Greenville News* (27 August): 1A

——. 1994e. "Ravenel, Backers Change Their Tune." *Greenville News* (28 August): 1G.

——. 1994f. "Beasley Plan Focuses on 'Growing Our Existing Industries'." *Greenville News* (6 October): 1A

——. 1994g. "State Christian Coalition Foresees Big Spending." *Greenville News* (24 October): 2A.

——. 1994h. "Beasley Leads GOP Tidal Wave." *Greenville News* (9 November): 1A.

——. 1994i. "Beasley: GOP Congress Can Push Both Prayer, Fiscal Issues." *Greenville News* (21 November): 1A.

Key, V. O. 1949. *Southern Politics in State and Nation*. New York: Alfred A. Knopf.

Kleppner, Paul. 1970. *The Cross of Culture*. New York: The Free Press.

Lamis, Alexander P. 1984. *The Two-Party South*. New York: Oxford University Press.

Pope, Liston. 1942. *Millhands and Preachers*. New Haven: Yale University Press.

Smith, Oran P. 1994. "Revisiting the Two Party Thesis: The Several Faces of South Carolina Fundamentalist Politics, 1976–1994." Presented at the annual meeting of the South Carolina Political Science Association, Clemson, S.C., 13 March.

——. 1995. "The Christian Coalition: The Evolving Unity of the Fundamentalist Right." *Journal of Political Science* (forthcoming).

Wilcox, Clyde. 1992. *God's Warriors: The Christian Right in Twentieth-Century America*. Baltimore: Johns Hopkins University Press.

8

Michigan: Veering to the Right

Corwin Smidt and James Penning

Although Michigan is a relatively urban and industrialized state, its history reveals a periodic influx of conservative, populist forces. In 1972, for example, George Wallace won the Michigan Democratic presidential primary, and in 1988 supporters of Pat Robertson threw the Michigan GOP into a state of chaos with their aggressive efforts on his behalf. According to one study, Michigan's GOP continues to have a "substantial" level of "religious right" strength within its state organization (Persinos 1994, 22).[1]

This chapter will analyze the 1994 election in Michigan to see what role groups of the religious right played. A variety of religious right groups have organized in Michigan over the past several decades and have become politically active, generally working on behalf of conservative GOP candidates. What factors have contributed to their rise? How active were they? What was the nature of their activism? What was their political impact?

To answer these questions, we begin by examining the changing political context which has contributed to the emergence of such groups. We then discuss the historical context of the 1994 Michigan elections. We conclude by examining the 1994 election and assessing the nature of the impact of such organizations on election outcomes within the state.

The Changing Political Context

Over the past decade, political analysts have frequently written the obituary of the so-called religious right. This was particularly true after Jerry Falwell, in June 1989, announced that the Moral Majority was to be dis-

147

banded. In reality, the decade of the 1980s helped to set the stage for the proliferation and growth of many political organizations with ties to conservative Christians, not the demise of such organizations. In particular, three distinct factors should be noted: (1) the impact of the Reagan revolution, (2) the candidacy of Pat Robertson, and (3) the changing political agenda.

The Reagan Revolution

Although the Reagan administration did not implement many of the policy objectives of conservative Christians, it did help to set the stage for further mobilization of many voters within their ranks. One important legacy of the Reagan administration was that power began to shift back to state governments. The emphasis was on greater local control and "returning power to the people."

This recognition that "one size does not fit all" and that attention must be given to state and local differences produced "a shift in emphasis from the White House to the grassroots" (Reed 1994b, 81). As political power devolved to the states and localities, organizational decentralization was becoming increasingly important for achieving political success. Groups such as the Christian Coalition recognized this situation and began creating organizational structures that provided considerable autonomy for local and regional units and that were built from the precincts upward. Organizations of this nature were thought best able to monitor rapidly changing political conditions in the various states and to respond effectively to those changes.

The Candidacy of Pat Robertson

Ralph Reed, national director of the Christian Coalition, has contended that Robertson's presidential campaign in 1988 served as "the political crucible" for the proliferation of many local groups supported by conservative Christians (Reed 1994a, 193). This certainly was true in Michigan politics. Some of the organizations that arose in the wake of his candidacy have direct ties to his presidential campaign efforts; others have little direct relationship, but arose in the political climate that existed following his statewide efforts. Of the four major statewide religious right organizations described below, three originated during or after Robertson's candidacy.

The Changing Political Agenda

A final reason for the growing success of these organizations is the development of a broader political agenda. Initially, the abortion issue dominated the agenda of conservative Christians. But as the political context changed, more issues were included. Euthanasia, the rights of homosexuals, pornography, and sex education in schools have become issues of concern to the "pro-family" movement. In Michigan issues related to "dismantling the monopoly of public education" have also become part of the agenda; legislative, judicial, and public attention have been given to policies related to home schooling and charter schools. Finally, the pro-family movement is also beginning to speak to various economic issues, particularly those related to taxation and the manner in which the tax code either punishes or fails to support the family as a social institution.

This proliferation of issues has facilitated increased policy specialization on the part of Michigan's religious right groups. For example, while some organizations focus primarily on issues related to abortion and euthanasia, other organizations give more attention to the family or "traditional values." This policy specialization is increasingly associated with diversity in political activity. Thus, some organizations limit their attention (either by legal requirements or by choice) to providing information to lawmakers and constituents. Other organizations endorse and financially support candidates, hire paid lobbyists and engage in direct lobbying, or engage in grassroots lobbying by asking their constituents to write their legislators about pending legislation.

The Historical Context

The Political Environment of Michigan

Office of Governor. During the early years of this century, Michigan could be accurately classified as a one-party Republican state. However, the Great Depression stimulated a revival of the Democratic Party in Michigan (Stollman 1978, 10). Ironically, it was political conservatives in Michigan who helped usher in one of the longest periods of Democratic Party control of the Michigan statehouse. In 1948, archconservatives, offended by the incumbent GOP governor, Kim Siegler, refused to support his reelection, preferring instead the election of Democratic challenger G. Mennen ("Soapy") Williams. After narrowly winning reelection in 1950, Williams went on to become one of Michigan's longest-serving (twelve years) and most popular governors. Williams, in cooperation with United Auto Workers president Walter Reuther, "sought to make Michigan a laboratory for social democracy" (Peirce and Keefe 1980, 185). So successful were the Democrats, operating in conjunction with big labor, that by 1957 virtually all top statewide offices were held by members of that party (Peirce and Hagstrom 1984, 255).

If the 1950s were a time of Democratic Party control of the Michigan statehouse, the 1960s and 1970s were a time of GOP dominance. GOP victories were created, in part, by voter concern over Williams's progressive—and very costly—social policies. Moreover, in the election of 1962 internal party divisions once again played a role in ushering in a new era, this time within the Democratic Party, as labor-backed candidate John Swainson, while progressive, was opposed by university liberals. Although Swainson won the governorship, he was left with a seriously divided party (Peirce and Keefe 1980, 185). Swainson was succeeded first by maverick GOP governor George Romney and later by progressive GOP governor William Milliken, whose twelve years in the statehouse equalled the record previously set by "Soapy" Williams. After Milliken's retirement, the Democratic Party regained control of the statehouse for eight years (1983–1990) under the leadership of James Blanchard before giving up control to John Engler and the GOP.

Michigan Legislature. In the first three decades of this century, the Republican Party dominated both state legislative chambers. The Great Depression, however, enabled the Democratic Party in 1937 to gain control of both houses of the Michigan legislature. This Democratic legislative dominance proved short-lived; only ten years later the Democratic Party was able to win only 4 of 32 senate seats and 5 of 100 house seats. During the 1950s, the Democrats gradually improved their legislative position, but it wasn't until the mid-1960s that, aided by post–*Baker v. Carr* reapportionment, they were once again able to control both houses of the legislature. Democrats continued to control both houses of the Michigan legislature throughout the 1970s, though the GOP was usually able during the 1980s to win control of the senate with small majorities (*Michigan Manual, 1991–92*). This pattern continued into the 1990s with one major change—the Republicans were able to achieve a 55–55 tie in the house of representatives during the 1993–94 legislative session, leading to a period of bitter partisanship and political gamesmanship as the parties traded control of the position of speaker of the house on a monthly basis.

Michigan Parties. Michigan political parties are rooted in differing patterns of social class, race, religion, ideology, and region. The contrasts are stark and meaningful; the parties don't like each other very much and have a difficult time finding common ground. Michigan's GOP finds its primary bases of support among small businesspersons, farmers, and the growing numbers of professionals in suburban areas. It also receives substantial support from conservative Protestants and traditional middle-class, WASP sectors of the population. GOP support tends to be centered in the more prosperous agricultural regions, in the small and medium-sized cities of west Michigan, and in the ring of counties surrounding Detroit.

In contrast, the core of the Michigan Democratic Party can be found in organized labor, particularly the powerful United Auto Workers Union and the Michigan Education Association. It receives considerable support from university liberals, working-class Roman Catholic "ethnics," and African Americans. It finds its greatest support in Wayne County (Detroit), in the cities of the I-75 corridor, and in the economically depressed Upper Peninsula.

In recent years, groups associated with the religious right have become increasingly active, particularly in the Republican Party. In 1988, for example, supporters of the religious right presidential candidate, Reverend Pat Robertson, threw the Michigan GOP into chaos with their aggressive efforts on his behalf. The chief intra-party split was between the religious right supporters of Robertson and the more moderate supporters of George Bush. At least twenty-six of Michigan's counties produced competing conventions controlled by the warring factions, with each voting to send its own slate of delegates to the state convention. The state Republican convention also split into two groups—a regular convention dominated by Bush delegates and a rump convention dominated by Robertson's supporters (Penning 1994, 329). The resulting ill will has taken a long time to dissipate.

The bitter 1988 campaign created some serious internal divisions within the GOP, pitting Robertson supporters and other members of the religious right against the more traditional elements of the party which had largely supported George Bush. The intra-party conflict had the potential to seriously weaken the GOP, particularly in view of evidence that demonstrated that support for the GOP in Michigan was more conditional among Robertson supporters than among party regulars (Penning 1994). Nevertheless, time has healed at least some of the wounds so that members of both factions were able to work together to defeat a common foe, candidates of the Democratic Party.

No doubt this healing process was enhanced, in part, by the withdrawal of some of Robertson's most ardent supporters from GOP activity. In addition, the rift between the Bush and Robertson forces may not have been as deep as it initially appeared. Spencer Abraham had served as the state GOP chairperson during the 1988 campaign when this influx of Robertson supporters occurred. Some of the criticisms of the GOP raised by Robertson supporters in the 1988 campaign were directed toward Abraham, and some important policy differences were clearly evident between Bush and Robertson supporters in 1988. Yet, some of the conflict between the party regulars and the Robertson forces centered more on strategy than on differences in policies or goals. Bush was simply seen by the regulars to be more electable than Robertson. That the policy differences might not have been as great as they initially appeared could be inferred from the fact that Abraham left his post to assume a position working for Vice President Dan Quayle, a person who enjoyed relatively strong popularity within the ranks of the religious right.

Finally, the election of John Engler in 1990 and his combination of economic and moral conservatism helped to unify the different wings of the party. Engler did not arise as a candidate of the religious right; he was a party regular and professional, who was serving as majority leader of the Michigan senate when he chose to seek the governor's seat, and thus the party regulars could stand behind him. However, Engler's policy positions and issue stands were such that they had appeal to the more socially conservative segment of the party as well. Thus, Engler's leadership position within the party and the issue stands that he staked out (coupled with his political skills and legislative successes) were such that they helped to forge better relations between the different segments of the party as well.

The Organizations of the Christian Right

The Michigan Right to Life. Begun in the late 1960s, Michigan Right to Life (RTL) successfully organized to handily defeat a 1972 state referendum that would have legalized abortion for the first twenty weeks of pregnancy. The Supreme Court's ruling the following year in *Roe v. Wade* made the referendum moot.

Michigan RTL is nonsectarian and has made no effort to assess the religious affiliation of its membership. Other organizations with a distinct religious base, such as Baptists for Life, operate alongside the Michigan RTL effort. Michigan RTL has a strong base of support in Kent and Ottawa Counties in the west side of the state, Grand Traverse County in northern lower Michigan, Bay County in the Saginaw Bay region, and

Oakland and McComb Counties on the southeast side of the state. Currently, Michigan RTL has a membership of approximately 160,000 households in its database and a mailing list of approximately 500,000 households throughout the state.

The Michigan Family Forum. Michigan Family Forum (MFF) was founded in late 1989 and is headquartered in Lansing. Its executive director is Randall Hekman, a former probate judge who resigned from the bench to head the organization. While MFF associates closely with Focus on the Family, it is not legally or financially tied to the national organization. The parent organization was founded and is led by psychologist James Dobson, whose radio program, "Focus on the Family," is aired on over 1,450 radio stations throughout the country (Moen 1992, 61). Headquartered in Colorado Springs, Focus is a parachurch organization dedicated to fostering traditional family values based on biblical teachings. Focus is loosely associated with the Family Research Council in Washington, D.C., headed by former Reagan staffer Gary Bauer, and produces a monthly political publication, *Citizen*, that has more than a quarter of a million subscribers (Steinfels 1990).

The MFF was created to function as a family policy council to address issues related to the family within the state of Michigan. About thirty such state organizations currently exist around the country, each functioning independently. The organization seeks to provide information to government leaders and the general public on "critical family issues of the day."[2] The MFF is one of the most influential family policy councils in the entire network, and its publications are widely distributed in other states.

Citizens for Traditional Values. Headquartered in Lansing (Ingham County), this organization traces its roots to Robertson's presidential bid in 1988. First organized in 1986 as the Michigan Committee for Freedom, the organization quickly became involved in Robertson's presidential bid. However, after Robertson's efforts faded and as the Robertson bid incurred huge debts, the Robertson organization withdrew its national people from the organization. At that time the board of directors of the Michigan Committee for Freedom invited James Muffett to become its executive director. Muffett, who had been involved in the Robertson campaign in Vermont, assumed the responsibility of executive director in 1988 and the task of eliminating a debt of $200,000 incurred by the organization in the Robertson effort. Muffett's initial effort was to eliminate the debt and develop a distinct niche for the organization.

In 1991, the organization changed its name to Citizens for Traditional

Values (CTV). In seeking to develop a distinct niche, CTV chose not to become a mass-based membership organization. Likewise, it decided to pull away from attempting to be a high-profile organization and, in the words of James Muffett, to adopt "a servant" rather than a "confrontational" mode. Neither did it choose to become an affiliate of some national organization (such as the then-emerging Christian Coalition). Rather, it decided to constitute an independent organization that focused on state rather than federal campaigns. Thus, CTV sees itself as a broad-based organization in that it (1) engages in both educational and campaign activities through endorsements, PAC contributions, and voter mobilization efforts and (2) addresses a range of issues rather than a single issue or narrow range of issues.

The 1992 election was the first election in which it mounted a major effort. This election proved to be critically important, as Republicans gained control of the senate and were able to obtain an even split in the house. With limited resources, CTV utilized its resources strategically. The organization sent a questionnaire to 110 candidates for public office in order to ascertain whether their issue positions merited the support of the organization. After analyzing the responses, CTV concluded that 64 candidates were worthy of support. However, CTV decided to focus only on the 17 most competitive races. Within those 17 districts, the organization conducted voter registration drives within churches, distributed candidate information (approximately 10,000 to 20,000 voter guides per district), and organized voter turnout efforts, primarily through phonathons targeted to particular churches. Of the 17 races targeted by CTV, 3 were decided by fewer than 120 votes.

The Christian Coalition of Michigan. Though this organization also traces its history, in part, to the Michigan Committee for Freedom, the Christian Coalition (CC) of Michigan was officially created in 1991. According to Ralph Reed, national CC director, the organization was built in terms of a "Field of Dreams strategy: build it and they will come" (Reed 1994a, 197). The CC of Michigan is an affiliate of the national CC, but it remains a separate legal entity. While the national and state organizations share similar missions, no edicts are given—nor are state affiliates necessarily in a position to carry out any particular suggestions provided by the national organization, as state organizations were created at different points in time and are at different stages of organizational development.

The CC is organized as a tax-exempt organization, and therefore cannot legally endorse candidates. Instead, its activities must be primarily educational in nature, and thus the CC has expended considerable energy in developing and distributing voter guides for election campaigns. The first Michigan CC voter guide appeared in the 1992 election and was prepared and distributed totally on a voluntary basis, as the CC had no paid staff at the time.

In August 1994, Glen Clark was hired as the state director of the CC and helped oversee the publication and distribution of its second voter guide as well as engineer its recent move to an office in suburban Detroit. While the organization claims to be statewide in nature, its primary focus has been on areas located close to its headquarters. This is done for strategic as well as organizational reasons. No other major organizations geared to conservative Christians are headquartered in that region of the state, and both McComb and Oakland Counties, which surround the Detroit metro area, are major population centers with many competitive electoral districts.

The Michigan CC presently is organized primarily on a county basis, but it seeks to move toward an organizational structure that would include city and township chapters. So far the organization has focused on federal rather than state races, but it does hope in the future to provide voter guides for state legislative races as well. The Michigan CC presently boasts 55,000 contributors—people who have contributed either time or money.

The Election

The Campaign

In Michigan, nominating primaries are held in August of each statewide election year. These primaries are followed by party conventions some weeks later. At the party convention, the party's gubernatorial candidate announces his or her choice for lieutenant governor (which requires approval by the convention) and the party selects its candidates for various positions on the ticket (e.g., secretary of state, attorney general, Michigan Supreme Court justices, and various boards that govern state universities). In addition to selecting the party's candidates for such offices, these conventions are intended to motivate and energize party activists.

Although Michigan party conventions rarely attract a great deal of media coverage, the 1994 GOP convention did attract some critical media attention. Newspaper accounts revealed that "while party officials say they don't support litmus tests for candidates, they are being applied nevertheless" and that the net result was that "moderates who test wrong shouldn't even bother to apply . . . if there are any left" (Luke 1994, C3). Just as former president George Bush never seemed to fully recover from the "cultural wars" rhetoric of the 1992 GOP convention in Houston, questions were raised about whether Engler could gain re-election with his conservative base, agenda, and record.

Engler had won a surprise victory in 1990, narrowly defeating incumbent Jim Blanchard. Engler ran as a pro-life candidate, and benefited from organized efforts by pro-life groups in the 1990 election. As governor, Engler has cut spending on most programs except education, privatized many public services, cut property taxes, and reformed the state welfare system.

Engler faced a seemingly formidable challenger in Howard Wolpe, who had served in Congress from 1978 to 1992. Wolpe, who chose not to seek reelection following reapportionment, captured the August Democratic primary to win his party's bid to challenge Engler. Wolpe won the nomination in a four-way race, capturing 35 percent of the Democratic vote. At the state Democratic Party convention several weeks later, Wolpe named Debbie Stabenow, his closest challenger in the primary, as his running mate. Stabenow had received 30 percent of the Democratic primary vote and was known as an aggressive campaigner.

Governor Engler, who had no opposition in the August primary, campaigned on the theme of his accomplishments as governor, particularly the economic climate of the state of Michigan and his welfare and education reform measures. In addition, Engler sought to paint his opponent as a "tax-and-spend liberal," focusing primarily on Wolpe's voting record during his years in Congress. A staunch opponent of abortion, Engler had received the endorsement of Michigan RTL in 1990, his first campaign for election, and again in 1994.

Wolpe, on the other hand, sought to cast Governor Engler as out of touch with the common man and insensitive to the needs of women. In particular, Wolpe attacked Engler's education reform package, contending that Engler not only undermined the health of the public school system but indirectly funded religious schools by means of the charter school provision of his reform package. In addition, Wolpe argued that Engler unwittingly had been the "tool" of the public utilities industry, particularly with regard to the state's supposed failure to regulate nuclear power plants adequately. Wolpe also attacked Engler's stand on abortion and on that basis secured the endorsement of Helen Milliken, wife of popular former Republican governor Milliken.

However, from the start of the campaign in September, public opinion polls indicated that Engler enjoyed a substantial lead; subsequent polls indicated that his lead never narrowed in any significant fashion. As a result, the Wolpe campaign suffered serious financial problems. Monies which might have been spent on the Wolpe campaign were diverted to other, more closely contested state legislative campaigns in the hope of preventing the Republicans from capturing control of the Michigan House. In fact, by the close of the campaign, the radio and television airwaves were dominated by Engler ads; few, if any, Wolpe ads were aired.

In Michigan's U.S. Senate race, Senator Don Riegle, politically tainted by the savings and loan scandal, decided not to seek reelection. With a popular governor and a discredited retiring Democratic senator, the GOP was hopeful that it could win the seat.

Both parties had contested August primaries for their respective U.S. Senate nominations. In the Democratic primary, Congressman Bob Carr won the Democratic nomination by capturing 24 percent of the vote in a six-way race, narrowly defeating state senator Lana Pollack by less than one percent of the vote. In Carr, who had served for eighteen years as a congressman from the Lansing area, the Democratic Party had a formidable candidate, despite the supposed disadvantages the party confronted.

Spencer Abraham, former state GOP chairperson (1983–1990) and aide to Vice President Dan Quayle (1990–1992), faced talk-radio host Ronna Romney in the GOP primary. Romney, though divorced from her husband, was the daughter-in-law of former governor George Romney. Ronna Romney not only enjoyed the political capital of the Romney name, but sought to challenge the conservative credentials of Abraham. While Abraham received the support of much of the party's organization and was viewed as the front-runner, Romney ran a surprisingly strong campaign.

Abraham won the nomination, but not before questions were raised about his ability to defeat Carr in November.[3] Thus, when the campaign began in September, the race was viewed largely as a toss-up. Not only was the GOP recovering from a relatively divisive primary, but questions also remained about Abraham's abilities as a candidate. The Republican campaign quickly sought to link Carr with Riegle; television ads early in the campaign portrayed images of Riegle and Carr in which, as the voice-over discussed Carr's record, the image of Carr morphed into Riegle, and vice versa. As the campaign wore on, the Abraham campaign endeavored to paint Carr as an entrenched liberal congressman and criticized him for accepting numerous expense-paid trips to the Caribbean while serving as chair of the Transportation Subcommittee of the House Appropriations Committee. Abraham, who sought to portray himself as a strong defender of the family, received the endorsement of Michigan RTL.

On the other hand, Carr sought to portray Abraham as lacking in political independence and unwilling to serve the unique needs of the people of Michigan. Carr's television ads portrayed Abraham, former state GOP chairman, as a "party boss" accustomed to "smoke-filled rooms" and as one who had sold his "political soul" and political independence by signing the GOP Contract with America.

In the congressional campaigns, fourteen candidates (eight Democrats and six Republicans) were seeking reelection. Two contests, the Eighth (Lansing) and the Thirteenth (Ann Arbor), were open races, as Congressman Ford (D-13) chose to retire and Congressman Carr (D-8) sought to become the state's next U.S. Senator. The 1992 election, the first under the newly reapportioned House districts, revealed several competitive congressional races within these newly created districts. Several Democratic seats, in particular, appeared vulnerable. The First Congressional District embodies the vast but sparsely populated region of the Upper Peninsula and portions of the upper regions of lower Michigan. An open seat in 1992, it was captured by the Democratic Party, and the GOP was hoping to unseat Congressman Stupak before he became fully entrenched as an incumbent. However, Michigan RTL endorsed Stupak in 1994 as it did in 1992. In fact, Michigan RTL provided Stupak with the crucial organizational and financial support needed to win his seat initially in 1992 (Gruenwald 1994, 3029).

The Eighth Congressional District, which Carr had won by less than 4,000 votes in 1992, was now an open seat. Moreover, Dick Chrysler, who had challenged Carr in 1992, was seeking the seat once again, and Republicans were hopeful of capturing the seat in 1994. Likewise, the Ninth and Twelfth congressional seats were viewed as within GOP striking distance. Congressmen Kildee (D-9) and Levin (D-12) each had captured their districts with less than a 25,000-vote margin, and both districts were far from being Democratic strongholds. Moreover, in both congressional districts, the two Republican challengers in 1992 (Megan O'Neill in the Ninth and John Pappageorge in the Twelfth) were again challenging in 1994. However, Congressman Kildee, a Roman Catholic who opposes abortion, received the Michigan RTL endorsement.

Finally, the Thirteenth Congressional District, which incorporates the city of Ann Arbor, was also an open seat. The GOP candidate, John Schall, a former Bush administration official, opposed abortion rights while supporting school choice, tax cuts, and reduced government spending. Michigan RTL had made Schall's primary race one of its top priorities (Groppe 1994, 2277), but he won the August primary by only 209 votes. The Democratic candidate, state representative Lynn Rivers, dismissed Schall as a "privileged Washington insider" and campaigned in support of abortion and gay rights. While optimistic, Republicans were far from confident that they could capture the Thirteenth District, because Democrats had held the district congressional seat since 1964.

Organizational Activity

The activity of religious right organizations in Michigan was not limited to a single level of government or type of political involvement. They were active both in the nomination process (Luke 1994) and in supporting the general election activities of candidates at both the state and local levels. Given their different goals and legal statuses, it is not surprising that the organizations surveyed in this chapter engaged in a variety of electoral activities, including disseminating political information, mobilizing voters, endorsing political candidates, and providing volunteers and funding for particular candidates and campaigns.

One of the major endeavors of these organizations in 1994 was to provide information to their members (or likely constituents) about the candidates' issue positions and (where legal) the organization's endorsement. All four organizations discussed here reported that considerable effort was made to accomplish this task. However, the strategies pursued and the amount of information provided varied, as did the particular races covered.

The MFF, for example, reported that it distributed approximately one million voter guides in the 1994 election, half during the primary election and half during the general election. MFF generally sent the guides to its county coordinators, who were responsible for distributing them within the county. Approximately two thirds of the guides were distributed to churches, with the remaining one third going to businesses, public libraries, and community groups.

The voter guides distributed by MFF during the general election campaign provided both responses given by the candidates to questionnaires sent to each candidate and incumbents' voting records on certain roll-call votes.[4] For the U.S. Senate and the U.S. House races, the guides reported the candidates' responses to twelve different questions. Three addressed issues related to the budget, the deficit, and taxation; three addressed issues related to education and abortion; two addressed environmental issues; others addressed such issues as the civil rights of homosexuals, terms limits, allowing women to fill combat positions in the military, and government growth. Likewise, for federal races, the guides provided the voting record of the candidates on a motion to require federally funded family planning clinics to notify parents forty-eight hours in advance of any abortion to be performed on a minor, the federal budget with its retroactive income tax hikes, the lifting of the ban on homosexuals from serving in the military, the GOALS 2000 educational proposal, and cutting the federal budget by $26 billion in discretionary spending over the next five years. Similar information was obtained and reported for the two gubernatorial candidates and for each state legislative candidate. As required by their legal status, no endorsements were given by MFF. Moreover, neither did MFF report those endorsements given the candidates by other organizations entitled to do so (Michigan RTL, CTV, Michigan Educational Association, and others).

The CC of Michigan also claimed to have distributed one million voter guides. However, these voter guides were distributed only for the general election and related primarily to federal offices. Due to the more limited nature of the CC voter guides (in terms of offices and scope of issues covered), these guides were much smaller and easier to distribute. These guides were sent to individuals, churches, and businesses (e.g., Christian bookstores). Moreover, the CC claimed that these guides "frequently took on a life of their own." People would take them, recopy them, and distribute them on their own. The guides were reportedly later found in mass quantities in places where the CC of Michigan had not originally distributed them.

On the other hand, CTV did not seek to engage in the massive distribution of voter guides. Rather, it followed a more narrowly focused but strategic plan in disseminating information. This plan involved preparing bulletin inserts for churches located in its targeted legislative districts.[5]

Finally, although Michigan RTL does not publish voter guides in the strictest sense, it nevertheless sent mailings containing information about its endorsements to individual members and even to prospective members. In addition, on the weekend before the election, Michigan RTL mailed to all its contributors sample ballots listing all endorsed candidates at all levels of government.

Because of their particular legal status, most of the election activity of MFF and the CC of Michigan involved the distribution of voter guides. One goal of the dissemination of such guides is to provide voters with information for making electoral decisions. A second goal is to motivate certain citizens to vote who might otherwise not have done so. Moreover, interest groups seek to mobilize voters in other ways. Toward that end, for example, CTV encouraged their members to become deputy registrars, legally able to register people.

Michigan RTL claims that its primary electoral activities are endorsements and volunteer work, rather than financial contributions. Nevertheless, in the 1994 elections the Michigan RTL PAC distributed $250,000 to $300,000 to candidates in the primary and general elections. Each candidate who wished endorsement and funding had to fill out a questionnaire and (optimally) submit to an interview conducted by the local RTL affiliate. Each affiliate then recommended one name to the state PAC for endorsement and funding.[6] RTL incumbents are automatically endorsed regardless of their opponent's pro-life credentials. However, if there is no incumbent, then the best candidate, regardless of party, is chosen. In 1994, the state PAC made funding decisions based on the closeness of the races and financial need, with close races being targeted. However, the races were monitored, and funding for races which began to look lopsided was reduced or stopped.

The Results

Michigan's 1994 general election provided a stunning victory for the GOP. For the first time in over a quarter of a century, the Republican Party gained control not only of the governor's mansion but also of both houses of the state legislature. Furthermore, the GOP succeeded in ousting longtime Democratic secretary of state Richard Austin, a Michigan "institution." The only major Democratic candidate for statewide office to survive the GOP onslaught was veteran attorney general Frank Kelly. This victory was not necessarily aided by a low turnout rate, conventionally thought to work to the GOP's advantage. The turnout rate in 1994 was estimated to be 44 percent, up from 37 percent in 1990 (*America at the Polls 1994*, 14).

The 1994 Michigan election revolved largely around the person and record of Governor Engler, and Engler led the way, receiving an impressive 61.5 percent of the total vote. This result contrasted markedly with his razor-thin victory (less than 20,000 votes out of 2.5 million cast) in 1990. Just as impressive as the magnitude of the victory was the geographical dispersion of his support. Engler carried all but 2 of Michigan's 83 counties! This scope of victory is evident in table 8-1 which shows the vote totals within those counties contributing the largest number of total votes in 1994, with the 17 counties listed contributing 75

Table 8-1
Percent of Vote Cast for Engler by County
(seventeen largest counties only)

County	Percent of Vote Cast for Engler	Percent of Vote Cast in County of All Votes Cast in State
Bay	60.27	1.3
Berrien	71.71	1.4
Calhoun	63.06	1.4
Genessee	49.96	4.8
Ingham	54.79	3.1
Jackson	70.00	1.5
Kalamazoo	60.30	2.4
Kent	74.36	5.3
Livingston	76.46	1.5
Macomb	69.89	8.0
Muskegon	59.80	1.6
Oakland	66.50	13.1
Ottawa	82.85	2.3
Saginaw	59.80	2.4
St. Clair	70.47	1.6
Washtenaw	53.58	3.0
Wayne	42.96	20.3

percent of all the votes cast. Engler carried all but Wayne (Detroit) and Genessee (Flint) Counties—with his loss in Genessee County coming by a margin of only 114 votes out of nearly 148,000 votes cast. Even in traditionally Democratic Wayne County, Engler garnered approximately 43 percent of the votes cast—a level far too high to enable Wolpe to offset his losses outside of Wayne County.

Engler's substantial margin of victory probably assisted Spencer Abraham in his bid for the Senate seat. Abraham garnered 1.58 million votes (51.9 percent) compared to Carr's 1.30 million votes (42.7 percent), with third party candidates capturing 170,000 votes (5.4 percent). Abraham's margin of victory, while not matching Engler's, was significant in that it gave Michigan Republicans their first victorious Senate candidate in twenty-two years.

Additional losses for the Democrats occurred at the congressional level, with the Republicans picking up one seat in the House (leaving the Democrats with a slim 9–7 edge). Democrats did manage to hold on to four of the five targeted congressional races, but continue to be more vulnerable than Republicans to losing congressional seats in the future.[7] As can be seen in table 8-2, the results of the 1994 congressional elections revealed four races in which the victor enjoyed less than a 10 percent margin of victory. Two of these races occurred in the races with the open seats (the Eighth and Thirteenth Districts), with Republicans

Table 8-2
Michigan Congressional Election Results

Congressional District	Winner	Party	Percent Total Vote	Margin (Percent)
1	Stupak	Dem	57	15
2	Hoekstra	Rep	75	51
3	Ehlers	Rep	74	50
4	Camp	Rep	73	48
5	Barcia	Dem	65	33
6	Upton	Rep	73	47
7	Smith	Rep	65	32
8	Chrysler*	Rep	52	7
9	Kildee	Dem	51	4
10	Bonior	Dem	62	14
11	Knollerberg	Rep	68	38
12	Levin	Dem	52	5
13	Rivers*	Dem	52	7
14	Conyers	Dem	82	65
15	Collins	Dem	84	70
16	Dingell	Dem	59	19

*Indicates race had no incumbent candidate.

capturing one seat (the Eighth) and Democrats capturing the other (the Thirteenth). However, the other two competitive races were ones in which Democrats were the incumbents (the Ninth and the Twelfth), suggesting that Democrats may be more vulnerable than Republicans to the loss of additional congressional seats in the 1996 election. Furthermore, the margins of victory obtained by GOP candidates in several of the congressional races were staggering, with the Republican candidates capturing nearly 75 percent of the votes cast within their districts. These margins of victory approximate the level of victory Democratic candidates have traditionally enjoyed in the heavily black congressional districts within the Detroit area.

How did the Republicans secure such a lopsided victory? In brief, Republicans were able to hold the loyalties of those who identified as Republicans, capture the support of those who labeled themselves as independents, and secure substantial defections among those who identified as Democrats. This is exactly what is suggested in table 8-3, which reports the votes cast for Republican candidates by the party identification of exiting voters in Michigan.[8]

Table 8-3 reveals that well over 90 percent of all Republican identifiers indicated that they voted for Engler, Abraham, and their party's congressional candidate. Democratic Party identifiers, on the other hand, moved away from their party as the races shifted from congressional races to the U.S. Senate race to the gubernatorial race (with 17 percent of Democratic identifiers indicating that they had voted for Engler). Independent voters broke in the Republican direction regardless of office, but the extent to which they did so varied by office. Whereas barely a majority of independents cast their ballots for Spencer Abraham, well over two out of three voted for Governor Engler.

Did the organizations of the religious right help to mobilize voters and provide the crucial margin of victory for GOP candidates? Although we are unable to answer that question directly, there are several pieces

Table 8-3
Percent of Vote Cast for Republican Candidate by Party Identification

Office	Democrat	Independent	Republican
Governor	17	73	93
Senate	11	51	97
House	6	57	97

Source: Election News Service Exit Poll.

of evidence that may help us to answer that question. First, white evangelical Protestants constitute one of the major target constituencies of these organizations, and those within their ranks voted Republican in overwhelming numbers in 1994. Table 8-4 reveals that more than four out of every five white evangelical Protestant voters cast a GOP ballot both for governor and for their congressional representative, and three out of four did so for the U.S. Senate race. On the other hand, mainline Protestants, historically the bedrock of the Republican coalition, were far less Republican in their voting patterns. White mainline Protestants cast a bare majority of their vote for Michigan's GOP congressional candidates. Even Governor Engler only managed to capture approximately 60 percent of white mainline Protestants. Thus, it appears that white evangelical Protestants provided the major foundation upon which the GOP built its winning Michigan team in 1994.[9] To the extent that organizations of the religious right were able to mobilize this target constituency and/or help frame their voting decisions through such means as voter guides, such organizations helped to contribute to the GOP success in Michigan.

Conclusion

Several conclusions can be drawn from the analysis of this chapter. First, there has been a growth and proliferation of organizations tied to the religious right within Michigan over the past decade. This proliferation has enabled such organizations to develop distinct niches within which to market themselves as they appeal to their target constituencies. In addition, it appears that these organizations are growing in political sophistication and are finding ways to use their resources more strategically.

Table 8-4
Percent of Vote Cast for Republican Candidate by Religious Tradition
(whites only)

Office	Evangelical Protestant	Mainline Protestant	Roman Catholic
Governor	83	61	68
Senate	76	57	56
House	81	53	57

Source: Election News Service Exit Poll.

Second, the target constituencies to which these organizations appeal have become the major base upon which the winning GOP coalition is built. White evangelical Protestants provide the starting base for the GOP coalition, just as blacks do so for the Democratic Party. And while the loyalty of white evangelical Protestants to the GOP does not as yet match that of blacks toward the Democratic Party, it is beginning to approximate such loyalty. However, this lower level of loyalty is more than offset by the fact that the starting base for the GOP coalition (white evangelical Protestants) is far larger than the starting base for the Democratic coalition (blacks).[10]

Third, in terms of the major races (governor, U.S. Senate seat, and U.S. House seats), the votes of supporters of the religious right must certainly be viewed as having been an important factor contributing to GOP victories. Nevertheless, such votes cannot be viewed as having been the determining factor. The margins of victory that the GOP candidates enjoyed were generally far too great for any one group to be able to claim that they provided the particular margin of victory.

Finally, it is likely that the religious right and its political organizations are likely to play a continuing role in Michigan electoral politics. As Leege (1992, 203) argues, its public agenda is cultural politics and its agenda is one that is likely to exhibit some staying power: "its materiel are norms about identity and meaning, responsibility and boundary maintenance." The religious right appears to have entered the electoral arena and is unlikely in the near future to withdraw from the political fray. Thus, it is not surprising that both the MFF and the CC of Michigan have begun to initiate citizen action training seminars. These day-long workshops are designed to train people how to become politically involved and organized at the grassroots level. Some seminars are designed to be leadership schools in which those receiving training can, in turn, equip others to become effective activists. Other seminars are designed for those who do not seek political leadership but simply desire to organize their precinct, get their voter guides distributed, and address issues of local concern. As Leege (1992, 203) notes: "As the moral agenda in American politics increasingly decentralizes . . . so will the religious right's involvement take on new intensity—at home." Because of its extensive (and difficult to achieve) cultural agenda, the size of its membership, and its political cohesiveness, it is not likely that the role of the religious right will diminish greatly in electoral politics, either nationally or in Michigan, any time soon.

Notes

1. Some caution must be exercised in the use and interpretation of terms such as "religious right" or "Christian Right." First, not all organizations would accept such a label. Some would claim that they are part of the "Christian mainstream" and attempts to label them as part of the religious right are simply a political ploy to frame the manner in which the organizations are viewed by those outside their ranks. Other organizations would note that although they may focus on an issue such as abortion that is tied to the agenda of those in the religious right, their membership is politically diverse and it is misleading to place them in that category.

2. To that end, it offers the following services: (1) Info Paks—materials which contain research, essays, and articles on various issues related to families, (2) LegiService—a newsletter which provides in-depth analysis of eight to twelve important state bills each month as well as voting records of state legislators on two or three selected key legislative votes on family issues over the month, (3) voter guides each year—to assist citizens in ascertaining where candidates for state and national office stand on a variety of issues, and (4) research publications—documents based on the efforts of the Research and Public Policy Division of the Michigan Family Forum.

3. Romney carried the three counties with the largest turnout (Oakland, Wayne, and McComb Counties, where her radio show was heard), with over a 14,000-vote margin. Abraham, however, made up most of Romney's metro Detroit advantage by carrying Kent County on the state's west side with a 12,000-vote margin.

4. Challengers were asked how they would have voted had they been present. Actual votes were indicated by capital letters; hypothetical votes by lowercase letters.

5. No information was provided, however, concerning how many such inserts were distributed within these targeted districts.

6. The state organization never selects someone else, but it may in rare cases withold funding and endorsement.

7. However, Michigan's term-limit requirement conditions this statement somewhat. Given its three-term limit for House members, even those congressional districts in which GOP incumbents amassed huge electoral victories will become "open" seats within a relatively short period.

8. It should be noted that the data presented in Tables 8-3 and 8-4 should be viewed as simply suggestive in nature. The particular precincts in which exiting voters are surveyed are not randomly chosen within the state, but instead are usually selected for "strategic" reasons. Only the particular voters exiting the polls are randomly chosen. Consequently, the results do not necessarily reflect a random survey of all voters casting ballots within the state.

9. These exit poll data reveal that nationally the same patterns tend to pre-

vail. Among all exit poll voters nationally, 75 percent of all white evangelical Protestants voted GOP in congressional elections, as did 56 percent of white mainline Protestants and 53 percent of white Catholics.

10. The size of the evangelical bloc of voters varies, in part, by how one chooses to measure them (i.e., by doctrinal beliefs, by self-identification, etc.). Roughly, however, the size of the white evangelical Protestant bloc is approximately twice the size of the black component of the electorate.

References

America at the Polls 1994. 1995. Storrs, Conn.: The Roper Center for Public Opinion Research.

Groppe, Maureen. 1994. "Michigan: It's the 'Year of the Incumbent' As Three Women Lose Narrowly." *Congressional Quarterly* (6 August): 2276–277.

Gruenwald, Juliana. 1994. "Michigan." *Congressional Quarterly* (22 October): 3029–30.

Leege, David. 1992. "Coalitions, Cues, Strategic Politics and the Staying Power of the Religious Right, or Why Political Scientists Ought to Pay Attention to Cultural Politics." *PS: Political Science and Politics* 25 (June): 198–204.

Luke, Peter. 1994. "Conservatives Control GOP." *The Grand Rapids Press* (4 September): C3.

Michigan Manual, 1991–1992. 1991. Lansing, Mich.: Legislative Council, State of Michigan.

Moen, Matthew. 1992. *The Transformation of the Christian Right*. Tuscaloosa: University of Alabama Press.

Peirce, Neal R., and Jerry Hagstrom. 1984. *The Book of America*. New York: Warner Books.

Peirce, Neal R., and John Keefe. 1980. *The Great Lakes States of America*. New York: W. W. Norton.

Penning, James M. 1994. "Pat Robertson and the GOP: 1988 and Beyond." *Sociology of Religion* 55 (Fall): 327–44.

Persinos, John. 1994. "Has the Christian Right Taken Over the Republican Party?" *Campaigns and Elections* 15 (September): 20–24.

Reed, Ralph. 1994a. *Politically Incorrect: The Emerging Faith Factor in American Politics*. Dallas: Word Publishing.

———. 1994b. "The Future of the Religious Right." Pp. 81–85 in *Christian Political Activism at the Crossroads*, ed. William R. Stevenson, Jr. Lanham, Md.: University Press of America.

Steinfels, Peter. 1990. "Dobson Counsels Way to Influence on Right." *The Grand Rapids Press* (9 June).

Stollman, Gerald H. 1978. *Michigan State Legislators and Their Work*. Washington, D.C.: University Press of America.

9

Minnesota: Christians and Quistians in the GOP

Christopher P. Gilbert and David A. Peterson

In the post–World War II era, Minnesota has staked out a reputation as one of the nation's most progressive states. Its distinguished tradition of liberal leadership, exemplified by Democratic-Farmer-Labor (DFL) party figures such as Hubert Humphrey, Eugene McCarthy, and Walter Mondale, has guided both the development of an activist state government and the ideals of the national Democratic Party. With this history as backdrop, the dramatic rise of the Christian Right as a potent force in Minnesota politics might seem to be an anomaly. In fact, the political culture of the state makes it well suited for electoral movements founded on social or moral grounds. Moreover, as the 1994 elections demonstrate, issues with strong social or moral foundations have the capacity to produce religiously motivated candidates and activists across the political spectrum.

Such issues and movements also have the capacity to lead the press and pundits to overreact. When Minnesota's popular sitting governor, a moderate Independent Republican (IR), was denied his own party's endorsement for reelection in June 1994, political analysts nationwide took notice of the shock waves emanating from St. Paul. But although a little-known fifth-generation farmer named Allen Quist may have embodied the national emergence of Minnesota's Christian conservatives, by no means did he represent its sole power base. In the wake of Quist's spectacular failure to win the party primary three months after his triumphant endorsement, many observers jumped the gun again, concluding erroneously that in Minnesota the electoral strength of the Christian Right was vastly overstated.

Following the November elections, a much more accurate portrait of Minnesota's Christian conservative movement has emerged, however. In looking beyond the gubernatorial race, it becomes clear that the Christian Right played a pivotal role in elevating a first-term U.S. representative to the Senate and driving substantial IR gains in the state legislature. Moreover, these successes—and Quist's failure—provide important clues for predicting the future of the movement in Minnesota and elsewhere. We will investigate the Christian Right's influence in contemporary Minnesota politics through a review of recent electoral history, a description of Minnesota's endorsement and nomination processes, and a thorough examination of the 1994 gubernatorial and Senate races that includes analysis of media coverage and county-level voting patterns.

The Background

Christian conservatives have been active and influential in Minnesota politics since the early 1980s, gaining strength within the IR party and forming a reliable core constituency for several prominent conservative officeholders (Haas 1992). The state Republican Party took on the name Independent Republican in 1974 to distance itself from the Watergate scandal, and indeed the label has come to represent two very distinct and conflicting worldviews—a primarily secular constituency advocating moderate to progressive social policies combined with fiscal restraint (the "I" side) and the increasingly Christian Right–dominated "R" wing that stresses a social agenda centered on opposition to abortion and the restoration of traditional values and family structures.

Some leaders have successfully merged these two strains of IR ideology. By the late 1980s the state's acknowledged key IR figure was Second District U.S. representative Vin Weber, a member of the House minority leadership and an articulate, effective spokesperson for both wings of the state party. The conceptual leadership of Weber, married to a vigorous set of pro-life activists and organizations, provided the foundation for the strong emergence of the Christian Right in the 1990s. Though not publicly a Christian conservative, Weber understood the importance of cultivating ties and incorporating the concerns of Christian Right voters into the party:

> In Minnesota, we have had this phenomenon for over 10 years. . . . By and large I have found that the vast majority of those folks become good, solid, responsible Republican activists and they don't give up their beliefs but they learn in the course of one election cycle the role of compromise, a proper understanding of the separation of church and state and they become very responsible activists in the process. (Haas 1992)

The commitment of the IR's newest "responsible activists" was sorely tested by the state's election results in 1990 and 1992. From a Christian conservative point of view, these two elections represented a near-complete disaster. The only incumbent U.S. senator to lose in 1990 was the well-financed (a nearly five-to-one fund-raising advantage) Rudy Boschwitz; although not regarded as a strong conservative, Boschwitz was nevertheless clearly preferable to the liberal college professor and political activist Paul Wellstone, who defeated him by a narrow margin after a bitter and contentious campaign (Barone and Ujifusa 1993, 683).

At the same time that Boschwitz was managing to turn certain victory into defeat, the conservative IR challenge to vulnerable incumbent DFL governor Rudy Perpich also managed to sink its own chances. IR gubernatorial candidate Jon Grunseth, with solid pro-life conservative credentials and the endorsement of the party convention, easily defeated state auditor Arne Carlson and four other contenders in the September IR primary. But in October 1990, Grunseth was accused of sexual improprieties involving teenage girls. Later that month a woman alleged in print that she had carried on a nine-year affair with Grunseth. Carlson declared himself a write-in candidate after the initial allegations; following the second disclosure, Grunseth withdrew and the IR party named Carlson its official nominee (Barone and Ujifusa 1993, 681; Hoium and Oistad 1991). Carlson subsequently defeated Perpich in November, but from the Christian Right's point of view the election of an IR governor who supported abortion and gay rights, day care, and handicapped access legislation was hardly a cause for celebration, regardless of Carlson's unquestionably solid record as a fiscal conservative.

The elections of 1992 proved little better for the Christian Right. Its supporters gained even more influence in the state party apparatus, while its desired candidates fell in alarming numbers statewide. The most visible loss was in the Second Congressional District. Vin Weber chose not to seek reelection, concerned about the probable focus on his House bank overdrafts. The IR nominee to replace Weber was farmer and former state legislator Cal Ludeman, who had run unsuccessfully for governor in 1986. Ludeman had more name recognition, more money, and solid conservative, anti-abortion credentials in the predominantly rural district. However, he lost by 569 votes to Montevideo lawyer David Minge, who received substantial assistance late in the race from Wellstone's grassroots organization (Barone and Ujifusa 1993, 690–91).

While not all IR candidates with ties to the Christian Right met a similar fate—the victory of newcomer Rod Grams in the sixth District House race is a notable exception—overall the Ludeman defeat was typical of a weak showing. Thanks primarily to independent candidate Ross Perot's strong campaign (24 percent of the vote, one of his best states), President Bush received only one third of the state's presidential vote and several other prominent conservative candidates lost in congressional and state legislative races.

In the wake of these results, many IR officials called for moderation of the party platform to reduce the Christian Right's influence (Smith 1992a). Despite fears that wealthy contributors and independent voters would desert, the response of Christian Right party activists was to oust the moderate state party chair in 1993 and to install a new chair with solid ties to the party's conservative core, thus setting the stage for the 1994 intraparty battles (Smith 1992b; Smith 1993).

Structural Factors

The structure of Minnesota's candidate selection process is particularly advantageous for well-organized factions. In late February or early March, both the IR and DFL parties hold local precinct caucuses, which adopt amendments and choose delegates to county conventions that are held a few weeks later. The county conventions in turn select delegates to each party's state convention, and are also charged with endorsing candidates for local legislative seats. In June, the two state conventions endorse candidates for the major statewide offices.

The primary election is not held until September. Most non-endorsed candidates pledge to drop out of the primary after the state conventions, but increasingly the primary has been contested; the Grunseth–Carlson IR primary battle of 1990 is an excellent example, with Carlson virtually ignoring the endorsement process to concentrate on the primary. The rules of the primary election encourage challenges as well—voters may take either party's ballot in the primary, and crossover voters are often crucial to the outcome.

The party endorsement carries several obvious advantages. Endorsees have a built-in organization ready to serve. Lists of campaign contributors and poll data are more readily available. Sample ballots assist with name recognition. Even the State Fair in late summer serves to enhance the stature of the party's chosen; nonendorsed candidates cannot distribute literature or have their photos displayed at either party's booth.

With fewer than one percent of the state's citizens participating in the precinct caucuses, mobilization of a small core of committed followers allows one group to dominate the entire process. After the frustration of the 1990 and 1992 races, this is precisely what Christian conservatives maneuvered to do in 1994 within the IR party, and their efforts centered on Allen Quist, a St. Peter farmer and former state legislator noted for his fervent faith and conservative social agenda. A member of the Evangelical Lutheran Synod, a small and independent denomination with Norwegian origins (Allen 1994), Quist declared his candidacy against Governor Carlson in July 1993, declaring his fellow party member to be "left of center" on social issues and a poor fiscal manager (Whereatt 1993).

The IR Gubernatorial Race—Caucuses to Convention

As the standard-bearer of the IR party's independent wing, Arne Carlson's first term lived up to modest expectations. His record as a prudent fiscal manager and his frequent use of the veto to counter the DFL legislative majorities earned Carlson favorable ratings (60 percent approval) among Minnesotans by late 1993 (Smith 1993). However, his longtime support for abortion rights and ending discrimination against homosexuals continued to make Carlson anathema to the conservative wing of the IRs, who of course had rejected him soundly in the 1990 primary in favor of the staunchly conservative Jon Grunseth.

Officeholders with such obvious strengths rarely would face a primary challenge, let alone an endorsement fight. Ironically, this is exactly what occurred—there was no endorsement fight because the race for the endorsement essentially ended with the opening night of local caucuses. Quist's supporters routed the Carlson forces and installed their own people as delegates, thus ensuring success at the county and state conventions to follow (Baden 1994a; Smith 1994d). The numerical strength and superior cohesion of the "Quistians" meant that almost no one who did not adhere to the Christian Right's positions on abortion, gay rights, school prayer, and related issues could even hold a delegate seat at any level of the process.[1]

For this faction that had seen its agenda largely bypassed inside and outside the IR party in the previous decade, the caucus and convention process represented a public "takeover" of the party by Christian conservatives, and they made sure to follow through at the state convention. Carlson made a half-hearted appeal to state IR delegates at the convention—many in the audience were openly hostile—and generally saved his resources for the primary, as Quist easily won the endorsement and generated national attention in the process (Whereatt 1994a; Berke 1994).

The success of the Quist race for the IR endorsement rested primarily with his superior organization, melded to the unique characteristics of the Minnesota endorsement process. Absent the insular caucus system in which access could be restricted to the political and religious faithful, however, Quist's June victory proved to be short-lived.

Rod Grams—the "Other" Christian Conservative Candidate

Somewhat lost in the attention that the Quist candidacy garnered in the spring of 1994, the Christian Right succeeded in gaining endorsement for another figure who was a natural ally to the movement. In his one term as U.S. representative, Sixth District Congressman Rod Grams had received a 100 percent rating from the Christian Coalition, higher than any other Minnesota representative (Schmickle and McGrath 1994). A former television anchor, Grams embodied the Christian conservative vision of the IR Party of the 1990s. His views and core constituency stood in marked contrast to the retiring incumbent David Durenberger (Schmickle and McGrath 1994).

Grams also presented convention delegates with a clear contrast to his principal opponent, Lieutenant Governor Joanell Dyrstad. Like her 1990 running mate Arne Carlson, Dyrstad drew support from the independent wing of the IR party, favoring abortion rights and prudent fiscal conservatism. Also like Carlson, Dyrstad recognized that Christian conservative dominance in the convention meant that she would have to focus resources on the September primary, effectively conceding the endorsement to Grams (Baden 1994b).

Beyond his obvious connections with the Christian Right, Rod Grams deserves even more attention as an amazing political success story. The 1992 congressional campaign was his first run for office, and while the name recognition from his television career certainly helped, Grams also benefited from a scandal surrounding his DFL opponent, plus a strong third candidate who served to split the pro-abortion rights vote— implying that Grams was simply lucky to be in the right district at the right time. Thus analysts and more moderate IRs tended in 1992 to underestimate the nature and strength of Grams's appeal, a mistake apparently repeated in the 1994 endorsement process, as the Quist phenomenon drew most of the public and media attention while Grams rather quietly dominated a crowded and well-regarded field of endorsement challengers.

The IR Primary

The three-month lag between the state convention and the primary proved too long for Quist's campaign. The tactics of conservative IR loyalists in excluding moderates and exploiting their control came off as arrogant and mean-spirited. A widely publicized Quist remark about men being "genetically predisposed" to head families became an albatross-like tag, forever attached to his media coverage regardless of the content of his stump speeches and anti-Carlson ads (Smith 1994d). Ultimately, Quist proved unable to expand his social conservative base of support despite an economic platform designed to present him as mainstream to the larger core of IR and crossover voters (Smith 1994c, 1994d).

The end result on primary election day was that the Quist candidacy mobilized substantial numbers of IRs and crossover voters; unfortunately for Quist, almost two thirds of the IR primary voters mobilized for the opposition, rejecting Quist in favor of Governor Carlson. Quist received over 160,000 votes, an impressive total in an ordinary primary year.[2] But Carlson's strategy of saving energy, resources, and political capital for the primary campaign proved to be prescient. Carlson trounced Quist in the Twin Cities suburbs, where the swing voters in a Minnesota state election reside, and managed to hold his own in outstate counties. Quist generated substantial support from self-described born-again Christians, according to exit polls, but moderates and independents overwhelmingly supported the governor (Smith 1994c; von Sternberg 1994a). An estimated 100,000 voters may have crossed over to vote in the IR primary; most did so exclusively to oppose Quist (von Sternberg 1994a).

While the Quist defeat received most of the attention on primary night, the quieter success story for IRs was endorsed Senate candidate Rod Grams, who received a larger share of the vote from born-again IR primary voters than did Quist (von Sternberg 1994a). Grams handily defeated Joanell Dyrstad, whose one-third share of the primary vote can be attributed to crossovers and Carlson supporters, and thus probably overestimates her true support among IRs. Grams was one of many Christian Right candidates who triumphed in the primaries despite the

Carlson landslide; Christian conservative candidates won two key congressional primaries and several state house races (Smith 1994d).

Overall, primary night represented a mixed bag for the leadership of the IR party. Five of its six endorsed candidates for state constitutional offices—all of whom had close ties to Allen Quist—were defeated, an embarrassment to the party (Smith 1994d). The wins by Grams and other conservatives, however, suggest a crucial point when interpreting the Christian Right's influence in the state. While Quist, Grams, and their allied candidates all supported virtually the entire party platform, no other candidate was as open or aggressive as Quist in stressing social issues in religious terms (Smith 1994d). It would seem that *support* for the agenda of Christian conservatives worked to a candidate's advantage, whereas *identification* of a candidate with the Christian Right became a clear disadvantage. The nature of this distinction is made clearer by an analysis of media coverage during the formative stages of the 1994 campaign.

Media Effects on Perceptions of Candidates

An analysis of *Minneapolis Star Tribune* coverage of the primary campaign supports this interpretation of the obstacles Quist confronted in appealing to non-Christian conservative voters. We consider the *Star Tribune* to be the best source for our purposes, because it has the largest readership throughout the state and therefore the largest probable effect on voter attitudes. The time frame covered is the defining part of the campaign, beginning roughly one month prior to the state conventions and continuing through the end of June, following the conventions. It is during this period that the effect of the media is the most prevalent (Polsby and Wildavsky 1991, 75–79); the major IR and DFL candidates are being covered intensively for the first time, and the conventions are clearly the signal events of the initial stages of the election.

The initial hypothesis is that coverage of Allen Quist will include a significantly higher religious content than coverage of either Rod Grams or DFL gubernatorial candidate John Marty, both of whom also campaigned with substantial church-based core constituencies. Further, the differences in coverage should lead to conclusions regarding the relative success of the three candidates. One apparent consequence of the newspaper's coverage would be that in the minds of many voters, Quist becomes marginalized as a fringe candidate.

Indeed, it is ironic that Quist received so much attention for the religious motivations behind his political beliefs, while the DFL primary victor ran a campaign that was also based substantially in churches. State senator John Marty, a member of the Evangelical Lutheran Church in America and son of the prominent Lutheran theologian and historian Martin Marty, made no secret of his own strong faith and liberal politics, and his father became a frequent presence who assisted with fund-raising and networking among Lutheran congregations (Allen 1994).[3]

Coding

Star Tribune articles were coded to differentiate among sections of the paper, news stories versus columnists and letters to the editor, and length of stories. Word counts were used to balance the discrepancies in the number and length of articles that cover the three candidates; not surprisingly, Quist received far more coverage in this time period.

Once articles were identified and sorted by type, the data base was analyzed to find religious references to Quist, Grams, and Marty. The terms selected for testing were: *religion* (or any word with the root *relig*), *Christian* (or any word with the root *Christ*, excluding Christmas), *church*, *Lutheran*, *Evangelical*, *fundamentalist*, *theology* (or any word with the root *theol*), *pray/prayer/praying*, *Bible/biblical*, *born-again*, *worship*, *zealot*, *God*, and *cult*. With appropriate controls for article length and type, the results of the analysis are presented in tables 9-1, 9-2, and 9-3.

Frequencies of Religious References

Within the time frame of the study, a total of 134 uses of the chosen terms are found. Table 9-1 shows that 78 percent of the religious term references come from the coverage of Quist; 13 percent describe Grams; and 9 percent are found in Marty's coverage. Controlling for the amount of coverage each candidate receives, religious references about Quist occur 3.32 times as often as those for Marty and 1.92 times as often as those for Grams. Marty articles have a religious reference once every 3,000 words, Grams articles every 1,700, indicating that the newspaper does pick up on some connection between religion and these candidates. By not emphasizing this connection to the same extent as for Quist (one reference every 900 words), the *Star Tribune* effectively defines Quist as a far more religious candidate than Marty, and Grams to a lesser extent, even though the motivations of all three men, their issue positions, and the voting patterns of their supporters suggest that this distinction is not fully justified.

Table 9-1

Frequency of Religious References for Quist, Grams, and Marty, May–June 1994, *Minneapolis Star Tribune*

	Quist	Grams	Marty
Number of references	105	17	12
Number of words	93,518	29,063	35,509
Words per reference	890.65	1,709.59	2,958.08
Ratio of Quist religious references to other candidates' references	—	1.92:1	3.32:1

Source: Authors' calculations from *Star Tribune*.

Location of References

The findings outlined in table 9-2 illustrate that the religious component of Quist's candidacy is presented throughout the *Star Tribune*, not merely isolated to one section. There are no references to Grams or Marty in articles by columnists, and Marty has none in the rest of the State/Metro section where the columnists appear. Quist, by contrast, has 21.9 percent and 34.3 percent, respectively, of his references in these two parts of the paper; Grams has only 12 percent in the Metro/State

Table 9-2

Percentage of Religious References by Type of Story, Month, and Location, May–June 1994, *Minneapolis Star Tribune*

	Quist	Grams	Marty
Type of story			
Columns (B section)	21.9	0.0	0.0
Letters to the Editor (A section)	6.7	0.0	2.2
Month			
May	18.1	29.5	0.0
June	81.9	70.5	100.0
Location in paper			
A (main) section	65.7	88.0	100.0
B (metro/state) section	34.3	12.0	0.0

Source: Authors' calculations from *Star Tribune*.

section. Only a small share of Quist's references come in letters to the editor (6.7 percent), but this is still three times as large as the letters references to Marty (2.2 percent), while no letters refer to Grams at all.

The variety in distribution of references translates into a stronger definition for Quist in two ways. First, not everyone reads all sections of the paper. Thus, the greater the variety of places to find references, the more likely people are to read and be influenced by them. If all references had appeared in the first (A) section of the paper, they would be missed by the readers who skip that section. Secondly, those who read all sections of the paper and find references laced throughout would have the references reinforced. The number of different locations for the references should amplify the definitions of the candidates that emerge from the references.

Specific Content of References

Table 9-3 indicates the differences in the content of the religious references made about the three candidates. Seven of the twelve references made about Marty (58.3 percent) are either *Lutheran* or some variation

Table 9-3
Content of Religious References, May–June 1994, *Minneapolis Star Tribune*

	Quist		Grams		Marty	
Bible/biblical	2	(2.0%)	2	(11.8%)	0	(0.0%)
Born-again	0	(0.0%)	0	(0.0%)	0	(0.0%)
Christ/Christian	11	(10.4%)	3	(17.6%)	1	(8.3%)
Church	8	(7.6%)	2	(11.8%)	1	(8.3%)
Cult	16	(15.2%)	0	(0.0%)	0	(0.0%)
Evangelical	4	(3.8%)	1	(5.9%)	0	(0.0%)
Fundamentalist	3	(2.9%)	0	(0.0%)	0	(0.0%)
God	6	(5.7%)	1	(5.9%)	1	(8.3%)
Lutheran	3	(2.9%)	1	(5.9%)	4	(33.3%)
Pray/prayer	3	(2.9%)	3	(17.6%)	0	(0.0%)
Religion/religious	41	(39.0%)	4	(23.5%)	0	(0.0%)
Theology/theologian	0	(0.0%)	0	(0.0%)	3	(25.0%)
Worship	1	(1.0%)	0	(0.0%)	0	(0.0%)
Zealot	7	(6.7%)	0	(0.0%)	2	(16.7%)

Source: Authors' calculations from *Star Tribune*.

of *theology*. These terms denote biographical references to Marty. In fact, each use of *theology* is actually a reference to Marty's father. Such terms are innocuous because they do not carry the political and emotional baggage of terms such as *cult*. We also note that *cult* represents 15 percent of the references to Quist, while the term is never used to reference Grams or Marty.

Additionally, terms that describe the Christian conservative movement (*religious*, *Christian*, *Evangelical*, *fundamentalist*, *cult*, and *born-again*) are used much more often to describe Quist and Grams than Marty. These terms account for 71.3 percent of the references about Quist, 47.1 percent of the references about Grams, and only 8.3 percent of the references for Marty. This is notable partly to show accuracy (most of the above terms are not appropriate for any DFL candidate) but also to show that the Grams references differ from Quist references both quantitatively and qualitatively.

Initial Conclusions

The findings outlined in the tables indicate not only how the media perceived the religion of the candidates in Minnesota's 1994 elections, but also how the media, and by extension voters, perceived candidates. While Grams and Quist are equally deserving of the "religious right" description based on their views and voter support, and Marty certainly can be accurately described as religious, Quist is the only candidate with whom such terms are strongly associated. Media framing of Quist in religious terms appeared to contribute to his marginalization among voters who do not belong to the Christian conservative movement. It is these voters, turning out in force, who ultimately propelled Arne Carlson to his landslide win in the IR primary.

General Election Results

Governor

The gubernatorial race proved to be no contest. Arne Carlson held a commanding 28-percentage-point margin over John Marty in the initial postprimary poll, a gap that widened through election day (McGrath 1994a). Carlson rolled to a record victory margin of more than a half million votes (almost a two-to-one advantage) over Marty, who suffered the worst gubernatorial defeat in DFL history. Exit polls show that Carlson simply overwhelmed Marty among nearly all categories of voters, save strong liberals and committed DFLers (Whereatt 1994b; von Sternberg 1994b).

Without a clear choice in this race, the interests and behavior of Christian conservative voters are difficult to identify. Exit poll data indicate that Quist primary voters favored Carlson over Marty by 55 to 35 percent in the general election (von Sternberg 1994b). Given Carlson's otherwise strong support among self-identified conservatives and Republicans, these figures suggest that many Quist supporters could not bring themselves to back Carlson after the bitter primary defeat. Many stayed home, while a few Quist loyalists publicized a write-in effort for their candidate in the week prior to the general election. But little attention was paid; Quist received an estimated 24,000 write-in votes in the end (1.3 percent of the total vote) (Whereatt 1994b).

Senate

In the lopsided gubernatorial election the behavior of Quist primary voters is interesting but certainly could not be considered decisive. Far more intriguing is the impact of the Christian Right on the U.S. Senate race. As demonstrated in the May-June media analysis, there were few cues that could lead voters to attach any pejorative, faith-related attributes to Rod Grams as opposed to Quist. Whether this was due to shrewd political maneuvering by Grams or to the failure of Grams's opponents to publicize and exploit such a connection (it was tried in both the primary and general election races, with little apparent success) remains an open question (McGrath and Baden 1994; Baden 1994c).

Grams turned a small postprimary deficit into a slim 42–38 edge over his DFL opponent, former state representative Ann Wynia, in the final preelection poll (McGrath 1994a). After a contentious general election campaign laced with attack advertisements from both sides and little substantive debate, Grams defeated Wynia by 49 to 44 percent (McGrath 1994b).[4] In the exit poll data there is substantial evidence of the Christian Right's strength. Grams won substantial majorities among voters opposing abortion (77 percent support among those opposed to all abortions), gun owners (59 percent), and voters who wanted new people in government (58 percent) (von Sternberg 1994b). An election eve poll also showed that voters who considered family values and morals as the most important issue would favor Grams over Wynia by 59 to 23 percent (McGrath 1994a). This category represented 27 percent of the total electorate, further evidence of the connection between Grams and the issue positions most salient to the Christian Right.

State Legislative Races

Given the substantial attention paid by the media and citizens to the nasty senate race between Grams and Wynia, there was little focus on local races where the Christian Right had notable success. In state legislative races, IRs gained thirteen seats, and in eleven of those districts they replaced DFL legislators with Christian Right–backed candidates. Most of the gains came in suburban Twin Cities communities, heretofore considered unwinnable by social conservatives. A massive voter turnout and information drive sponsored by the Christian Coalition, Minnesota Concerned Citizens for Life, and other affiliated organizations greatly assisted these IR victories (Baden 1994d).

More importantly, the state house gains demonstrate the importance of controlling the party apparatus. With Christian conservatives dominating the endorsement process and the allocation of general election campaign resources, the state legislative outcome was no accident. No moderate IR candidate defeated a DFLer for state legislature; moreover, all of the defeated DFL incumbents had been supporters of abortion and gay rights (Baden 1994d). The ability to use the party organization to target rivals outside (and within) the party means that the Christian Right will have an active voice for years to come.

County-Level Vote Analysis

The selective importance of the Christian Right in the general election outcomes is clearly demonstrated by an analysis of aggregate voting patterns in Minnesota's eighty-seven counties. Aggregate patterns do not necessarily indicate individual motivations; however, county-level models of Carlson and Grams voting supplement the exit poll data in revealing some nonobvious patterns that reflect Christian conservative strengths and weaknesses in 1994.

Data for this analysis were gathered from several sources. County vote totals are widely published for both the primary and general elections. We add to this the 1992 county presidential returns, as well as a series of measures of the religious composition of Minnesota counties. This latter data set comes from the 1990 national church census conducted by the Glenmary Research Center and the National Council of Churches of

Christ (NCCC) (Bradley et al. 1992). Tables 9-4 and 9-5 present multiple regression models assessing the impact of county-level variables on Carlson and Grams voting across counties. All variables included in the regression models are expressed as percentages.[5]

Table 9-4 reports results from the county-level analysis of the Carlson vote. Carlson makes no appeals based on religion or morals, nor does he draw attention to his personal faith.[6] Hence the model predicts only 20 percent of the variance in the county Carlson vote. Moreover, the impact from religious factors is neither consistent nor easily explained. Increasing percentages of Methodists and nontraditional Protestants[7] correspond to higher percentages of Carlson voting, yet the presence of more Presbyterians drives Carlson voting lower. Further, a variable measuring the percent of a county population that belongs to a church is not a statistically significant predictor of county Carlson voting. The strongest statistical effect in table 9-4 comes from 1992 Perot voting, which is not a religious-based factor at all. It would seem that Carlson's county vote reflects his overall dominance (he carried all but three counties) and indicates no specific connection to the Christian Right.

Table 9-5 presents a very different picture regarding correlates of

Table 9-4
Estimated 1994 General Election County Vote for Arne Carlson (OLS Estimates)

Independent Variable	Coefficient	
Intercept	37.98	(6.36) ***
Percent religious adherents in county	0.05	(0.05)
Percent 1992 Perot vote in county	0.70	(0.20) ***
Percent Methodists in county	0.40	(0.21) *
Percent nontraditional Protestants in county	2.33	(1.23) *
Percent Presbyterians in county	–0.61	(0.24) **
Number of cases	87	
Adjusted R²	.20	

Source: Bradley et al. 1992; authors' compilation of 1992 and 1994 county votes in Minnesota.
Standard errors in parentheses.
*Significant at 0.10 level.
**Significant at 0.05 level.
***Significant at 0.01 level.

Table 9-5

Estimated 1994 General Election County Vote for Rod Grams (OLS Estimates)

Independent Variable	Coefficient	
Intercept	7.77	(4.05) *
Percent religious adherents in county	0.05	(0.02) **
Percent 1992 Perot vote in county	0.52	(0.12) ***
Percent Carlson general election vote in county	0.34	(0.06) ***
Percent Quist primary vote (Quist share of total primary votes, IR and DFL)	0.36	(0.06) ***
Percent Jewish adherents in county	−1.04	(0.42) **
Number of cases	86	
Adjusted R^2	.67	

Source: Bradley et al. 1992; authors' compilation of 1992 and 1994 county votes in Minnesota.
Standard errors in parentheses.
*Significant at 0.10 level.
**Significant at 0.05 level.
***Significant at 0.01 level.

Grams voting across counties. Increasing county support for Ross Perot in 1992 and Arne Carlson in 1994 leads to higher levels of Grams voting.[8] More important, counties with higher levels of religious adherence also tend to give more support to Grams. These three factors demonstrate the key trends that allow Grams to win a tight contest—partisanship (represented by Carlson voting), capturing independent and swing voters (represented by Perot in the model), and gaining votes in counties where more citizens belong to churches (the adherents variable). In such counties, we can reasonably hypothesize that a candidate espousing family values, social and moral issues, and a conservative Christian faith should be expected to attract more votes than a candidate identified with secular issues (Wynia's principal issue was health care reform) and liberal politics (Baden 1994c).

This hypothesis is buttressed by one more finding from table 9-5. After controlling for the above three factors, a fourth significant, positive influence on county voting for Grams comes from Allen Quist's primary support in the county. Quist primary support is defined as the share of the *total* primary vote for Quist; recall that Minnesota voters can take either party's ballot in the primary, hence it is necessary to use the total primary vote and not simply Quist's share of the IR primary vote. The model in table 9-5 shows that in counties where Quist received more support in September, Grams gains more support in November.

Thus there is clear evidence of underlying Christian conservative support for Grams based on factors beyond partisanship—most notably religion and perhaps support for Quist as well. Further, the negative relationship between the presence of Jewish citizens and county Grams voting may show something of a reaction against the base of Grams's appeal; as in most of the United States, Minnesota Jews tend to vote Democratic/DFL and may have been influenced by the frequent charge that Christian conservatives tend toward intolerance of opposing viewpoints (Smith 1994b). The bottom line is that lost in the debris of the Quist primary defeat, Christian Right voters continued to exert influence on the general election, but this influence did not extend very far beyond Christian Right–affiliated candidates.

Lessons

Based on the results of the 1994 elections, the Christian Right in Minnesota stands poised to maintain its influence in the near future. Although there were some significant setbacks in 1994, the process by which candidates are selected and endorsed has not changed,[9] and the presence of Christian conservatives in key IR party positions means that more moderate IRs will have difficulty attracting electoral support and resources from their leadership. It is estimated that only one in three IR partisans is a Christian conservative or self-described born-again individual (McGrath 1994b); clearly the institutional strength of the Christian Right exceeds its numerical strength, and thus the battle between the "I" and the "R" within the IR party is likely to rage on. To the extent, however, that the Minnesota citizenry comes to equate the IR party solely or primarily with its Christian conservative faction, Christian Right–affiliated candidates may face a backlash among independents and swing voters similar to the crossover turnout that decimated Quist last September.

This last point leads to three important conclusions to be drawn from Minnesota's 1994 results. First, successful efforts by the Christian conservative movement in Minnesota tend to be *issue-driven*, not candidate- or personality-driven. A close identification with religion or the Christian

Right appears to hurt candidates, while identification with specific social and economic issues, not all of which typecast candidates as religious conservatives on the fringes, appears to be a plus. At least in Minnesota, the weaker the visible link between the Christian Right and the candidates it supports, the better the chances such candidates have of winning general elections.

Second, the media play a key role in structuring this link in the minds of voters. Considering the consistency of the social agenda advocated by both Quist and Grams, it is clear that the apparent framing of Quist as religious (with negative or pejorative connotations implicit in the terms used) and Grams as secular had tremendous implications for the different outcomes of the two candidacies.

This points to two basic assertions about the media's coverage of religious and Christian conservative candidates. First, the press often seems to lack a framework for analysis that allows for the consideration of a religious basis for political attitudes. The newspaper polls referred to in this chapter, for example, subdivide voters' religious faith into "Protestant" and "Catholic," categories that many political scientists regard as having limited utility in analysis. The media are also slow to comprehend the religious nature of candidates, systematically ignoring the connections until or unless such connections can be related to a movement that does fall within their prevailing paradigm. Coverage of John Marty exemplifies this point: having conceded—because it could hardly be denied—that Christian conservative candidates like Allen Quist have religious motivations leading to political agendas, it became difficult for the *Star Tribune* to find the salience of religion within a non-Christian conservative such as Marty. The use of simplistic terminology and frequent non sequiturs (references to separation of church and state come to mind) also tends to muddle coverage and mislead citizens.

By underplaying the religious foundations of Rod Grams's candidacy, the *Star Tribune* demonstrates the second assertion regarding media coverage of religion and politics. In order to comprehend the Christian Right, the newspaper personalized it around a single candidate (Quist), and often a single issue as well (abortion). Much of the *Star Tribune* coverage implies that Quist is *the* motivating factor for the mobilization of Christian conservative voters. This is of course untrue. Both Quist and Grams benefited from a movement that had been well established for a decade and recognized as such by party insiders like Vin Weber. Why did the media not also make this connection with Grams? Probably because Grams was already established in media coverage as a sitting IR officeholder. With the party cue determining the framing of Grams, ignoring his religious base reinforced the perception that Grams represented something different from Quist, when in fact their policy positions and profiles of their voting constituencies suggest just the opposite.

Finally, in evaluating the strength of the Christian Right, analysts must continue to recognize that in Minnesota and across the nation the movement is involved not only in high-profile, media-intensive races but also in legislative, school board, and city council contests. Citizens mobilized to run and support candidates for such offices, when motivated by a belief that their communities have lost the sense of traditional values and common purpose that underlie the fabric of American society, are not likely to demobilize simply because a handful of candidates in one election happen to lose. Theirs is self-consciously a strategy for exerting and maintaining political influence in the long term, at all levels of government. Concentrating only or primarily on what happens at the top of the ballot carries the risk of missing the dynamism and fervor that mark the ascendance and the future of the Christian Right in contemporary Minnesota politics.

Notes

1. The stringent ideological standards of the Christian Right prevented a number of prominent IRs from becoming state convention delegates, including the previously acceptable Cal Ludeman and the venerable Harold Stassen; this prompted a modest backlash among party veterans (Triggs 1994).

2. Jon Grunseth, for example, received over 169,000 votes in winning the 1990 IR primary (Barone and Ujifusa 1993, 685).

3. After a turbulent three-way campaign, DFL endorsee Marty eventually won a narrow victory over his rivals in the primary. His general election fortunes are considered later in the chapter.

4. A third Senate candidate, Dean Barkley of the Independence Party, received 5.4 percent of the general election vote. Although poll data suggest that Barkley pulled more votes from Wynia than from Grams, it would be an overstatement to claim that Barkley's presence in the race was the deciding factor. Regardless, his impact on the outcome is highly ironic; it should be recalled that Grams's 1992 U.S. House victory was largely due to the DFL candidate losing a significant share of pro-choice voters to an independent candidate—Dean Barkley.

5. The dependent variables *Percent Carlson vote in county* and *Percent Grams vote in county* represent each candidate's respective share of the *total* county vote, including all candidates. The same is true for *Percent 1992 Perot vote in county*.

6. Biographical sketches list Carlson's religion simply as "Protestant" (Barone and Ujifusa 1993, 685).

7. The group *nontraditional Protestants* includes Latter Day Saints and Jehovah's Witnesses.

8. It is worth noting that county Grams voting is *not* a statistically significant predictor of county Carlson voting—Carlson clearly leads the IR ticket.

9. There is, however, a growing sense that change is necessary in Minnesota's candidate endorsement procedures, and that reducing the three-month lag from convention to primary would be beneficial for voters. To date, however, while several proposals have been forthcoming there has been little movement towards passage of significant reforms in the state legislature (*Minneapolis Star Tribune*, 25 August 1994).

References

Allen, Martha Sawyer. 1994. "Quist, Marty Have One Faith, but Two Political Directions." *Minneapolis Star Tribune*, 10 July.

Baden, Patricia Lopez. 1994a. "Election Season Begins in Trenches; Again, Foes of Abortion Show Force at IR Caucuses." *Minneapolis Star Tribune*, 2 March.

———. 1994b. "U.S. Senate Candidates Solid But Not Charismatic." *Minneapolis Star Tribune*, 4 September.

———. 1994c. "Grams Had Just the Right Message at the Right Time; Wynia Had Trouble Matching His Focus on Crime, Taxes." *Minneapolis Star Tribune*, 9 November.

———. 1994d. "Religious Right Sees Its Influence in IR House Wins." *Minneapolis Star Tribune*, 23 November.

Barone, Michael, and Grant Ujifusa. 1993. *The Almanac of American Politics 1994.* Washington, D.C.: National Journal, Inc.

Berke, Richard. 1994. "Advances Posted by Religious Right in Several States." *New York Times*, 3 June.

Bradley, Martin, et al., eds. 1992. *Churches and Church Membership in the United States.* Atlanta: Glenmary Research Center.

Haas, Cliff. 1992. "Life of the Party: Issues and Ideas Man Vin Weber Sets His Sights on Reviving GOP." *Minneapolis Star Tribune*, 22 November.

Hoium, David, and Leo Oistad. 1991. *There Is No November.* Inver Grove Heights, Minn.: Jeric Publications.

McGrath, Dennis. 1994a. "Senate Race Tight; Carlson Keeps Big Lead." *Minneapolis Star Tribune*, 6 November.

———. 1994b. "Republicans Win Across U.S.; Grams, Carlson Victors." *Minneapolis Star Tribune*, 9 November.

McGrath, Dennis, and Patricia Lopez Baden. 1994. "Wynia Made Missteps and Missed Opportunities." *Minneapolis Star Tribune*, 10 November.

Minneapolis Star Tribune. 1994. "Crossovers: Party Registration Would Foil the Spoilers." Editorial, 7 August.

Minneapolis Star Tribune. 1994. "Commission to Seek Ways of Improving Caucus System." 25 August.

Peterson, David. 1995. "And They Shall Know You by Your Coverage: Media Definition of Religious Candidates in Minnesota's 1994 Statewide Elections." To be presented at 1995 American Political Science Association annual meeting, Chicago.

Polsby, Nelson, and Aaron Wildavsky. 1991. *Presidential Elections* 8th ed. New York: Free Press.

Schmickle, Sharon, and Dennis McGrath. 1994. "Rod Grams [candidate profile]." *Minneapolis Star Tribune*, 25 August.

Smith, Dane. 1992a. "Tuesday's IR Losses Bound to Bring Changes in Strategy." *Minneapolis Star Tribune*, 8 November.

———. 1992b. " 'Golden Elephants' Shun Conservatives and IR Party Coffers." *Minneapolis Star Tribune*, 6 December.

———. 1993. "Carlson Must Speak Softly and Carry the IR Right." *Minneapolis Star Tribune*, 13 September.

———. 1994a. "Quist's Quest for Governor Hardly Quixotic." *Minneapolis Star Tribune*, 27 March.

———. 1994b. "Carlson's Mention of Hitler Draws Fire from Quist; Religious Right's Rise Is Focus." *Minneapolis Star Tribune*, 9 August.

———. 1994c. "Carlson Victorious; Marty Is Surprise Winner: IR—Win Quells Revolt of Party's Right Wing." *Minneapolis Star Tribune*, 14 September.

———. 1994d. "Primary Lessons: Caucuses Will Stay and the Right Is Healthy." *Minneapolis Star Tribune*, 18 September.

Triggs, Mike. 1994. "Zombie Conservatives Decimate IR Faithful." *Minneapolis Star Tribune*, 12 April.

von Sternberg, Bob. 1994a. "Undecided Voters Held Sway in Three-Way DFL Battle." *Minneapolis Star Tribune*, 14 September.

———. 1994b. "Different Election, Same Outlook: Exit Polls Show Minnesota Voters Haven't Changed Much." *Minneapolis Star Tribune*, 9 November.

Whereatt, Robert. 1993. "Ex-legislator Takes Aim at Governor's Job." *Minneapolis Star Tribune*, 29 July.

———. 1994a. "IR Delegates Give Quist a Historic Win." *Minneapolis Star Tribune*, 18 June.

———. 1994b. "Governor Hands DFL Its Biggest Defeat." *Minneapolis Star Tribune*, 9 November.

10

Iowa: Everything Comes up Rosy

Jeremy D. Mayer and Bruce Nesmith

They asked him "Who are you going to vote for?"
When he told them George Bush, three of them
got down on their knees and started praying for
his soul.

> —Rich Bond, Bush national
> political director, in 1987,
> referring to the Iowa Robertson
> campaign

This is not about religion, this is about politics.

> —D. J. Gribbin, Christian
> Coalition national field
> director in 1995

The story of the Christian Right's success in Iowa since Marion (Pat) Robertson's 1987 upset victory in the state's GOP straw poll is one of compromise, cooperation, and conquest. It is through following the dictum of Gribbin, to practice politics, rather than praying for the eternal souls of their political opponents, that the Christian Coalition and its allies in Iowa achieved such sweeping influence within the state and the Iowa Republican Party. As shown by Bond's comment, there has always existed the potential for conflict between traditional Republican forces in Iowa and the Christian Rightists. Following the shock of Robertson's triumph in 1987, the Christian Right has strengthened and evolved in Iowa, learning when to fight and when to negotiate. Their successes include the 1994 reelection of a prominent ally in Governor Branstad, the acquisition of all five Iowa house seats for the Republicans with the defeat of powerful incumbent Neal Smith in 1994, the 1992 defeat of a state ERA referendum, near-complete control of the state Republican platform, and the attainment of a solid majority on the party's central committee.

The power that they hold today in Iowa is impressive, but the explanation for their triumphs contains within it the outlines of potential cracks in their alliance with the mainstream Republicans of Iowa. It is only through careful management of their relations with the rest of the state Republican Party, as well as through skillful manipulations of national trends, that the Christian Right in Iowa achieved so much in the period from 1987 to 1995. The ability of the Christian Coalition and its ideological allies to maintain their position as "the most potent single force in the state GOP" (Von Drehle 1994) depends on their ability to prolong and deepen their ties to moderates and economic conservatives in Iowa.

The Iowa Republican Party and its experience with the Christian Right illustrates one pattern of how the party has adjusted to the influx of evangelical Christians in the past fourteen years. Beginning with the 1980 presidential campaign, the national Republican coalition became dramatically more heterogeneous with the incorporation of conservative social-issues Christians. The changes caused by this partisan shift among white evangelicals may have been even more dramatic in Iowa, which traditionally had two "almost indistinguishable" centrist parties (Schmidt 1990, 252). It was these centrist Republicans of Iowa that gave George Bush, at the time a moderate, pro-choice Republican, his unexpected caucus victory over conservative front-runner Ronald Reagan, probably leading to Bush's eventual selection as the vice presidential candidate.

In Iowa as in the nation, the Republican Party has undergone a great change in the last fourteen years with the influx of white evangelicals, many of whom had previously been apolitical or even leaned Democratic. These new Republicans eschewed libertarian ideologies and sought to use the power of the state to promote traditional moral values. The tensions between these two wings of the party were evident from the beginning.

Thus, in any state where the Christian Right seeks to have a voice in the Republican Party, two ideal types of outcomes are possible. The first might be termed the "rosy scenario," where economic and social conservatives, along with the still important Republican moderates, combine to pursue common electoral and policy goals (Nesmith 1994, 129–32). Examples of this scenario at the national level include Reagan's victories in 1980 and 1984 as well as George Bush's election in 1988. The Republicans in those years positioned themselves to take advantage of a "reaction against modernity" and the "moral emptiness of the public square" as well as a "general renewal of confidence in the market" (Reichley 1986, 35; Hutcheson 1988). This scenario requires that all party factions display a measure of pragmatism, accepting and supporting each other's candidates regardless of divisions over specific issues. The opportunity to defeat Democrats, either locally or nationally, cemented such interfactional cooperation.

The other possibility, the "bleak scenario" (Nesmith 1994, 132–36) results from white evangelical restiveness due to lack of progress on their policy goals, even after Republican victories. Some religious conservatives to this day express disappointment with the Reagan presidency, because they believe that social issues such as school prayer and abortion were placed on the back burner and economic and foreign affairs concerns dominated the Reagan agenda. This feeling was even more prominent among evangelical supporters of Bush, and may have been one explanation for the early strength of Patrick Buchanan's challenge in 1992. In a bleak scenario, conservative Christians, feeling alienated from the mainstream Republican Party, threaten to either abstain or defect from the coalition. Internecine primary battles among Republican factions split along religious lines pose an obvious threat to November victories.

In Iowa, fights in the past have erupted over such internal issues as state party platforms, the selection of Iowa's delegation to the national party convention, and state central committee membership. A modified form of the bleak scenario involves Christians mounting a third-party challenge in November, thus giving the Democratic candidate a great advantage and "punishing" the traditional Republicans. While bitter intraparty disputes and third-party candidacies hurt the Republican Party as a whole, they may serve a longer-range goal of the newer Christian Republicans, that of gaining respect from the party establishment. Gary Jarmin of Christian Voice complained as early as 1986 that Republican politicians "don't want to relinquish power and control to their Christian puppies. They just want to throw us a Milk-Bone every now and then" (Stern 1986).

Of course, traditional Republican moderates and economic conservatives may become equally frustrated when they feel that their policy stances and concerns are ignored by an ascendant Christian Right. Longtime Republican regulars in Iowa often reacted with disdain and anger to the influx of energized Christian activists; this response is typical of the nation as well (Wilcox 1995, 31). Such antipathy can have electoral effects. For example, Bush's 1992 election defeat is attributed by many to his loss of traditional Republican constituencies, although he substantially retained evangelical support (*New York Times* 1992). A local Bush supporter, Congressman Jim Leach, echoed this concern when he made his 1992 postelection analysis. According to this popular moderate Republican, if the Christian Coalition and the more traditional Republicans "cannot work together, we may well see a splintering of the two-party system" (Pins 1992). Holding the left and right wings of the Republican Party together is no longer a Rockefeller–Goldwater divide; now the ideological descendants of Goldwater and Rockefeller work together on one side, while Buchanan and Dan Quayle occupy the right. In Iowa and throughout the nation, the ability of Republicans to manage that divide will help to determine their electoral success (Connelly and Pitney 1994). While all of the factors pointing toward a "bleak scenario" of intraparty division have been present in the Iowa Republican Party in recent history, none of them surfaced in 1994, and this is the best explanation of the Republican surge in Iowa.

Steps in the Maturation Process: From Robertson for President to Stop the ERA in Iowa

The Christian Coalition, in Iowa and the nation, sprang forth from the remnants of Pat Robertson's 1988 run for the Republican nomination for president. From the first, Robertson supporters realized how Iowa's caucus system aided their efforts. Bush's unfortunate comment after his 1988 third-place showing, that his supporters were probably too busy attending debutante balls to spend all day at the Iowa caucuses, is illustrative of the differing socioeconomic backgrounds and levels of commitment between Iowa's traditional Republicans and the new Christian Rightists. This advantage led to Robertson's 1987 win in the Iowa straw poll and his second-place finish the following year in the Iowa caucuses. Both of these events sent shock waves through the state and national Republican Party (Dionne 1987).

The Robertson campaign, as seen through the eyes of media analysts and Republican mainstreamers, was limited to an enthusiastic group of religious activists. Supporters overwhelmingly tended to be white evangelicals with little political experience, and they often used blunt religious rhetoric to attack their opponents (Peterson 1987). While the Robertson campaign was extremely successful in mobilizing evangelicals in the Iowa caucuses, to achieve their goal of becoming the major force within the Republican Party they would have to expand their appeal.

This was the primary impetus for the founding of the Christian Coalition, which was formed after Robertson's failed 1988 campaign. Within Iowa, many of the twenty-six thousand Robertson caucus voters quickly joined the new group, providing the nucleus for its early activism. "You started with a certain core of evangelical conservative Christians. . . . what we've done in five years is blown way out beyond that. . . . we've got Orthodox Jews, we've got Catholics involved, Hispanics, African Americans, you name it" (Gribbin 1995).

Because of Iowa's demographic characteristics, the main focus of Christian Coalition outreach in Iowa had to be conservative Catholics; acquiring all of the Orthodox Jewish, African American, and Hispanic votes in Iowa is a negligible accomplishment for any political faction. Through its close association with Governor Terry Branstad, a Roman Catholic, and through its alliance with a number of Catholic pro-life groups, the Iowa Christian Coalition has begun to shed its strictly evangelical image.

The alliance with Governor Branstad may be crucial in this respect. Christian conservatives are typically portrayed as lower socioeconomic status (SES), southern white evangelicals. Although this stereotype was largely true of the Moral Majority and of the 1988 Robertson campaign, the Christian Coalition is actively working to confound that image. Moreover, to the extent that the Christian Coalition can appear to be different from that stereotype, the rhetorical efficacy of their opponents' attacks may be lessened. As National Field Director Gribbin puts it: "the press still tries, because of the unattractive message we're delivering . . . to marginalize us by saying that . . . you've got a few token this and token that, but basically it's just a white male Southern evangelical-charismatic group . . . (actually) it's becoming less so everyday."

In Iowa, where Gribbin characterizes the alliance between conservative Catholics and the Christian Coalition as "very effective," the presence at the top of the ticket of the Roman Catholic Branstad, with Christian Coalition support, may be a key hidden part of the Christian Right's success in the 1994 elections. Catholics, comprising 18 percent of the state's population, have played a prominent part in earlier elections as well, particularly the 1992 Second Congressional District race between redistricted incumbents Dave Nagle and Jim Nussle. Nagle had been a prominent supporter of abortion rights, and Nussle, a conservative Republican, apparently received the support of a number of conservative Democratic Catholics because of that issue (*Congressional Quarterly* 1992). Such crossover support has always been vital to Republicans in Iowa, because as recently as 1990 registered Democrats outnumbered registered Republicans by ninety-nine thousand (*Congressional Quarterly* 1991). Branstad's choice of moderate women as his running mates in his last three elections has also helped attract crossover votes. Building a coalition of conservative Catholics and other crossover Democrats has allowed the Christian Coalition to win many general elections that the old Christian Right would have probably lost.

Another statewide win for the right in Iowa was the 1992 movement against the Equal Rights Amendment (ERA), a victory that helped the Christian Coalition organize and mature politically through alliances with a number of local and national groups. This was the second attempt by women's groups and their allies to add an equal rights clause to the state constitution, and it was once again defeated, this time by a closer margin of 52 to 48 percent.

Robertson became personally involved in this fight, through his Christian Coalition, at one point releasing a letter which stated that the ERA "encourages women to leave their husbands, kill their children, practice witchcraft, destroy capitalism, and become lesbians" (Glover 1992). Although Robertson later disavowed the letter as not representing his own opinions, the battle lines had been decisively drawn. A number of prominent Republicans endorsed the ERA, as did, not surprisingly, most of the state's leading Democrats. Among the Republican supporters were popular former governor Robert Ray and sitting lieutenant governor Joy Corning.

Governor Branstad did not take a position on this burning political issue; neither did Republican senator Charles Grassley (Howard and Roos 1992), perhaps because for both experienced politicians, this was a lose-lose issue. By taking a stand, they risked losing support either among the Christian Right or among moderate Republicans, particularly women. The Christian Right mobilized through grassroots networks established by groups such as the Christian Coalition, the Eagle Forum, and Concerned Women for America. Additionally, the overall ideological leanings of Iowa played a part in the outcome; according to Arthur Miller, head of the Iowa Social Science Institute at the University of Iowa, of all Midwestern states, "Iowa is the most antifeminist, the most conservative on issues like abortion and women's rights" (Walsh 1994).

Even more important than the electoral outcome of the ERA fight for the Christian Right was the ability of religious conservatives to network and work together for a common goal. Phyllis Schlafly's Eagle Forum even cited the 1992 Iowa campaign to stop the ERA as the principal bright spot in a rather disappointing election year (Schlafly 1992). These groups worked hard against a referendum endorsed by many prominent moderate Republicans, once again exposing potential fault lines in the Republican Party that could have, but did not, prove costly in 1994. According to Iowa Christian Coalition chairman Ione Dilley, the Stop ERA movement was "one of our most productive means of organizing" (Pins 1994); clearly, the broad appeal of this campaign with the majority of Iowa voters in a Democratic presidential year was an encouraging sign for the various right-wing groups who rallied to defeat the ERA.

The Primaries: The Rosy Scenario Emerges, Barely

Like those in a number of other states, Iowa's traditional Republican Party organization has faced primary challengers supported by evangelicals and related Christian Right organizations. Beginning in 1986, evangelicals often packed state GOP conventions, fighting for the inclusion of several hot-button planks in the state platform. Over the next eight years, the Iowa platform, which had once been pro-choice and relatively moderate, evolved into a document that advocated the abolition of the National Endowment for the Arts, the dismantling of both the federal and state departments of education, the elimination of the Occupational Safety and Health Administration, the mandatory reporting of AIDS carriers, a cap on federal spending for AIDS research, the teaching of creationism in the public schools, and a constitutional amendment to ban abortion (Cranberg 1992).

After the formation of the Iowa Christian Coalition, with its broad policy agenda and national political coordination, the state Republican apparatus gradually became dominated by religious conservatives. By 1994, the Christian Right had achieved an absolute majority on the state party central committee. The friction caused by this increase in power was palpable; following the adoption of some of the aforementioned planks, former state representative Sue Mullins stated, "This is no longer a political party. This is a religious cult" (*Church & State* 1992). The potential for deep divisions among Iowa Republicans existed going into the 1994 primary season, and in fact, by some measures, the 1994 primary elections were divided along religious lines. Yet the impact was limited to the primaries and did not prevent a Republican sweep in November.

The stability of the Republican-evangelical alliance in any campaign results as much from the choices individual candidates make as from any contextual aspect. The 1994 governors' races in neighboring Iowa and Minnesota provide an instructive comparison. Both states had incumbent Republican governors who faced primary competition prior to taking on significant Democratic challengers. In Minnesota, insurgent evangelical Allen Quist won the party endorsement at a heated state convention, but then lost badly to moderate incumbent Arne Carlson in the Republican primary, in a campaign that was relentlessly focused on religion and social issues (*Daily Southtown* 1994). In Iowa, by contrast, incumbent Governor Branstad was supported early by the Christian Coalition and related groups in a tough primary campaign against Representative Fred Grandy. The religious content of the Branstad–Grandy contest was muted, particularly compared with the Minnesota race between Quist and Carlson. Yet the potential for a damaging rift was present throughout.

A three-term incumbent, Governor Branstad had been a successful politician without ever being particularly popular. Thus challenges from Democrats have always appeared viable at the outset. In 1994 he faced the additional hurdle of a strong primary challenge. Republican Fred Grandy, a former television star (likable Gopher from the "Love Boat"), had served four terms in Congress from a northwest Iowa district. While he received a 77 percent approval rating from the Christian Coalition in 1993 (Yepsen 1994b), his general reputation was that of a moderate conservative. His most visible stand in Congress was to sign on as an early sponsor of the bipartisan health care plan proposed by Representative Jim Cooper (D-Tenn.). Iowa's semiclosed primaries, in which only registered party members may vote in the primary but voters may change their party registration on primary election day, presented the possibility that Grandy might try to defeat Branstad by assembling a centrist coalition of moderate Republicans, independents, and crossover Democrats.

Instead, Grandy adopted a strategy of attacking Branstad from the right. He promised large tax cuts if elected, criticized the governor's taxing and spending record (Yepsen 1994a), and chided him for his failures in fiscal management (Yepsen 1994c; *Cedar Rapids Gazette* 1994). In May, he produced an anticrime plan that stressed more prison construction and an end to parole, along with the adoption of the death penalty (Yepsen 1994e). Even after Grandy began to court crossover votes from Democrats in the last three weeks of the campaign, he avoided raising hot-button issues that might attract anti–Christian Right voters, and he did not make a major issue of Branstad's strong support from the Christian Coalition.

The role of the Christian Coalition in the Branstad–Grandy contest was unprecedented in Iowa Republican politics; for the first time, the Christian Coalition passed out voter guides to their members and affiliated churches that distinguished between candidates in a Republican primary. As State Chairman Dilley put it:

> We've never gotten involved in primaries previous to that election . . . but we did this time simply because we thought that there was a difference in some of the issues and the values that the two candidates had and therefore we should get a voter guide out. . . . we did that, and Governor Branstad and Mr. Grandy said that it certainly influenced a lot of people. (Dilley 1995)

Given that the final tally was quite close, with Branstad winning by a scant four percentage points, it would be difficult not to attribute a large measure of credit for Branstad's victory to the unusual level of primary activism by the Christian Coalition and its supporters.

Grandy's rhetoric during the campaign was never raised in opposition to the Christian Right, as Carlson's was occasionally in Minnesota. He did say, somewhat cryptically, that "this campaign is to recapture the heart and soul of this party," and it may have been this sort of statement, combined with his moderate stance on some social issues, which convinced the Christian Coalition to break with tradition and support Branstad in the primary. In the aftermath of his narrow loss, Grandy did not lay blame directly on the Christian Right, although his wife was heard to lash out at the "lies" spread by the Christian Coalition as the cause of her husband's defeat (Boston 1994). Grandy's decision to avoid challenging the Christian Right during the campaign may have been a tactical mistake; perhaps Iowa would have followed the Minnesota pattern of Republican moderation had the Christian Coalition become a central issue in the primaries. Regardless, Grandy's reticence was one factor in preventing the fraying of the Iowa Republican coalition. Branstad was hard pressed to defeat Grandy, but the contest never became overly personal and did not involve a level of religious attacks that could have meant trouble in November.

At the lieutenant governor post, however, a different story emerged. The incumbent, Joy Corning, was a moderate, pro-choice Republican woman, who had supported the ERA movement. In many ways she was closer to the Carlson model of Republicanism than to that of Branstad. She was most assuredly not the candidate of choice for the Christian Coalition. In the last eight years, Branstad's running mate had been something of a contentious issue within the Republican Party. In 1986,

Branstad chose another moderate, pro-choice woman, Joan Lipsky, to run with him. This so angered one conservative Christian, Dean Arbuckle, that he chose to run as a third-party candidate on pro-life and other social issues. Branstad was reelected, but his running mate was defeated, due to the Arbuckle challenge as well as abstentions by religious conservatives, who voted for Branstad but could not support a pro-choice candidate for lieutenant governor. This led to four years of cohabitation with a Democratic lieutenant governor, an example to Republicans of how "bleak scenarios" of conflict within their coalition cause Democratic victories.

In 1990 the Iowa Constitution was altered, making it mandatory for the governor and lieutenant governor to run as a ticket. Thus, Branstad was given a certain amount of freedom in selecting his running mate, and he chose a woman quite similar to Lipsky, Joy Corning. Corning balanced the ticket in many ways, since she was far more urban and moderate than Branstad. However, Corning admits that her pro-choice position may have also played a role in her selection: "In the 1990 election, the abortion issue was more of an issue in Iowa, and the governor is a pro-life person and I am pro-choice, and that was, I think, one reason [for my selection]" (Corning 1995).

In 1994 Arbuckle, with the support of some other religious conservatives, mounted a late challenge to Corning, hoping to convince Branstad that he should not run with a pro-choice candidate beneath him. This potentially posed a problem for Branstad, and for the Republican Party as a whole. Branstad had a pro-life record going back a number of years, but he seemingly was continually trying to straddle the issue by running with pro-choice women on his ticket. However, at the convention itself Arbuckle chose to withdraw at the last minute, thus preventing Branstad from having to expend any political capital in defense of a pro-choice running mate.

In Iowa, Arbuckle is not merely speaking for himself when he labels Branstad "a big disappointment" for his support of Corning, Lipsky, and statewide gambling. Arbuckle has also become somewhat disillusioned with the Christian Coalition; "they're certainly not the pure group that Robertson envisioned. . . . they've lost a lot of their prestige in the state" (Arbuckle 1995). Yet it was arguably the decision of the Christian Coalition not to fight Corning that allowed them to profit so greatly in the November election. Had they made abortion an absolute litmus test, then Branstad's general election opponent, Bonnie Campbell, would have been much more effective in her attacks on Branstad as a pawn of the Christian Right (Barrett 1994). Allowing the convention to resoundingly endorse a pro-choice woman was a very strategic move by the Republican Party and by the Christian Coalition; it pleased Corning's moderate supporters among Republicans and sent a message to the general electorate that the Christian Right was not without its toleration of diversity. The presence of Christian Coalition executive director Ralph Reed as the keynote speaker at the Iowa convention that endorsed Corning may have enhanced that effect.

Another potentially divisive primary was defused by national political developments. First District representative Jim Leach, one of the most liberal Republicans in the U.S. Congress, had been a possible target of an evangelical primary challenge. Leach's defeat would have been extremely disappointing to many of the Republican Party's moderates, who see him as a natural leader. Many of them might imagine that there was no place for them in a party that had no place for a Jim Leach. In 1993, however, Leach's position as ranking Republican on the House Banking, Housing, and Urban Affairs Committee made him a prominent critic of President Bill Clinton's actions in the Whitewater scandal. Clinton had become such a bete noire to the Christian Right over issues such as abortion and homosexual rights that Leach's public criticism of Clinton enhanced his standing among potential opponents in his own district. Leach's own reputation for personal honesty did not hurt, either. Whatever the cause, no primary challenge to Leach was forthcoming in 1994, a nonevent that greatly aided Republican unity.

The 1994 primary season for the Iowa Republican Party was clearly a case of the Republicans dodging several bullets. If Grandy had challenged Branstad's position as an ally of the Christian Coalition and attempted to tar and feather him with some of the wilder policy stands and pronouncements of Pat Robertson, it is possible that Grandy could have become the nominee. Iowa's Christian Right might have reacted by staying home in November, or even by mounting a third-party challenge to Grandy, potentially handing the election to the Democrats. On the other hand, if Arbuckle had not dropped out, or if the Christian Coalition had successfully supported another challenger to Corning, moderate Republicans might have sat on their hands in November or voted Democratic. Finally, a primary defeat of Leach would not only have aroused the passions of both wings of the Republican Party, it is possible that a moderate Democrat could beat a conservative Republican in the First District, thus preventing the Republicans from achieving their clean sweep of Iowa's House delegation.

What is interesting about the Iowa primaries of 1994 is not only that none of these divisive events occurred, but how each primary or nonprimary was connected to the overall tenor of Republican politics in Iowa. Had Fred Grandy in the early stages of his race against Branstad made sweeping attacks based on Branstad's support from the Christian Right and his stance on certain social issues, this might have sent shock waves throughout all the other races. Once the knives were drawn at one level, it would be difficult to sheath them in other state races. The coalition between conservative Christians and moderate Republicans that was re-forged at the 1994 Iowa convention was extremely strong on the surface, but many of the tensions between, for example, Corning and the Christian Coalition, were merely papered over. The Republican coalition that Branstad led was undoubtedly wide, but the relationships among the various factions of the party may have been more fragile than they appeared.

The General Election: The Scenario Remains Rosy

Without any major rifts in its ranks in 1994, the Iowa Republican Party enjoyed the full benefits of the alliance between moderate Republicans such as Corning and conservative Christians such as Branstad. Incumbent governor Branstad fought off an aggressive campaign by Attorney General Bonnie Campbell to win a fourth term as governor by a surprisingly large fifteen-point margin. During the campaign, Campbell tried repeatedly to link Branstad to the Christian Right. She directly attacked certain Christian Right figures from out of state, and portrayed Branstad supporters as "extremist, fundamentalist Christians" (Roos 1994). At one point, she even questioned the sincerity of conservative Christians' religious beliefs: "I hate to call them Christian because I am a Christian, and I hate to call them religious because they're not. So I'll call them the radical right. . . . these are the people that get their orders directly from God, which is funny because I get contrary orders from God" (Mercer 1994). It is difficult to tell how much Branstad's Roman Catholicism or his selection of a pro-choice moderate as a running mate helped insulate him from Campbell's attacks, though Corning's presence on the ticket probably helped retain moderate Republicans who might have agreed with some of Campbell's issue positions.

As shown by table 10-1, the proportion of each candidates's support that came from respondents who identified themselves as either religious or secular differed greatly, with Branstad's coalition only one-quarter "secular," whereas Campbell's supporters were overwhelmingly "secular." The differences become even clearer when ideology is added to

Table 10-1
Proportion of Candidate Support by Religion and Ideology

	Branstad	Campbell
Religious right	39%	10%
Religious moderate	33%	19%
Secular moderate	15%	39%
Secular liberal	12%	31%
Total	99%	99%

Source: University of Iowa Social Science Institute Heartland Poll.

the mix. Additionally, the advantage Branstad enjoyed among the members of the Christian Right was far larger than Campbell's advantage with any of the secular groups (Muller 1994).

Perhaps even more revealing are the results of a *Des Moines Register* poll given in table 10-2. As expected, Branstad's support among fundamentalists and born-again Christians was overwhelming. His 33-percentage-point advantage among that group was two and a half times as large as his lead in the entire sample (Fogarty 1994). Furthermore, not only does Branstad receive more support than Campbell among mainstream Protestants (often identified as traditional constituents of the Republican Party), he and Campbell nearly split the Catholic vote evenly, with a sizable minority of Catholics undecided on whom to support a month before the election. This may be evidence of the success of the Christian Coalition's outreach campaign; an alliance with conservative Catholics and Catholic Reagan Democrats may be much more appealing when the top spot on the ticket is held by a Roman Catholic. Other Republi-

Table 10-2
Candidate Choice by Religious Group

	Branstad	Campbell	Undecided/ Other
Fundamentalist/ born-again Protestant	57%	24%	19%
Other Protestant	47%	37%	16%
Catholic	38%	41%	21%
Total	47%	34%	19%

Source: *Des Moines Register* Iowa Poll.

can coalition members, including farmers and the affluent, also showed high levels of support for Branstad, indicating that the alliance was holding together.

This shows that Branstad and Corning were able to retain the more traditional Republican social groups while integrating the Christian Right into their coalition, a feat that is certainly not accomplished in every election. Given the margin of Branstad's victory over Campbell and the number of groups that overwhelmingly supported him, it is likely that national forces were also at work in the Branstad landslide, and thus the Iowa Christian Coalition, along with its voter guides, may have had less to do with his 1994 victory than with some of his earlier general election triumphs. Ironically, Branstad's sense of indebtedness to the Christian Coalition and its allies may have been much greater following his comparatively narrow primary win over Grandy.

The GOP attained complete control of Iowa's U.S. House delegation when eighteen-term incumbent Neal Smith was defeated by Greg Ganske, a candidate whose issue positions mirrored those of the Christian Coalition. Smith, while something of an institution in Iowa politics and a legendary producer of federal spending in his district, was also highly vulnerable because of his position on abortion, occasionally voting for government funding of the procedure. Smith was once again targeted for defeat by the Christian Coalition, and its voter guides distributed at churches probably helped his relatively inexperienced challenger (Arbuckle 1995). Smith was one of several high-profile Congressional scalps collected by Republican challengers nationwide, so it is difficult to attribute his defeat to exclusively Iowa factors. Regardless, Christian Right groups were certainly active in the Ganske campaign and were not hesitant to take credit for Smith's fall.

In Iowa's state legislature, the Democrats managed to retain a narrow hold on the Iowa Senate. Republicans did increase their margin from a razor-thin 51–49 to a comfortable 64–36 in the Iowa House, and this may present Branstad with a number of opportunities and potential problems. Given that a number of the new state legislators, as well as some incumbents, belong to the Christian Right wing of the party, they can be expected to loyally support much of the governor's activist agenda for reforming state government and addressing issues such as welfare reform. However, if the newly strengthened house Republican majority puts issues such as the teaching of creationism on the front burner of the state agenda, Branstad may be forced to take positions that risk losing support from either the moderate Republicans or his friends in the Christian Coalition.

Conclusion: Increasing Fissures or Continuing Coalition?

The future of the alliance between the Christian Right and the traditional components of the Iowa Republican Party depends on a number of factors. First, the willingness of the Christian Coalition to continue to tolerate Republicans such as Corning and Leach, who may not follow their stance on a number of social issues, is central. Up to this point the Christian Coalition, in Iowa and the nation, has often followed the "big tent" advice of the late Lee Atwater on issues such as abortion. While the Iowa Christian Coalition may have disagreed with Corning on abortion or the ERA, it worked to elect her as part of a ticket with a pro-life candidate at the top. This is not entirely atypical of the Christian Coalition, which has supported, for example, Kay Bailey Hutchison in Texas, despite her stand on abortion. As their national field director, D.J. Gribbin, states:

> Sometimes you end up with a choice between two pro-abortion candidates but one of whom was willing to vote for parental notification, one of whom would vote against taxpayer funding. . . . Even though, ideally, you would have a candidate who agrees with you straight down the line on everything, I encourage people to vote for the candidate that most represents your views, and if he doesn't represent them a hundred percent, don't stay home! Then the other guy'll win. (Gribbin 1995)

This softer position on divisive issues was put more succinctly by Ralph Reed, who proclaimed at the 1994 Iowa convention that "we're adopting a Maoist strategy. . . . let a thousand flowers bloom" (Brownstein 1994).[1]

However, more recent statements by the Christian Coalition's leadership indicate that perhaps criticism from within the Christian Right has caused them to return to a less accommodating position on abortion. Reed and fellow conservative Christian leader Gary Bauer have warned the national Republicans that moderating the antiabortion plank in the party platform or nominating a presidential or vice presidential candidate with a pro-choice position would risk alienating Christian Right voters. Bauer, president of the Family Research Council, cautioned that such moves "would absolutely guarantee an explosion and perhaps even a third party" (Edsall 1995). Obviously, if such a litmus test on abortion, extending down to the number-two spot on the ticket, had been at work in the Iowa gubernatorial election of 1994, the alliance between Branstad and his running mate Corning would not have been nearly as successful.

It is doubtful that the surging Christian Right in Iowa would passively accept a gubernatorial ticket that was split on abortion the other way, with a pro-choice candidate occupying the top slot. Thus, the post-Branstad era looms over Iowa Republican politics. Branstad has announced that he will not seek reelection, and the jockeying to succeed him is already beginning. Corning herself admits to being interested in the post, but she sees the Christian Right as likely to actively oppose any gubernatorial candidate who is not pro-life. Corning does hope that "moderates in the Republican Party do exactly what the Christian Coalition has done" and organize at the precinct level (Corning 1995).

Another factor is the agenda selected by the Iowa Christian Coalition and its Republican allies. The alliance has been most successful when it had focused on economic and "inertial" social issues such as the anti-ERA movement. The Stop ERA campaign was inertial in that it was opposing a progressive change in the state's constitution, and the natural prairie conservatism of the mass electorate may have worked in the right's favor on the referendum issue. Issues such as the teaching of creationism and the banning of books in the public schools are the antithesis of the Stop ERA movement in that they actively seek to change, in some cases radically, the existing order.

A local school board election in Waterloo, Iowa, illustrates the difficulties facing that portion of the Christian Right's agenda. In September 1994 two high-profile Christian Right candidates, running on creationism and the promotion of textbooks that extol traditional values, lost elections with record high turnouts. This election, taking place scarcely a month before the Republican sweep of November, seems to indicate that when the issues involve the more extremist portions of the evangelical platform, the general electorate may not vote with them (*People for the American Way* 1994).

The ability to select its fights carefully and manage its intraparty alliance with Republican moderates and economic conservatives will be crucial to the success of the Christian Right in Iowa. The Christian Right must also, of course, hold together internally and avoid splintering between its own moderate and extremist forces.

The "rosy scenario" that prevailed in Iowa in 1994 was a product of national forces (such as the anti-Clinton tide), carefully crafted compromises among state Republican factions, choices by individual candidates such as Fred Grandy, skillful campaigning by Republicans and the Christian Coalition, and a great deal of luck. In 1996, when liberal Democratic senator Tom Harkin faces the electorate again, some or all of these factors could break the other way, producing a Harkin reelection, which would represent a sizable setback for the Iowa Christian Right. The attention of the nation has already begun to focus on Iowa for another reason: the presidential caucuses. Republican candidates such as Phil Gramm, Bob Dole, and Lamar Alexander have made extensive trips to this rural state with its tiny population and vitally important role in the selection of the nominee.

This makes the Christian Right of Iowa potentially the most influential group of conservative, politically active Christians in the country. As State Chairman Dilley points out, the Iowa Christian Right will not welcome the candidacies of pro-choice Republican governors Christine Whitman, William Weld, or Pete Wilson. Whether the spirit of ecumenical cooperation that characterized Iowa Republican politics in 1994, and produced such fruitful results for the party, can survive a bruising presidential caucus battle over abortion remains to be seen.

Note

1. Skeptics will recall that Mao used this strategy to ferret out dissent, for the "flowers" were all cut once they bloomed.

References

Arbuckle, Dean. 1995. Interview with the author. 7 February.

Barrett, Laurence I. 1994. "Christian Right Play Politics, Religiously." *New York Newsday* (25 September).

Boston, Rob. 1994. "Operation Precinct." *Church & State.* (July/August): 8–10.

Brownstein, Ronald. 1994. "Iowa GOP Gears Up For '96 With Presidential Poll." *Los Angeles Times* (25 June): A13.

Cedar Rapids Gazette. 1994. "Grandy Calls Branstad 'Master Card Governor'." 1 April: B2.

Conn, Joseph L. 1992. "Robertson Roulette." *Church & State* 46 (October): 14–16.

Connelly, William F., and John J. Pitney. 1994. "The Future of House Republicans." *Political Science Quarterly* 109: 577–78.

Corning, Joy. 1995. Interview with the author. 8 February.

Cranberg, Gilbert. 1992. "Even Sensible Iowa Bows to the Religious Right." *The Los Angeles Times* (17 August): 10.

Daily Southtown. 1994. "Religious Right Takes Aim at November Election." 18 September: A23.

Des Moines Register. 1994. "Conservative Platform Shows Clout of GOP Right." 23 May: A3.

Dilley, Ione. 1995. Interview with the author. 3 February.

Dionne, E. J., Jr. 1987. "Robertson's Victory in Ballot Shakes Rivals in GOP Race." *The New York Times* (14 September): 1.

Donovan, Beth. 1991. "Democrats Tug on GOP Roots as Iowa Adapts to New Times." *Congressional Quarterly* 49 (17 August): 2288.

————. 1992. "Special Report: Iowa." *Congressional Quarterly* 50 (29 February): 52–53.

Edsall, Thomas B. 1995. "GOP Warned Not to Forget Family Values." *The Washington Post* (12 February): A27.

Fogarty, Thomas A. 1994. "Branstad Has 13-Point Lead Over Campbell." *Des Moines Register* (6 November): A1.

Glover, Mike. 1992. "ERA's Defeat." *Associated Press.* 11 November.

Gribbin, D. J. 1995. Interview with the author. 1 February.

Howard, Phoebe Wall, and Jonathan Roos. 1992. "ERA Backers Vow Issue Will Not Die." *Des Moines Register* (November 5): A1.

Hutcheson, Richard G., Jr. 1988. *God in the White House: How Religion Has Changed the Modern Presidency.* New York: Macmillan.

Mercer, Marsha. 1994. "Nobody's Laughing Now: Christian Conservatives Are Potent Force in GOP Politics." *Richmond Times Dispatch* (9 September): A1.

Muller, Lyle. 1994. "U of I Poll Gauges Religious Support." *Cedar Rapids Gazette* (4 November): A1, 10.

Nesmith, Bruce. 1994. *The New Republican Coalition: The Reagan Campaigns and White Evangelicals.* New York: Peter Lang.

New York Times. 1992. "Portrait of the Electorate." 5 November: B9.

People For the American Way. 1994. "The Religious Right and the 1994 Election." Election Report II: 12.

Peterson, Bill. 1987. "Robertson Followers Puzzle Iowa GOP." *Washington Post* (31 October): A7.

Pins, Kenneth. 1992. "Shrewd Religious Right Attains Clout in GOP." *Des Moines Sunday Register* (20 December): A1.

————. 1994. "Religious Right Flexes Its Muscle, Decries Bigotry." *Des Moines Register* (18 September): A1.

Reichley, A. James. 1986. "Religion and the Future of American Politics." *Political Science Quarterly* 101: 23–47.

Roos, Jonathan. 1994. "Campbell: 'Religious Right' Hampers Change." *Des Moines Register* (16 October): A1.

Schlafly, Phyllis. 1992. "We Defeated ERA in the Iowa Referendum." *Eagle Forum Newsletter,* November.

Schmidt, Steffen W. 1990. "Challenges for the Future." In *Issues in Iowa Politics,* ed. Lee Ann Osbun and Steffen W. Schmidt. Ames: Iowa State University Press.

Stern, Marcus. 1986. "Religious Right Takes Its Lumps in the Polls." *Wheaton Daily Journal* (18 November): 15.

Von Drehle, David. 1994. "Coalition Reaching to the Middle." *The Washington Post* (15 October): A1.

Walsh, Edward. 1994. "Iowa Governor and Rival Wield Dueling Themes." *The Washington Post* (21 October): A6.

Wilcox, Clyde. 1995. "Premillenialists at the Millenium: Some Reflections on the Christian Right in the Twenty First Century." Pp. 21–39 in *The Rapture of Politics: The Christian Right as the United States Approaches the Year 2000*, ed. Steve Bruce, Peter Kivisto, and William H. Swatos, Jr. New Brunswick: Transaction Publishers.

Yepsen, David. 1994a. "Grandy Proposes Sweeping Tax Cuts." *Des Moines Register* (16 February): A1, 6.

———. 1994b. "Will Crossover Voters Show Up?" *Des Moines Register* (7 March): A5.

———. 1994c. "Grandy: Branstad Cooking the Books." *Des Moines Register* (1 April): A2.

———. 1994d. "State GOP Undergoes 'Silent Revolution'." *Des Moines Register* (19 April): A1, 3.

———. 1994e. "Grandy: End Parole, Build More Prisons." *Des Moines Register* (3 May): A1, 5.

11

California: Christian Conservative Influence in a Liberal State

J. Christopher Soper

The role of the Christian Right in California politics is a study of contrasts. Conservative Christians are the dominant force in California's Republican Party and many candidates supported by Christian Right activism won office in the 1994 election. None of the Republican Party's nominees for statewide office in 1994, however, clearly aligned themselves with the Christian Right, and the two most prominent Republican Party candidates, Pete Wilson for governor and Mike Huffington for U.S. Senate, were both pro-choice and social moderates. Membership in the Christian Coalition of California and the Traditional Values Coalition has grown in recent years and both have become politically powerful interest groups in the state, but California has liberal policies on abortion and gay rights and the state is disproportionately secular and unchurched.

This chapter examines the paradoxical influence of the Christian Right in California politics. First, I show how California's political culture and institutions provided strategic opportunities for the mobilization of the Christian Right in the late 1980s and early 1990s. California's weak party system favored Christian Right activism and enabled conservative Christians to gain control of the state Republican party; once in power, however, those structures limited the ability of conservative Christians to shape party policy and affect policy outcomes. Second, I evaluate the political strategy of the Christian Right leadership in the 1994 election and assess the influence of conservative Christian voters on the races for governor and senator. Leaders of the Christian Right chose not to make abortion or gay rights key issues in the general election and Wilson and Huffington did very well among white evangelical voters. I conclude the chapter with a discussion of the future prospects for the Christian Right in California politics.

Political Institutions and Christian Right Activism

It is hard to imagine a state whose political institutions and culture were more amenable to conservative Christian activism in the late 1980s than California. Since the Progressive reforms of the early twentieth century, California's political parties have been weak and thereby open to the mobilization of active, dedicated voters and organizations. Among the most important Progressive regulations limiting the power of California's parties are nonpartisan city elections, political primary elections to nominate party candidates, nonexistent precinct and ward organizations, and a ban on preprimary endorsements by the party.[1] Further compounding the weakness of California's political parties has been the influx of voters to the state and a healthy tradition of voter independence (Ross 1984; Culver and Syer 1984; Mayhew 1986; Gerston and Christenson 1991).

This antipartyism provided the ideal context for the leaders of the Christian Right when they decided at the end of the 1980s to move from national to state and local political activism (Moen 1994). The two most important statewide groups, the Christian Coalition of California and the Reverend Lou Sheldon's Anaheim-based Traditional Values Coalition, forged an alliance, and conservative Christians stepped up their political involvement in state party politics. The religious convictions of conservative Christians provided clear positions, priorities, and a well-integrated network of churches, television programs, and associations that made them relatively easy to mobilize. Preexisting religious institutions made it easier for group leaders to organize evangelical Christians who shared the group's moral conservatism (Liebman 1983).

In terms of political institutions, California's fragmented and weak party structures allowed newly mobilized conservative Christian voters to translate those resources into political power. The Christian Right, particularly the Christian Coalition, pursued two political strategies. First, they mobilized support within the Republican Party to wrest control from party moderates and, second, Christian groups recruited and supported candidates for elective offices (Lozana and Frammolino 1992). Conservative Christians did what groups always do if they want to gain party power: they committed time, energy, and resources and turned out for party leaders' elections to county and state committees, to which few party members pay attention. Because turnout in these party elections is low, the Christian Right exaggerated its popular following and won important positions within the party. According to one estimate, conservative Christians controlled thirty-eight of the fifty-eight county GOP central committees by the end of 1992 (Nollinger 1993). By 1993, Christian conservatives controlled California's Republican Party and they used their newfound authority to help draft the party platform and make appointments to the party's state central committee.

There was never much serious consideration that Christian conservatives would mobilize within California's Democratic Party, which is firmly committed to social policy liberalism. The Democratic Party cannot win over this religious constituency because there is no conservative wing in the state Democratic Party on the issues of abortion and gay rights, as there is in a number of other states. Not one of California's thirty Democratic U.S. House members voted with the Christian Coalition on the abortion and gay rights issues the group highlighted in its 1994 congressional scorecard, and only one received a scorecard ranking above 30 percent on a scale of 100. The *average* score for Ohio's ten Democratic house members, by contrast, was 33, while Texas's twenty-one Democrats averaged a score of 42 (Christian Coalition 1994).

The Christian Right also stepped in to fill the void created by weakened political parties by endorsing candidates and providing the financial resources necessary for a successful campaign. Money from Allied Business PAC, a political action committee formed in 1991 by four wealthy southern California businessmen with ties to established religious communities, has helped the political mobilization of the Christian Right in California. In 1992, Allied funneled over one million dollars to Republican candidates supported by the Christian Right. In addition, the Christian Coalition educated and mobilized voters by distributing hundreds of thousands of voter guides the week before the election in churches throughout California. This campaign literature listed the candidates' positions on key issues for races at all levels. In 1992, candidates backed by the Christian Right won several U.S. House seats, scores of state assembly and state senate races, and a significant number of city council and school board elections (Barber 1994). In some races, particularly nonpartisan school board elections, conservative Christians ran as "stealth candidates" who minimized their ties to the Christian Right (Shogren and Frantz 1993).

California's party system encouraged Christian Right grassroots activism at the same time that it intensified tensions between socially conservative, moderate, and libertarian factions within the Republican Party. The Christian Right challenged moderate party leaders with insurgent candidates in primary elections in the late 1980s and early 1990s. State party elites were powerless to stop this threat to party power because they did not control the most important party processes, including party nominations and candidate endorsements in primary elections. Conservative Christian candidates became a prominent feature of local elections, particularly in the suburbs, which are the power base of the Christian Right in California.[2]

A notable primary battle between the two wings of the Republican Party occurred in 1992 for the nomination to the U.S. Senate. The primary pitted John Seymour, a social moderate, against William Dannemeyer, a seven-term congressman and outspoken opponent of abortion and gay rights. Pete Wilson had appointed Seymour to fill the Senate seat that Wilson vacated when he became governor in 1991. Conservative Christian groups actively supported Dannemeyer's candidacy while party moderates campaigned for Seymour. Divisions within the party spilled over at the party's summer convention where hundreds of delegates walked out during Seymour's speech, protesters gathered to tar and feather the governor in effigy, and resolutions opposing abortion rights and gay rights divided party delegates (Peterson 1991).

Seymour's convincing victory over Dannemeyer in the primary election, 51 percent to 27 percent, demonstrated the political limits, even within the Republican Party, for candidates closely tied to the Christian Right in statewide races. Religious conservatives are growing in number and influence in California, but they still constitute a minority in the state and the party. According to a field poll conducted in 1993, 21 percent of Californians can be categorized as part of the religious right—people who are both religious and political conservatives. A large majority of these voters oppose homosexual rights and gays in the military and support prayer in school, stricter laws against abortion, and stricter laws against pornography. According to the same poll, however, more than half of Californians, 54 percent, are secularists—people who are not religious or are not religiously active. Large majorities of secularists are liberal on the social issues of abortion and homosexual rights (California Opinion Index, 1993).

California is also among the most pro-choice states in the union. In 1972, a year before the decision in *Roe v. Wade* that legalized abortion, Californians approved an amendment to the state constitution that specifically added the right of privacy to the other inalienable rights of individuals. Pro-life candidates do not do well in statewide races because there is broad public support for abortion. A 1992 field poll reported that 75 percent of the adult public either advocated no change in the existing abortion laws (41 percent) or favored legislation that would make it easier to obtain abortions (34 percent) (Russo 1995). There are similar political limits for the Christian Right within the Republican

Party. While a majority of Republican Party voters describe themselves as conservative, most are also pro-choice and have a negative impression of candidates closely associated with the Christian Right.

The Christian Right discovered that control of the Republican Party had few direct political benefits. In states with stronger parties, control of party posts can be politically significant. In Virginia, Christian Right delegates to the Republican Party convention helped to nominate Oliver North to the U.S. Senate in 1994, while in Minnesota the Christian Right secured the Republican Party's preprimary gubernatorial endorsement for Allen Quist. In California, the Christian Right could do neither because parties do not nominate candidates or provide preprimary endorsements. Control of the Republican Party has been a symbolic victory for the Christian Right with few political benefits. Conservative Christians have been unable to use party power to press their conservative agenda on abortion and gay rights on a recalcitrant electorate or on pro-choice party leaders such as Pete Wilson who ignored or opposed the Christian Right until the 1994 gubernatorial election (Persinos 1994).

The Christian Right and the 1994 Election

The limits of party control were evident in the 1994 election, in which the Republican Party's two most prominent statewide candidates, Pete Wilson for governor and Mike Huffington for senator, were both pro-choice. The 1994 midterm election presented conservative Christian voters with a dilemma: would they support Republican candidates who were better than their Democratic challengers on moral issues but far from ideal candidates from a conservative Christian perspective? Since taking control of the party and becoming party regulars, the Christian Right has tempered its political action and rhetoric for statewide races. The Christian Right continued to support conservative candidates in primary and local elections, but group leaders demonstrated a willingness to work with the party to elect moderate candidates in the races for Senate and governor. In both races, group leaders shifted away from the politically contentious abortion issue to the electorally appealing issues of illegal immigration, family values, crime, and lower taxes. Wilson and Huffington courted evangelical Christians on these social issues, and both candidates retained the support of conservative Christian voters in the 1994 election.

Pete Wilson had credibility problems to overcome with the Christian

Right as he entered the 1994 gubernatorial race. As a social moderate, Wilson's pro-choice stance had been a fundamental source of friction with Christian conservatives in the past. He appointed fellow moderate John Seymour to the Senate in 1991, signed a bill into law prohibiting job discrimination against gays and lesbians in the same year, and has historically supported Republican moderates in party primary battles with religious conservatives. Wilson faced a surprisingly strong primary challenge from Ron Unz, who attacked the governor for the record $7 billion tax increase he signed his first year in office. Unz, who won 34 percent of the primary vote, shared Wilson's moderate views on social issues and did not appeal to the Christian Right. With the state mired in an economic slump and the incumbent governor trailing his Democratic challenger, Kathleen Brown, in the early polls, Wilson needed to secure the support of all the factions within the Republican Party to win the general election.

Wilson spent the months leading up to the election mending fences with conservative Christians and finding a social issue that had broad conservative appeal. Through a combination of good fortune and political skill he successfully did both. The California legislature presented Wilson with three bills that allowed him to placate the leadership of the Christian Right without alienating moderates within the party. A week before the party's convention in September, Wilson vetoed a bill that would have made California the first state in the country to legally recognize domestic partners by allowing them to register with the state (Lucas, 1994). Less than a week later, Wilson signed into law a bill that doubled the penalty for disrupting a church service (Bailey 1994). Assemblyman Gil Ferguson wrote the bill after his friend the Reverend Lou Sheldon, founder of the Traditional Values Coalition, had a church service interrupted by gay rights protesters. At the end of the month, Wilson vetoed a bill that would have preserved the California Learning Assessment System (CLAS), a test roundly criticized by leaders of the Christian Right as ineffective and intrusive (Schrag 1994).

During the campaign, the governor shifted to the right on selective social issues and championed causes that concerned the leadership of the Christian Right (Lesher 1995). The bills that Wilson vetoed or signed concerned issues where public support for the values of the Christian Right is highest. While a majority of Californians do not share the pro-life or anti–gay rights views of the Christian Right, there is much greater support for the emphasis on traditional moral values. Wilson justified his veto of the gay rights bill by saying that he did not want to undercut traditional values and marriages: "We need to strengthen, not

weaken the institution of marriage" (Walters 1994). When Wilson vetoed the CLAS bill, Lou Sheldon began referring to the governor as his
good friend.

It would have been foolish for Wilson to ignore groups within the
party that can mobilize voters as effectively as the Christian Coalition
and the Traditional Values Coalition. The Christian Coalition has been
among the most politically active interest groups in California for the
past several years. It distributes its voter guides in thousands of churches
the week before the election. In addition, conservative Christian voters
are a significant percentage of the electorate. Exit poll data on the 1994
election from Mitofsky International show that 29 percent of voters described themselves as born-again/evangelical Christians, and an impressive 17 percent were white born-again or evangelical Christians who attend church weekly. This group constitutes the core constituency of the
Christian Right. Wilson knew that white evangelical Christians would be
a sizable percentage of the electorate and that in a close race their support could provide the winning margin.

Wilson also discovered a social issue with extensive conservative appeal: illegal immigration. Wilson strongly supported the popular Proposition 187, an initiative that proposed to make illegal immigrants ineligi-
ble for public social services, public health care services, and public
school education at elementary, secondary, and postsecondary levels.
Wilson linked the moral idea of personal responsibility to support for
Proposition 187; the governor asserted that it was morally wrong for
immigrants to enter the state illegally to receive benefits and drain state
resources. In addition to illegal immigration, Wilson stressed other issues with strong resonance among conservative voters including tax and
welfare cuts, smaller government, personal responsibility, and crime.
Kathleen Brown, who opposed Proposition 187, tried to make the election a referendum on education and Wilson's handling of the state's
economy (Schneider 1994). Wilson accomplished both of his campaign
objectives: he made the race a contest about illegal immigration and he
secured the support of the Christian Right. Proposition 187 passed with
a large majority (59 percent), and illegal immigration ranked highest
among voters as the issue that determined their vote for governor. Forty
percent of those polled listed immigration as the most important issue
and Wilson won 77 percent of those votes. Illegal immigration also
ranked as the most important issue to Christian Right voters, at 47 percent. Wilson's moral appeal on Proposition 187 appears to have been
particularly salient for white evangelical voters, who supported the initiative by over 65 percent.

The governor clearly was a vulnerable incumbent, with nearly two thirds of all voters (62 percent) and 72 percent of white evangelicals saying that the state was seriously off on the wrong track. Brown was not, however, an acceptable alternative for the Christian Right; 78 percent of these Christians voted for the incumbent governor; nearly one quarter (22 percent) of Wilson's vote total came from white evangelical Christians. It is possible that they voted for Wilson because he was the lesser of two evils; the data, however, do not seem to lead to this conclusion. Christian Right voters were more likely to approve of Wilson's job performance as governor (65 percent) than was the general electorate (52 percent). Despite the historically uneasy relations between Wilson and the Christian Right, white evangelical Christians turned out enthusiastically for the incumbent governor. The absence of a credible alternative and Wilson's turn to the right on family values, immigration, and taxes ensured conservative Christian support for Governor Wilson.

The Republican candidate for the Senate, Mike Huffington, faced even more formidable hurdles than did Pete Wilson to win the support of the Christian Right. Huffington was pro-choice, supported gays serving in the military, and faced William Dannemeyer—a candidate with close ties to the Christian Right—in the 1994 Republican Party primary. While Huffington's libertarian views appealed to a wing of the Republican Party, as a congressman he received only a 50 percent approval rating in the 1994 Christian Coalition's congressional scorecard, which placed him second from the bottom among California's twenty-two Republican House members (Christian Coalition 1994). In addition, Huffington's wife, Arianna, received criticism because of her past involvement with the controversial Church of the Movement of Inner Spiritual Awareness, a new age church that places its founder, John Rogers, in a position more mighty than Christ. It was clear that Huffington had much work to do to gain the confidence of evangelical Christian voters.

Huffington easily defeated Dannemeyer in the party primary, 55 to 29 percent, and began to court the Christian Right vote. He appeared several times on Christian radio stations, where he advocated restoring prayer to public schools, and gave a speech before San Francisco's Commonwealth Club where he said that America should "welcome God back into our lives and into the public square" (Lappin 1994). Arianna took the remarkable step of securing a letter from a Greek Orthodox bishop and her Santa Barbara priest testifying to her devout Christianity. She also described her born-again experience on her cable television program, an admission meant to please conservative Christian voters (Lieblich 1994). Huffington also benefited from a widely publicized National Abortion Rights Action League (NARAL) report that denounced the Republican candidate as one of six "great pretenders" on the abortion issue. NARAL intended to challenge Huffington's appeal to moderate Republican women by highlighting his opposition to federal funding for abortions. The report had the unintended consequence of increasing his support among conservative Christians who did not initially trust his socially moderate views (Doyle 1994).

Huffington did nearly as well among white evangelical Christian voters as Wilson; 70 percent voted for Huffington over Feinstein. Twenty-four percent of Huffington's vote total came from the Christian Right. The Senate race was so close that Huffington might have won the election had he done as well as Wilson among white evangelical voters. Given his socially moderate views, however, and his low 1994 congressional scorecard ranking by the Christian Coalition, it is remarkable that Huffington did so well among conservative Christian voters.

The Christian Right in the Republican Party

The level of support Huffington and Wilson received from the Christian Right is an indication of how firmly attached evangelical Protestants are to the Republican Party. Sixty percent of white evangelical Christians surveyed described themselves as Republican in 1994 (see table 11-1). The 1994 election solidified a religious and cultural cleavage between the parties at the state level that a number of analysts have noted for the national parties. The Republican Party increasingly represents conservative religious voters whereas the Democrats win the support of religious liberals and secularists (Green, Guth, and Fraser 1988; Kellstedt, Green, Guth, and Smidt 1994). Voters who attend church frequently and identify themselves as evangelical or born-again Christians are very likely to

Table 11-1
Selected Religious Voting Blocs for the Democratic and Republican Parties, 1994

	Percent of Survey	Percent Republican	Percent of Rep. Total	Percent Democratic	Percent of Dem. Total
White evangelical	17	60	24	25	9
Weekly church	40	51	49	35	37
Jewish	4	4	1	83	9
None	11	24	6	46	13

Source: Mitofsky International.

be Republicans; those who attend church less frequently or not at all identify with the Democratic Party. In terms of party politics this means that the salience of religion for voters is as important for determining party affiliation as is denomination (Guth and Green 1993). The Republican Party appeals to religious conservatives of various Protestant denominations for whom religion is particularly salient.

As table 11-1 shows, California's Republican Party did very well in 1994 among white evangelical Christians and frequent church attendees. Sixty percent of white evangelicals and 51 percent of frequent church attendees described themselves as Republicans. In terms of political ideology, these are the most conservative religious voting groups in the electorate (see table 11-2). The religious mainstays of the Republican Party are the Christian Right and mainline Protestants and Roman Catholics who attend church frequently and are likely to be more conservative. One of every four Republican partisans was a white evangelical Christian (24 percent); one in two in the GOP attended church at least once a week (49 percent).

The most partisan Democratic religious voting groups, by contrast, were also the most politically liberal: Jews and those with no religious affiliation. Eighty-three percent of Jewish voters and 46 percent of secularists described themselves as Democrats. Both groups are far more liberal than the general electorate. With 9 and 13 percent of all Democratic partisans in the survey, respectively, Jews and secularists are as important a faction within the state Democratic Party, as are evangelical Christians in the state Republican Party.

The widespread support by white evangelical voters for moderate Republican Party candidates confirms that the divisions within the party between moderate and conservative factions have waned somewhat. Evangelical militancy has cooled considerably in the past several years; in 1994, at least, leaders of the Christian Right and conservative Chris-

Table 11-2
Religion and Political Ideology

	Percent of Survey	White Evangelical	Weekly Church	Jewish	None
Liberal	20	8	13	48	30
Moderate	40	32	35	39	50
Conservative	40	61	52	13	20

Source: Mitofsky International.

tian voters within the Republican Party put aside their differences with moderate candidates for the goal of partisan victory.

The Politics of Pragmatism in 1994

The 1994 elections witnessed a more pragmatic strategy on the part of a Christian Right leadership that did not seem interested in making abortion or gay rights a litmus test for the election (Wilcox 1994). Given the Republican identification of evangelical Protestants, the leaders of the Christian Right concluded that they could exercise more power by becoming an active, loyal voting bloc within the GOP rather than continuing their political militancy. Conservative Christians within the Republican Party did not propose divisive propositions on abortion or gay rights at the party's 1994 state convention as they had done in previous years, and neither issue was an important factor during California's general election campaign (Lesher 1994). Taking a cue from national leaders of the Christian Right, state groups broadened their agenda to include issues that had extensive conservative appeal (Reed 1993; Seib 1993). In the process, conservative Christian groups supported socially moderate party candidates in statewide races, while they continued to back more conservative Republicans in local elections where their bargaining power and strength were much greater.

In its 1994 voter guide on the U.S. Senate race, for example, the Christian Coalition compared the candidates' views on term limits for Congress, federal government control of health care, and raising federal income taxes. The scorecard avoided moral issues that would have exposed Huffington's moderate views (gays serving in the military); highlighted issues where Huffington's libertarian values coincided with the Coalition's policies (voucher program for education); and worded issues in a way that would differentiate the candidates as much as possible. On abortion, the voter guide focused on taxpayer funding for abortion, which Huffington opposed and Brown supported. In the governor's race, the voter guide similarly portrayed Wilson in a favorable light by highlighting issues that separated him from his Democratic counterpart, Dianne Feinstein (Christian Coalition 1994). This is not to suggest that the Christian Coalition was duplicitous in how it presented issues; Huffington and Wilson supported the Coalition on a number of issues and they certainly came closer to the Coalition's social agenda than their Democratic opponents. The Coalition chose to highlight the social policy differences between the candidates instead of their similar views on abortion and gay rights.

There are a number of reasons why the Christian Right leadership adopted this policy pragmatism. This moderation is in part a natural response by a faction that has adapted itself to a party culture that stresses accommodation and compromise for the good of the party. As Jo Freeman has noted, unity is a key value in the political culture of the Republican Party. As conservative Christians have become more active in party politics, they have adopted party values and minimized their differences with moderate party members (Freeman 1986).

It is also apparent that Christian Right leaders made a conscious decision to broaden their social agenda because they concluded that they benefit from their alliance with the Republican Party. The GOP provides a conduit into a political system that discourages third-party candidates and rewards politically active groups within the party. What governs the Christian Right alliance with the California Republican Party is the understandable belief that the party provides conservative Christians with greater influence over policy than a state Democratic Party that advocates social policy liberalism. The Republican Party has not ignored the Christian Right. Wilson and Huffington courted evangelical voters and the party has helped the Christian Right to elect numerous candidates to public office, particularly in local races where support for a conservative social agenda is highest. Candidates endorsed by the Christian Right ran for local elections with the blessing and support of the party in 1994, and the Allied Business PAC once again spent millions of dollars on conservative Republican candidates. Dozens of candidates identified with the Christian Right won office in 1994, including Andrea Seastrand and Robert Dornan for the House of Representatives, Rob Hurtt for the State Senate, and Phil Hawkins and Tom Woods for the state assembly, to name a few.[3]

Finally, pragmatism and local activism were tactics born of necessity. It is unlikely that the Christian Coalition or the Traditional Values Coalition could mobilize its membership to abandon a Republican Party with which most of its members have identified since 1984 (Smidt 1987). Evangelicals care about issues other than abortion and gay rights; their economic and foreign policy views coincide with the Republican Party (Guth, Green, Kellstedt, and Smidt 1993). In addition, the voting public does not share the Christian Right agenda on abortion and gay rights, and conservative Christian voters rarely prove decisive in statewide races. There is greater public support and political appeal for the moral traditionalism that the Christian Right represents and that the GOP is happy to endorse.

The Future of the Christian Right in California Politics

The Christian Right is at a political crossroads in California. As they have integrated into the Republican Party, evangelical Protestants have lost their original militancy and their electoral independence. Like numerous social movements before it, the Christian Right has discovered that time and involvement within a party lead inevitably to political accommodation and moderation (Wilson 1973). The Christian Right could choose to return to a purist ideological strategy and nominate candidates in political primary elections, challenge the party leadership on the moral issues of abortion and gay rights, and threaten to abandon the GOP if moderate candidates run for statewide office. It seems, in California at least, that there are always some local leaders of the Christian Right who want to take extreme political positions. This is not likely to succeed, however, because candidates identified with the Christian Right do not win statewide races in California, a majority of party members do not share the pro-life and anti–gay rights views of the Christian Right, and there are no attractive electoral alternatives to the GOP for evangelical Protestant voters. William Dannemeyer might run for a third time in the GOP Senate primary, but his sound defeats in the past two elections surely will dampen the enthusiasm of his evangelical Protestant supporters, who must recognize by now that a candidate as politically extreme as Dannemeyer cannot possibly win the party primary, let alone a general election.

The Christian Right could, on the other hand, continue to pursue its political accommodation within the Republican Party. The advantage of this approach is that it allows evangelicals to retain access and influence within the political system. The potential danger is that moderation risks alienating Christian activists for whom the social issues of abortion and gay rights are particularly salient and who will not want to always support pro-choice party candidates. These evangelical activists might wonder what it profits them to gain influence within a political party if they must lose their soul in the process. The Christian Right also faces a threat to the distinctiveness of its religious appeal. In the past, evangelicals have supported the Christian Coalition and the Traditional Values Coalition because they share the religious beliefs and values espoused by the groups on the issues of abortion, gay rights, and family values (Wilcox 1992; Soper 1994). It is not clear if evangelicals will continue to support groups that emphasize such nonreligious issues as a balanced budget amendment and term limits for members of Congress.[4]

The Christian Right's political accommodation in 1994 appears to be a harbinger of things to come. Given the partisan attachment of evangelicals to the GOP and the tendency of social movements to moderate their appeal over time, tactical accommodation is politically attractive and inevitable. The state Republican Party will remain pro-choice, but it will not abandon the Christian Right or most of its conservative political agenda. Conservative Christians are too powerful a party faction and too significant a force in local elections for the party to ignore. The party needs the resources and votes of evangelical Christians nearly as much as the Christian Right needs the Republican Party. Tony Blakely, spokesman for Newt Gingrich, correctly concluded after the 1994 elections that the evangelical vote is roughly to the Republican Party what organized labor was in past years to the Democratic Party. A good indication of the importance of the Christian Right in the state party is the political transformation of Pete Wilson in the past four years. Wilson is still pro-choice, but he is far more conservative on other social issues than when he first ran for governor in 1990. He is no longer battling the religious wing of the state Republican Party and in his recent inaugural address he embraced the conservative viewpoint on family values, personal responsibility, crime, and illegal immigration.

The paradoxical political influence of the Christian Right in California will continue for the near future. Conservative Christians might retain control of the state Republican Party if they remain as politically active as they have been in the past two years. This party power will give them some leverage, but it will not allow the Christian Right to nominate its own candidates or impose unpopular policy positions on abortion and gay rights on socially moderate party members. California is still a liberal state, but the Christian Right will continue to exercise political power, particularly in localities where conservative Christian political views are more popular and in local races where Christian Right resources can make a greater impression.

Notes

1. In 1989, the United States Supreme Court overturned the 1913 Progressive ban on preprimary endorsements. As a result, California's parties now have the right to endorse candidates in primary elections. In the aftermath of the court's decision, however, California's Republican Party officially banned preprimary endorsements.

2. John C. Green, James L. Guth, and Kevin Hill have noted that congressional candidates associated with the Christian Right have tended to come from suburban communities. See Green, Guth, and Hill 1993, 80–91.

3. For a district-by-district analysis of congressional, state senate, and state assembly races see, A.G. Brock, *California Journal*, December 1994.

4. Ralph Reed, the Christian Coalition's executive director, has said that the coalition will support the GOP's Contract with America despite the fact that it does not mention abortion or school prayer (Harwood 1995).

References

Bailey, Eric. 1994. "Law on Disrupting Worship Draws Fire," *Los Angeles Times* (15 September).

Barber, Mary Beth. 1994. "Rob Hurrt: New Power on the Right," *California Journal* 35 (February).

California Opinion Index. 1993. "Religion and Politics." September.

Christian Coalition, 1994. "1994 Christian Coalition Congressional Scorecard."

Culver, John C., and John C. Syer. 1984. *Power and Politics in California.* New York: John Wiley and Sons.

Doyle, Michael. 1994. "Senate Race a Matter of Choice," *The Fresno Bee* (14 October).

Freeman, Jo. 1986. "The Political Culture of the Democratic and Republican Parties." *Political Science Quarterly* 101: 327–56.

Gerston, Larry N., and Terry Christenson. 1991. *California Politics and Government.* Pacific Grove, Calif.: Brooks/Cole Publishing Company.

Green, John C., James L. Guth, and Cleveland R. Fraser. 1988. "Apostles and Apostates? Religion and Politics Among Party Activists." Pp. 113–38 in *The Bible and the Ballot Box: Religion and Politics in the 1988 Election,* edited by James J. Guth and John C. Green. Boulder, Colo.: Westview Press.

Green, John C., James L. Guth, and Kevin Hill. 1993. "Faith and Election: The Christian Right in Congressional Campaigns 1978–1988." *The Journal of Politics* (February): 80–91.

Guth, James L., and John C. Green. 1993. "Salience: The Core Concept?" Pp. 157–76 in *Rediscovering the Religious Factor in American Politics,* edited by David C. Leege and Lyman A. Kellstedt. Armonk, N.Y.: M. E. Sharpe.

Guth, James L., John C. Green, Lyman A. Kellstedt, and Corwin E. Smidt. 1993. "God's Own Party: Evangelicals and Republicans in the '92 Election." *The Christian Century* 110 (17 February).

Harwood, John. 1995. "Religious Right Plans to Use Tax, Budget Battles to Start Reshaping the Nation's Moral Landscape." *Wall Street Journal* (17 January).

Kellstedt, Lyman A., John C. Green, James L. Guth, and Corwin E. Smidt. 1994. "Religious Voting Blocs in the 1992 Election: The Year of the Evangelical?" *Sociology of Religion* 55 (3): 307–26.

Lappin, Lisa. 1994. "Huffington Courts Religious Right Among Some Doubts." *Sacramento Bee* (19 October).

Lesher, Dave. 1994. "Huffington Under Spotlight as GOP Meets." *Los Angeles Times* (26 February).

———. 1995. "Political Winds Driving Wilson's Shift to the Right." *Los Angeles Times* (28 January).

226   *J. Christopher Soper*

Lieblich, Julia. 1994. "Politics and Religion: When are Questions Justified about a Candidate's Beliefs?" *The San Diego Union Tribune* (30 October).

Liebman, Robert. 1983. "Mobilizing the Moral Majority." In *The New Christian Right*, edited by Robert Liebman and Robert Wuthnow. New York: Aldine.

Lozana, Carlos V., and Ralph Frammolino. 1992. "Christian Right Tries to Take over State GOP." *Los Angeles Times* (18 October).

Lucas, Greg. 1994. "Governor Vetoes Bill on Domestic Pairs." *San Francisco Chronicle* (12 September).

Mayhew, David. 1986. *Placing Parties in American Politics.* Princeton, N.J.: Princeton University Press.

Moen, Matthew. 1994. "From Revolution to Evolution: The Changing Nature of the Christian Right." *Sociology of Religion* 55:3 (Fall 1994): 345–57.

Nollinger, Mark. 1993. "The New Crusaders—The Christian Right Storms California's Political Bastions." *California Journal* 34 (January).

Persinos, John C. 1994. "Has the Christian Right Taken over the Republican Party?" *Campaigns and Elections* 15 (September): 20–25.

Peterson, Larry. 1991. "The Dannemeyer-Seymour Race—Fruitcake or Jell-O? Do Republicans Face an Unpalatable Choice?" *California Journal* 32 (July).

Reed, Ralph. 1993. "The Religious Right Reaches Out." *The New York Times* (22 August).

Ross, Michael. 1994. "GOP Congress Forces Assail Fazio over Religious Right." *Los Angeles Times* (24 June).

Ross, Michael J. 1984. *California: Its Government and Politics.* Monterey, Calif.: Brooks/Cole Publishing Company.

Russo, Michael A. 1995. "California: A Political Landscape for Choice and Conflict." Pp. 168–81 in *Abortion Politics in American States*, edited by Mary C. Segers and Timothy A. Byrnes. Armonk, N.Y.: M. E. Sharpe.

Schneider, William. 1994. "In 1996, It's as California Goes." *The National Journal* (3 December).

Schrag, Peter. 1994. "Politics and CLAS Bias." *Sacramento Bee* (30 September).

Seib, Gerald F. 1993. "Christian Coalition Hopes to Expand by Taking Stands on Taxes, Crime, Health Care and NAFTA." *The Wall Street Journal* (7 September).

Shogren, Elizabeth, and Douglas Frantz. 1993. "School Boards Become the Religious Right's New Pulpit." *Los Angeles Times* (10 December).

Smidt, Corwin. 1987. "Evangelicals and the 1984 Election: Continuity or Change?" *American Politics Quarterly* 15: 419–44.

Soper, J. Christopher. 1994. *Evangelical Christianity in the United States and Great Britain: Religious Beliefs, Political Choices.* New York: New York University Press.

Walters, Dan. 1994. "Wilson Cans Domestic Partner Measure." *The Fresno Bee* (13 September).

Wilcox, Clyde. 1992. *God's Warriors: The Christian Right in Twentieth-Century America.* Baltimore: The Johns Hopkins University Press.

———. 1994. "Premillenialists at the Millenium: Some Reflections on the Christian Right in the Twentieth-First Century." *Sociology of Religion* 55 (3): 243–62.

Wilson, James Q. 1973. *Political Organizations.* New York: Basic Books.

12

Oregon: Identity and Politics in the Northwest

William M. Lunch

In 1994, as they had in 1992, Oregon voters rejected an antihomosexual ballot initiative sponsored by the Oregon Citizens' Alliance (OCA), an organization of the Christian Right in Oregon. Both of the initiatives— Measure 9 in 1992 and Measure 13 in 1994—would have amended the state constitution to deny civil rights protections to homosexuals and otherwise restrict their legal rights, but the language used in the 1994 initiative was less severe than in 1992. Perhaps as a result, the 1994 initiative, Measure 13, came closer to passage, losing by only 51 to 49 percent of the vote, while Measure 9 had lost by 56 to 44 percent. These measures have given the OCA high visibility—though not popularity—in the Northwest, and even some national attention.[1]

In 1992, Measure 9 attracted national and even international attention. Had it passed, Measure 9 would have overturned existing local laws in three Oregon cities protecting homosexuals from discrimination[2] and the state constitution would have been amended to add a provision stating that the state could not "promote, encourage, or facilitate" homosexuality. This was an extraordinarily broad and vague provision which would have required hundreds, if not thousands, of specific policy changes, had it been enacted. The OCA sponsored the measure and collected more than a million dollars, mostly in small contributions, for the campaign. But there was also an intense opposition campaign. The measure passed in twenty-one of Oregon's thirty-six counties, and in 1993 and 1994, a number of local antigay initiatives at the city and county levels passed in areas where Measure 9 had been successful (see figure 12-1). In the general election in 1994, Measure 13 did not receive as much attention as Measure 9 had, but it came closer to passage, winning in twenty-five of the counties of the state.

Table 12-1

Comparing National and State Attitudes toward Homosexuals

Level and Date: Source:	National, Sept. '92 Gallup, for *Newsweek*	National, Feb. '93 *New York Times*/CBS	State, Nov. '92 *Oregonian*
Answers reflecting anxiety/ mistrust of homosexuals:			
Homosexuality is an acceptable lifestyle.	53% no	54% no	na
Homosexuals should be able to legally marry.	58% no	na	58% no
Homosexuals should be able to adopt children.	68% no	na	59% no
Answers reflecting tolerance of homosexuals:			
Homosexuals should have equal opportunity in employment.	78% yes	78% yes	82% yes
It is acceptable to include homo- sexuals in the president's cabinet.	64% yes	na	69% yes
It is acceptable to have a doctor who is homosexual.	59% yes	na	69% yes

Sources for these figures are the Gallup Poll conducted for *Newsweek*, reported in the February 14, 1992, edition; the *New York Times*/CBS poll reported March 5, 1993; and the state poll commissioned by the *Oregonian*, reported in its October 11, 1992, edition. Question wording varied slightly between the Gallup and *NYT*/CBS polls; the state pollsters in Oregon used the same question wording as Gallup when they asked about the same subject.

Cultural Politics in 1992 and 1994

The antihomosexual activity in Oregon is not unique to the state. In 1992, a less inflammatory antihomosexual measure was approved by voters in Colorado as Oregon voters rejected Measure 9. And as the Oregon campaign was becoming nationally visible, the Republican national convention in Houston featured a number of speakers who warned of a cultural "war" brewing in the United States. It can be argued that cultural conflicts in politics were more prominent in 1992 than at any time since 1928, when religious differences between Catholics and Protestants were the focus for much of the election. Although cultural conflict has reemerged in national politics, unlike the twenties, when the Democrats were deeply divided between northern and southern factions, cultural conflicts today are being fought largely within the Republican Party.

In 1994, the Christian Right was very active in the Northwest. Though antihomosexual initiatives failed in both Oregon and Idaho, in many other respects it was a banner year for the sponsors. In Washington Republicans scored the largest reversal of congressional fortunes in any state, with the Washington House delegation going from eight-to-one Democratic to seven-to-two Republican. Christian Right activists could claim credit for at least helping almost all the GOP victors and had a direct role for at least three of the six successful challengers. Moreover, in Idaho, the last major Democratic elected official in the state, Larry LaRocca, was defeated by a woman, Helen Chenowith, with strong ties to the Christian Right. In Oregon, two Republicans were elected to open congressional seats—Jim Bunn in the mid–Willamette Valley Fifth District and Wes Cooley in the huge eastern and southern Oregon First District—both with active support by the OCA and other religious conservatives. And in the First District, in northwest Oregon (including most of suburban Washington County, west of Portland), Bill Witt, a small businessman who was once active in the OCA, came within a few hundred votes of unseating incumbent Democratic representative Elizabeth Furse (Berke 1994). These gains were mirrored in state-level elections: in the Washington state legislature Republicans seized control of the state house, and in Oregon, Republicans swept to power in the state senate for the first time in forty years.

Within the party structure, Christian conservatives have come close to winning control of the Oregon Republican Party state central committee, though they lost narrowly to more traditional business conservatives in both 1993 and 1995. Nonetheless, it is clear that the OCA and its allies in Washington and Idaho will be back in 1996.

The Christian Right in the Northwest has become, in a relatively short time, a major force in party, interest group, and electoral politics. It is worth asking how and why organizations as far to the right as the OCA could come to exercise such political influence, particularly in a relatively liberal state such as Oregon.

Social Control: Conceptualizing Cultural Politics

Economic issues ask how far government should intervene in the economy and on behalf of whom, while social control issues ask how far the government should intervene in regulating private moral behavior. All governments impose at least some social controls; they are legal restrictions, sometimes supplemented by extralegal means, routinely imposed to restrict personal behavior and limit social relationships. Social controls enforce individual conformity with standards of behavior established by dominant groups; though such conformity may serve economic purposes, enforcing at least outward acceptance of the standards set by dominant groups is the prime goal for social control policies, even if they are economically costly. Some social controls restrict everyone in society; for example, prohibitions on public nudity or on harmful drugs apply to all citizens. But social controls are often applied to disfavored groups, which are often, but not always, defined by ascribed status, that is, characteristics established at birth, such as race and gender.

Historically, social controls in the United States have increased in each of three conservative periods during this century: the 1920s, when prohibition of alcohol was attempted, with disastrous consequences; the 1950s, when conformity was a cultural norm reinforced by cold war anxieties during the McCarthy era; and the 1980s, when attempts were made to reverse the relaxation of social controls that had taken place during the sixties and seventies (Schlesinger 1986).

African Americans have been subject to very strong social controls, starting with slavery. Even after the abolition of slavery, blacks were treated, at best, as second-class citizens—virtually all were effectively banned from advanced education, limited to a few undesirable occupations, and otherwise restricted. The controls to which they were subjected limited even where they could eat a meal or get a drink of water. After a long struggle, the national government forced state and local governments and private businesses to lift at least the legally sanctioned social controls against blacks when the Civil Rights Act of 1964 was passed. Other disfavored groups, such as religious minorities, were also protected by the Civil Rights Act, but the egregious mistreatment of blacks was the reason for the law. The national government then guaranteed access to the polls in the Voting Rights Act in 1965. Today, some of the most intensely debated social control issues concern civil liberties for homosexuals. Christian Right groups have found that gay and lesbian rights issues motivate their supporters into political action with an intensity normally reserved for the abortion controversy.

Oregon provides an excellent microcosm for understanding such cultural conflicts, in part because the state—along with some other "Northern tier" states, such as Minnesota and Vermont—has anticipated national trends on noneconomic issues such as the environment and women's rights, and in part because racial conflicts have not been as divisive in a state with a black population of less than 2 percent.

That an antigay measure should have appeared on the Oregon ballot at all was disconcerting to many Americans. The state is often perceived as one of the most culturally liberal in the nation. For example, the well-known *Almanac of American Politics* had once described Oregon as characterized by "liberal positions on cultural issues" (Barone and Ujifusa 1987, 1024). But after the events of 1992, the *Almanac of American Politics* revised its description of Oregon to: ". . . a quintessentially American state thousands of miles from where most Americans live, an experimental commonwealth and laboratory of reform, home of angry owl-hating loggers and crusaders against homosexuality: all these things are Oregon" (Barone and Ujifusa 1994, 1052). Political developments in Oregon prior to 1992 show that the antigay measures were not as peculiar as many observers thought; indeed, they were related to aspects of Oregon politics quite familiar to regional observers and nationally, to changes within the Republican Party.

The Political Roots of the Oregon Citizens' Alliance

The origins of the Oregon Citizens' Alliance can be traced to a challenge by the Christian Right to Republican senator Bob Packwood in 1986. During the eighties, Packwood was a dissenter among Republicans due to his moderate to liberal positions on issues concerning women, notably his pro-choice position on abortion. At the time, Republicans controlled the U.S. Senate and Packwood was the chairman of the Senate Finance Committee. But in 1981 and 1982 he led Senate opposition to efforts to recriminalize abortion, and national antiabortion leaders had promised to punish him in his next reelection campaign.

Back in Oregon, most mainstream Republicans did not take the challenge to Packwood very seriously. After all, Packwood was not only the chairman of a powerful Senate committee, he was a politician with a record striking in its sensitivity to shifts in public opinion and willingness to adapt to such changes. But religious conservatives recruited a handsome, energetic Baptist minister named Joe Lutz to run in the GOP primary. Supported by hundreds of volunteers, most of whom were new to politics, Lutz ran a visible, active campaign and was stronger than he appeared to be.

Turnout among Republican voters in the primary was low—fewer than 300,000 votes were cast, out of almost 600,000 registered Republicans. Packwood's experience and superior financing could not generate the intensity found among the activists supporting Lutz, who drew more than 126,000 votes, or 42 percent. The surprised press in Oregon used the time-honored phrase "better than expected" to describe the support for Lutz. Given this initial success, Lutz and his key campaign staff (notably Lon Mabon) decided to form a political organization, hoping to extend the influence of the Christian Right in Oregon politics in general while looking forward toward a future election in which Lutz might run successfully for high office. The Oregon Citizens' Alliance was organized with those goals in mind (Ota 1988b).[3]

Initially, it appeared that Lutz himself might have a bright future as a rising conservative star. With the visibility he had gained as a result of the Senate campaign, he was discussed as a potential candidate for a variety of important posts, from mayor of Portland to governor of Oregon. But the personal pressures of being a public figure were evidently too much for Lutz. He left his wife and family to go to California with another woman; though he later returned to Oregon, Lutz had fallen off the political radarscope (Ota 1988a). But although Lutz had disappeared, the OCA survived.

In the meantime, the Democratic governor of Oregon elected in 1986, Neil Goldschmidt, had issued an executive order extending to homosexuals in state government protection against discrimination that already existed for race, gender, and religious belief. The OCA leadership opposed the order by Goldschmidt and may have seen a political opening to move against a minority about which the public has, at best, ambivalent feelings. OCA leaders responded with an initiative that proposed to amend state law to overturn the governor's order and prohibit civil rights protections—described as "special rights"—for gays in state employment. Asked what he meant by special rights, Mabon claimed that homosexuals have a "political agenda," including establishment of "minority status," which he as a Christian was bound to oppose.

At the time, neither the gay community nor the political establishment in the state took the OCA initiative very seriously. Later, both mainstream and gay leaders would say that they did not believe that Oregonians would vote for such a measure. But once again, as in 1986, they underestimated the appeal of the OCA's arguments. Without much of a campaign against it, the initiative passed, with 53 percent of the vote. The statute that resulted from the vote in 1988 was overturned in 1993 by the state supreme court as violating the state constitution, but the OCA had shown that it could organize a statewide petition drive, qualify a measure, and conduct a successful campaign. Those were substantial political accomplishments; political observers in Oregon began to realize that the OCA would probably have continuing political influence.

The good showing in 1986 and the success in 1988 had come, in no small measure, through the emulation of organizing techniques that had earlier been used—albeit for very different purposes—by the civil rights movement in the South. As in Mississippi and Alabama among disenfranchised blacks during the early 1960s, so in Oregon a quarter of a century later, white religious conservatives organized by persuading ministers who would exhort their often initially reluctant congregations to become politically active. Unlike the civil rights movement, the most visible political leaders among the Christian Right in Oregon were not themselves ministers—at least, not after Reverend Lutz disappeared. Lon Mabon, who had been the chief lieutenant to Lutz, effectively recruited evangelical ministers to alert the potential constituency to issues and, once alerted, to mobilize the troops. One key to the success of the OCA in qualifying measures for the ballot may well be access to churches where large numbers of the faithful are conveniently—and inexpensively—gathered.

There was a national model for these efforts. National voter registration drives were conducted among evangelical congregations in the early 1980s and had substantial success, particularly in the South and the Midwest. National organizations on the Christian Right, such as the now-defunct Moral Majority, claimed, for example, that they had registered as many as eight million new voters for the 1980 election; although this was clearly exaggerated, Christian Right organizations registered at least two million new voters, almost all of them for the Republicans.[4]

Oregon provided a formal opening for this form of mass political mobilization; among states that allow for direct democracy measures such as initiatives and referenda, Oregon has one of the lowest qualification thresholds. The Christian Right, although a sizable cultural group, does not represent even a quarter of the Oregon electorate.[5] In a state such as Arizona—which is far more conservative than Oregon but requires that a larger fraction of the electorate sign petitions before initiatives appear on the ballot—the OCA or a similar organization would find getting access to the ballot more difficult.[6]

Mabon was, for a time, less successful at raising money; his is a predominantly working-class and lower-middle-class constituency that is not accustomed to political giving and that has been economically squeezed for at least a decade in Oregon and longer in the nation. Economic reverses in the state and the region have been particularly sharp in rural areas, such as eastern Oregon and Washington, dependent on natural resource industries such as timber, mining, and fishing. It is those areas that have consistently provided the strongest support to the OCA's initiatives (Lunch 1995).

Nor did Mabon have a good financial track record himself; he had gone bankrupt in small business dealings before becoming a political operative. He has admitted that initial fund-raising efforts were clumsy and ineffective (and though Mabon has not said so, early fund-raising letters were couched in language extreme enough to put off all but the most intense potential supporters). Eventually, the OCA leadership became more adept at using direct-mail fund-raising techniques but in the first few years, the OCA had constant financial problems (Neville 1993a, 1993b).

Nonetheless, the organization was clearly connecting with deeply held feelings among its constituency, so in 1990 the OCA returned to the issue that was largely responsible for its founding: abortion. Though the OCA had failed to defeat Bob Packwood, it had shown that at least within the Republican primary, numerous voters would respond to an antiabortion appeal. In 1988, perhaps somewhat to the surprise even of the OCA's own leaders, the organization had passed a statewide initiative. Seen from the perspective of the OCA leadership, the organization had built success upon success; in 1990, they went for what their active members clearly regarded as the big brass ring in politics—restoring the legal prohibition on abortion that existed prior to *Roe v. Wade*. It seems clear that opposition to abortion and, more broadly, to the changing status of women is central to the motivations of leaders and activists. And in 1989, after their success in the 1988 elections, OCA leaders were undoubtedly encouraged by a decision of the U.S. Supreme Court, *Webster v. Reproductive Services*. The court, with a large Republican majority, had given the states far greater latitude to regulate abortion than at any time since 1973. For activists on the Christian Right, it seemed a propitious time to act.

The OCA drafted, circulated petitions for, and qualified for the 1990 ballot a very strict antiabortion amendment to the state constitution that would have banned abortion except in cases posing a threat to the mother's life. At the same time, moderate elements in the antiabortion movement qualified a measure that would have required parental notification for minors seeking an abortion. The two measures were placed on the 1990 ballot as Measures 8 (sponsored by the OCA) and 10 (sponsored by Oregon Right to Life). But the OCA had overplayed its hand and misread public opinion. Measure 8 was resoundingly defeated, by a margin of more than two to one; Measure 10 lost narrowly, as pro-choice opponents of both measures successfully tied the two together in the minds of voters.

Still, the OCA could claim at least a partial success in 1990 because its "independent" candidate for governor, a retired federal employee named Al Mobley, was responsible for the defeat of a moderate Republican, Dave Frohnmayer, who was the state attorney general at the time.

Frohnmayer started his campaign for governor thinking that he would be running against Neil Goldschmidt, the Democrat who had issued the executive order to protect gays. But in February 1990, Goldschmidt abruptly announced that he would not run for reelection. Democrats were momentarily thrown into disarray, but after hurried meetings among party leaders, the secretary of state, Barbara Roberts, a gregarious Portland liberal, became the consensus candidate of the party. Roberts was probably the most liberal credible candidate who could have been selected at a time when Oregonians were in a rather cranky, antigovernment mood, so her prospects did not seem at all bright. In part because of this expectation, the Democratic nomination was hers without serious primary opposition; that would prove significant later. But at the time, Frohnmayer was widely expected to win.

On the Republican side, the perception that Frohnmayer was all but elected increased the internal party pressures on him. Leaders of the OCA met with Frohnmayer, asking that he reverse his position on abortion; he refused. They then asked him to shift in the direction of greater social control on other issues; again he refused. Finally, the OCA leaders asked Frohnmayer for a substantial contribution to their legislative campaign fund, to be used ostensibly to support Republican candidates who met their standards as acceptable; offended, Frohnmayer ended the discussion and left the meeting. When he did so, his chance to become governor departed with him.

The OCA leadership was, in turn, offended by Frohnmayer's rejection of their proposals, but also, more generally, by what might be described as "lack of respect"[7] for them by mainstream Oregon Republicans. They resolved to punish Frohnmayer and, in so doing, to serve notice on other Republicans that without OCA support the party could not win statewide.

Why would the OCA—almost all of whose members are Republicans—want to cause the defeat of another Republican? If the Christian Right could be seen as capable of *defeating* Frohnmayer, they might gain effective veto power over GOP candidates. Moderates in the party could be sent a message that it was unsafe to oppose the Christian Right. In time, OCA leaders could hope that state Republican leaders would tire of internal battles over social control issues and would cede control over such questions to them.

Because Frohnmayer was opposed in the primary by a moderate, the OCA chose not to back either candidate. Instead, after the primary, the OCA named a candidate, Al Mobley, a recently retired middle manager from the Army Corps of Engineers. Mobley announced that he would run as an independent for governor. Even with Mobley in the contest, however, in the early fall it was widely believed within the political community that Frohnmayer would win easily. Both public and private polls during the summer showed him with a substantial lead over Roberts, with Mobley scarcely visible.

Roberts decided to take a gamble in early September by running a number of statewide television ads, spending a substantial part of her small campaign treasury. Statewide polls were scheduled for the period just after the Roberts ads had run—predictably, her standing improved notably. While this tactical move may not have had much long-term impact on voters, it persuaded a number of major Democratic donors who had been holding back that Roberts was a viable candidate; contributions to her campaign increased substantially. With the increased funding, Roberts was able to counter Frohnmayer's attack ads and launch a number of her own. Little noticed at first, Mobley was nonetheless able to assemble increasing support from Republicans unhappy with Frohnmayer, particularly those sympathetic to the Christian Right. By October, Frohnmayer's campaign became aware of the threat Mobley posed. As the election approached, in conservative eastern and southern Oregon his campaign ran radio and even television ads warning Republican voters that a vote for Mobley was the equivalent of a vote for Roberts.

But Frohnmayer's efforts were largely wasted on those who supported the OCA. Religious conviction reinforced political frustration among such voters; on election day Roberts received 46 percent, Frohnmayer 40 percent, a Libertarian 1 percent, and Mobley received 144,000 votes, or about 13 percent of the total vote cast for governor. Clearly, the vast majority of those who cast protest votes for Mobley would otherwise have voted for Frohnmayer. And among OCA activists, Frohnmayer's loss in 1990 was perceived as a victory. On election night, as returns came in showing Mobley in third place, the mood was jubilant at OCA headquarters. Around midnight, the assembled OCA activists, in high spirits, cheered as new returns came in; they began chanting, "Packwood, Packwood, Packwood . . ."

The Mobley campaign was a success in the sense that it demonstrated to Oregon Republicans that it would be very difficult if not impossible for moderates to win statewide elections without the support, or at least acquiescence, of the Christian Right and that a precondition for such acceptance was opposition to legal abortion.

But the vote for Mobley also showed the limits of the opposition politics of the OCA. In 1986, in a poorly attended Republican primary, Joe Lutz had received about 126,000 votes. Four years later, with a formal organization, extensive publicity, better financing, and a candidate with better credentials, the Christian Right in Oregon was able to attract only slightly more—144,000 votes—in a general election, in which almost *four times* as many voters participated as in the 1986 primary. Quite clearly, the OCA has a disciplined, determined constituency, but just as clearly, there is a ceiling beyond which it cannot hope to reach very far. That ceiling currently appears to be about 12 to 13 percent of the total state vote; conceivably, in a low turnout election, it might reach 15 percent. But those limits describe only the explicit supporters of the OCA.

On certain issues the Christian Right can attract substantially more voters. The 1990 antiabortion initiatives had shown that, at least in Oregon, only about a third of the voters were prepared to return to the time when abortion was illegal and, in conjunction, Oregon voters even rejected comparatively mild increased restrictions on young women. With its committed followers the OCA could repeatedly qualify antiabortion measures for the ballot, and just as clearly, the measures would repeatedly lose. But the 1988 vote against protections for homosexuals showed that public opinion was more disposed to vote for restrictions on gays than on women.

The OCA in 1992

As soon as the 1990 returns were complete, political speculation in Oregon focused on the role the OCA would play in 1992 when Senator Bob Packwood was due to run for reelection. It seemed clear from the reaction of the OCA faithful on election night in 1990 that they had not forgotten the original raison d'etre for the organization. But by this point, unlike in 1986, Republican Party leaders were awake and alert. In 1991, as the state legislature was beginning its biennial session, moderate Republicans gathered for an annual meeting called the Dorchester Conference. Many years earlier, during the 1960s, when he was a young state legislator, Packwood had started the conferences, partially as strategy sessions and partially as social gatherings for moderate Republicans, even then beginning to feel outflanked by conservative elements in the party. Normally, Republicans as far to the right as the OCA leaders would not be invited to a Dorchester Conference, but Mabon, Mobley, and some others were invited in 1991. There they met with Packwood, moderate state Republican chairman Craig Berkman, and a number of other state GOP officials. Following these "bury the hatchet" meetings, everyone involved spoke vaguely of party unity; but within a few days, the details of a bargain leaked out. The moderates had agreed to at least one and perhaps a series of "unity dinners," which would raise money from major Republican contributors for the OCA, still suffering from financial difficulties. In return, the OCA would not run a spoiler candidacy by Mobley or anyone else against Packwood in 1992.

Unfortunately for the participants, the Dorchester deal began to fall apart as its outlines became public. Moderates were pressured to shun any public involvement with the OCA, which is widely disliked among mainstream Republicans. The unity dinners sank beneath the political waves. But those involved continued for some time to behave as if they expected the bargain to be completed. That may have been truer of OCA leaders—who saw their acceptance at Dorchester as evidence that they were finally being treated with respect—than among Republican Party officials. Months later, when the unity dinners had clearly been abandoned, OCA officials were flown to Washington to a closed meeting with a number of Republican U.S. senators, who reportedly promised to go out to Oregon after the elections for a series of fund-raising events, with the quid pro quo that the OCA would not sponsor a spoiler candidacy against Packwood. This deal, unlike the unity dinners, stuck.

During the time when the unity dinners were still anticipated, the focus of the OCA had already shifted away from efforts to defeat Packwood. Instead, OCA leaders announced that they would circulate petitions to put on the ballot an antihomosexual measure. This time, unlike 1988, the initiative would be drafted as a state constitutional amendment so, if passed, it would be beyond the reach of state courts.

In explaining their motivation for the antigay initiative, Mabon and other OCA leaders spoke of their opposition to public funds being spent for and public recognition being given to organizations of homosexuals. As far as such declarations went, they were accurate—both OCA leaders and supporters view homosexuality as morally wrong—but they do not explain the OCA's organizational need to have an issue that would attract volunteers and contributors. For an organization that had fund-raising troubles, the need to have a visible issue was acute. OCA supporters began to collect signatures for the initiative.

In May 1992, the OCA and its supporters in two Oregon communities rehearsed the arguments they would make throughout the state in the fall. In Oregon, state initiatives must appear in the general election in even-numbered years, but state law allows local initiatives to appear at other times, including the primary date in May. Local OCA chapters, with state support, had qualified antihomosexual initiatives in two Oregon cities, Corvallis and Springfield. They had also attempted unsuccessfully to qualify a parallel measure in the more progressive Portland.

Springfield and Corvallis, while both small cities in Oregon's Willamette Valley, are quite different economically and demographically. Springfield is a predominantly blue-collar town where the local economy was once dominated by timber mills. The town, near the more cosmopolitan Eugene, has traditionally voted Democratic, but many voters there have confronted economic stagnation if not reverses for many years; debates over social control issues often summon forth resentments that are close to the surface in Springfield.

Corvallis, home to Oregon State University, is quite different. The university is the largest employer in Corvallis; the second largest is Hewlett-Packard, the large electronics firm. A regional hospital and a national engineering firm are also major employers, so the city has a highly educated population; in the 1990 census it was found that 20 percent of the adult population held advanced degrees. Politically, in recent years Corvallis has shifted from its traditional liberal Republicanism toward the Democrats, in part because of a reaction against social control positions taken by the Republican Party. By 1992, the city council had adopted a law to ensure equal treatment for gays. Corvallis was one of only three cities in the state with such a law. The OCA initiative would have overturned the gay rights laws in Corvallis and in Springfield. As expected, the local OCA initiative failed in Corvallis by a vote of roughly two to one. Although the initiative was expected to fail—but by a closer margin—in Springfield it passed with 53 percent of the vote.

Arguments made in Corvallis and Springfield presaged arguments made statewide in the fall. When Mabon or other OCA leaders speak of "special rights" being granted to homosexuals, they mean that gays will become "another minority group," to be protected by civil rights laws. Proponents argued that homosexuals also have a cultural agenda that includes infiltration of the schools and recruitment of children to become gay or lesbian. They also objected to public funds being spent, even indirectly, to support gay organizations, such as gay student clubs at colleges. Voting in favor of the local antigay measures (and later, Measure 9) was a way for citizens to express their disapproval of these cultural trends, according to OCA leaders.

The opponents of the measures emphasized that the initiatives challenged civil rights protections and so a vote for the measures was a vote for discrimination and hate. The opponents pointed to the very broad and vague wording of the measures and regularly asked, "Who's next?" They emphasized, for example, that books by homosexual authors might well have to be banned from libraries along with music by homosexual composers from school orchestras if the OCA measures were to pass, that public employees who were gay would have to be fired, or that doctors, pharmacists, lawyers, or barbers—for that matter, anyone licensed by the state—would be at risk of losing their livelihood if they were homosexual or were accused of being homosexual. The opponents consistently emphasized *specific* consequences that the measures might have, while the proponents countered that the measures were mainly intended as broad *symbolic* statements of opposition to homosexuality. These themes reappeared in the fall campaign (Strinkowski 1993).

A poll published as a cover story in *Newsweek* in September helps to explain why each side in the Measure 9 debate attempted to frame the issue as they did. As table 12-1 shows, when asked general or symbolic questions about homosexuals and their lifestyle, most Americans reflected feelings from discomfort to hostility; when asked, for example, if "homosexuality [is] an acceptable alternative lifestyle," 53 percent of respondents said no and 41 percent said yes. Some specifics seemed to evoke similar disapproving attitudes, particularly if the question concerned aspects of family life; 58 percent of the *Newsweek* respondents disapproved of legal gay marriages, for example, and only 32 percent felt that gays should be able to adopt children. But when specific questions concerned economic or political opportunities, there was greater tolerance; for example, 78 percent felt homosexuals should have equal rights to job opportunities, and 64 percent felt that gays should not be barred from serving in the president's cabinet (Turque 1992, 34–41; Schmalz 1993, 1).

It is easy to understand why the OCA phrased their arguments in terms of "special" rights. In late September and early October, a state poll conducted for *The Oregonian* found that 82 percent of respondents agreed that homosexuals "should have equal rights in job opportunities," and 58 percent disagreed with the statement "Civil rights for homosexuals will result in special treatment." But only 36 percent of the Oregon respondents felt that homosexuals should have the right to legally recognized marriages, and only 35 percent felt that gays should be able to adopt children (Church 1992).

After the election, in February 1993, the same patterns appeared in a national poll by the *New York Times*/CBS polling organization; while only 36 percent of the respondents felt that homosexuality was "an acceptable alternative lifestyle," as in the earlier Gallup poll, 78 percent felt that homosexuals should have equal rights to job opportunities (Schmalz 1993).

The 1992 Statewide Campaign

Once the statewide campaign began in the fall, perceptions of the underlying attitudes revealed in the polling meant that proponents of Measure 9 de-emphasized practical effects of the initiative while opponents emphasized the likely consequences of it. The opponents also underscored Oregon's national reputation for tolerance and the potential damage to it if Measure 9 passed. Measure 9, as presented to Oregon voters, read:

> Amends Oregon Constitution. All governments in Oregon may not use their monies or properties to promote, encourage, or facilitate homosexuality, pedophilia, sadism, or masochism. All levels of government, including public education systems, must assist in setting a standard for Oregon's youth which recognizes that these "behaviors" are "abnormal, wrong, unnatural and perverse" and that they are to be discouraged and avoided. State may not recognize this conduct under "sexual orientation" or "sexual preference" labels, or through "quotas, minority status, affirmative action, or similar concepts."

The political establishment of the state opposed Measure 9 all but unanimously. Governor Barbara Roberts compared the measure and its sponsors to early efforts by the Nazi Party in Germany. Her opponent in 1990, Republican Dave Frohnmayer, was very active and visible in the "No on Nine" campaign. Both of Oregon's GOP U.S. senators—Bob Packwood and Mark Hatfield—announced their opposition to the measure, as did all five U.S. representatives. The opponents claimed that the initiative was not only bad policy but unconstitutional. They warned of the consequences for Oregon's reputation nationally, including possible economic boycotts.

Thus, framing the issue was fundamental to campaign strategy for both sides. To the extent that persuadable voters in the middle of the electorate saw the issue presented as largely symbolic disapproval of homosexuality, they would be inclined to vote yes. To the extent that such voters perceived the question as one of officially required or sanctioned discrimination against gays, they would be inclined to vote no. For this reason, both the OCA and its opponents in the No on Nine organization focused a great deal of attention on the press, in particular the state's largest newspaper, *The Oregonian*. The paper strongly editorialized against Measure 9, and Robert Landauer, the editorial page editor, who wrote a series of scathing editorials denouncing the measure, even received death threats. More important than the editorials, however, was the paper's news coverage, which framed the debate as being about officially sanctioned discrimination.

But such subtle distinctions were easy to lose in the emotional uproar over the measure. Because the campaign asked voters to pass judgment on the legal status and protection of citizens based upon their identity, it was ugly and divisive. Activists on both sides reported incidents of harrassment and threats, and one night in late September racist skinheads in Salem, the state capital, firebombed a house where a white gay man and a black lesbian lived. Both were killed. The OCA immediately denounced the attack and attempted to distance itself from those responsible, but opponents of Measure 9 claimed that the OCA had created a climate of opinion in which physical attacks on homosexuals were encouraged.

The 1992 Election Results

Measure 9 failed by a margin of 56 to 44 percent. There was a decided urban–rural split in the results; Measure 9 passed in 21 of Oregon's 36 counties, but with one exception every one of those where it passed was lightly populated, in southern or eastern Oregon. The major population centers in the state all voted against the measure, generally by very heavy margins. But perhaps most important, the suburban counties (Washington and Clackamas) that ring the city of Portland cast key votes against the measure, siding this time, at least, with their urban brethren. Regionally, Measure 9 did best in conservative southern Oregon. The measure was also quite successful in much of rural eastern Oregon, but lost badly in the more heavily populated Willamette Valley and overwhelmingly in the city of Portland. Religious differences were huge; in exit polling conducted for the Eugene *Register-Guard*, it was found that while 74 percent of self-identified "fundamentalist Christians" voted for the measure, only 25 percent of Catholics voted in favor, and all self-identified Jewish voters in the exit poll said they voted no (Esteve 1992). Exit polling conducted by *The Oregonian* and the Eugene *Register-Guard* showed that typical supporters of Measure 9 were Republicans from rural areas who were quite religious and who had low levels of education. Among the best educated segment of the Oregon electorate, those with postgraduate degrees, 22 percent voted in favor; among college graduates, 35 percent voted yes; but among voters with a high school education or less, the measure prevailed, with 55 percent of the vote.

1993-94: The Band Plays On

Within a few days of the loss in 1992, Lon Mabon announced that the OCA would return to the ballot in 1994 with a measure revised to appeal to moderate voters by eliminating the most extreme language of the original (Rubenstein 1992). Mabon blamed the 1992 loss largely on the fact that the opposition to Measure 9 outspent the OCA—and they did, by a margin of about two to one—but also admitted that the extreme language used in the measure had damaged its chances. For example, language linking homosexuality to sadomasochism and pedophilia, and ambiguous language that many lawyers read to require revocation of state occupational licenses for those accused of homosexuality, went too far even for some potential supporters, Mabon admitted. He then devised a two-pronged strategy for 1993-94; first, the OCA would attempt to pass a series of local initiatives containing antihomosexual provisions in cities and counties where Measure 9 had prevailed in the 1992 vote; second, another statewide initiative would be circulated, so that the local campaigns would overlap with signature gathering for the 1994 statewide effort. This approach also guaranteed continuing publicity and controversy for the OCA, which helped its direct-mail fund-raising.

The local initiatives strategy worked almost to perfection; local OCA chapters qualified sixteen local measures in 1993, primarily in localities such as Sweet Home, a depressed timber town in the foothills of the Cascade mountains, and counties such as Josephine County in southern Oregon, where the Ku Klux Klan was strong earlier in the century and populist resentment is currently a trademark of local politics. The antigay measures passed in every case except one in which modification of the city charter required a three-fifths margin, but the OCA measure received only a majority of the votes (Rubenstein 1993b, 2).

Meanwhile, in the state capital, concerns about civil liberties, the effect the OCA campaigns were having, and the potential for damage to tourism caused the 1993 legislature to pass a highly ambiguous law that prohibited local governments in Oregon from providing "special rights" based on sexual orientation but also prohibited any policy that "singles out" citizens on the basis of sexual orientation. What did this mean? It clearly meant that the local antigay measures the OCA was passing would be without legal effect, but beyond that, as state representative Tom Mason admitted, "nobody has absolutely any idea of what it does" (Mapes 1993b). The language of the almost laconic bill was unusually vague because it had to be in order to attract needed Republican votes; in 1993 the GOP controlled the state house but the Democrats controlled the state senate. Republican legislators from urban and suburban areas felt it necessary to get on record as being opposed to official discrimination, but rural Republicans would not vote for a gay rights proposal that had come close to passage two years earlier. Internal divisions within the party resulted in the watered-down, ambiguous bill that passed.

All the while, the OCA was collecting signatures for its statewide initiative, which it qualified easily in July 1994. The revised version stripped out some of the most inflammatory language in the 1992 measure, but the legal impact of the measure would have been largely the same because it retained the broad provision that public funds could not be used to "promote or express approval of homosexuality."

The campaign in the fall was largely dominated by a desultory repetition of the arguments that had been made in 1992. Again, political leaders opposed the measure; even conservative former representative Denny Smith, who was the Republican nominee for governor, announced his opposition after some pressure was applied by moderates in the party. Again, the OCA contended that the measure would mainly prevent homosexuals from receiving "minority status" and would stop public funds from being spent in support of homosexuality. And again, the opponents emphasized that the measure would require state and local governments to discriminate against citizens on the basis of sexual orientation. Polls again showed the measure losing, but given the publicity about the issue, there were a suspiciously large number of "undecided" respondents, even in October (Hill 1994).

There were two developments of note during the 1994 campaign. First, the Colorado Supreme Court ruled unconstitutional that state's antigay Amendment 2, which had passed in 1992. The decision did not come until October, when most voters had presumably decided how they would vote, but it did focus attention on the legal issues. The political effect of a ruling by a state court—even the supreme court—in another state, was probably minimal (Rubenstein and Bates 1994). As of this writing, the U.S. Supreme Court has accepted an appeal of the Colorado Supreme Court ruling and a decision is expected in summer 1995 (Greenhouse 1995).

Second, in what was surely the most bizarre development of the campaign, apparently in response to repeated charges that the OCA resembled the Nazi Party in its formative years, OCA officials claimed in October that homosexuals had been responsible for the Holocaust during World War II. Scott Lively, the OCA's membership director, claimed there was a connection between homosexuals in Germany and the

Nazis; leaders of the Oregon Jewish community were described as "struggling between surprise and outrage" (Rubenstein 1994a, B1). Rabbi Emanuel Rose, leader of the largest Jewish congregation in Portland, said that the OCA's charges ". . . turn truth on its head. Gays and lesbians and so-called 'enemies of the state' in addition to Jews were targets of the Nazis" (Rubenstein 1994b, D4).

Measure 13 lost, but very narrowly, winning in almost all of rural Oregon, but losing by large enough margins in the cities of Portland, Eugene, and Corvallis—and the Portland suburbs. Exit polls showed much the same pattern to the vote as in 1992, but that those in favor of the antigay measures had persuaded about five percent of the electorate to shift to a yes vote in 1994. Soon after the 1994 results were in, Mabon announced that the OCA would try again in 1996 and sent his followers another direct-mail fund-raising appeal (Suo 1994).

Whatever happens in 1996, it is clear that the Christian Right activists involved in these efforts feel very strongly that society should reimpose a variety of social controls weakened roughly during the past quarter century. Why?

Motivation Among OCA Activists

Since the great majority of citizens in democracies are usually little interested in politics or political issues, one of the great unresolved questions for political science is simple: why is the active minority active? The question is simple, but not easy to answer. When we consider economic issues, self-interest is the obvious answer, though that poorly explains the wealthy who favor income redistribution or the poor who oppose it. But social control issues evoke feelings rooted in strongly held convictions. That certainly has been the case among Christian Right activists in both Oregon and the nation.

One obvious way to find out why the activists are active is to ask them. I began trying to understand motivation among OCA activists rather early in the history of the organization; I was able to distribute questionnaires at the initial OCA state convention in Portland held on September 26, 1987. There is little to suggest that OCA activists have changed significantly since 1987. Indeed, the activities of the OCA in the eight years since then have reflected all of the concerns I heard mentioned that day (Rubenstein 1993a; Mapes 1993a). I counted seventy delegates present and received completed questionnaires from forty-six of them

(66 percent). I also interviewed eight delegates at greater length about their motivations and political views.

In some respects, the delegates to the 1987 OCA convention were quite similar to other political activists. A typical delegate to the 1987 OCA convention had "some college," not a degree, but median household income was relatively high—between fifty and sixty thousand dollars. This combination of relatively modest education and relatively high income has been found among strongly conservative groups in the past (Lipset and Raab 1970; Bell 1964).

All of the OCA delegates were white; while the Baptist Church is strong in black neighborhoods, the politically conservative views of the OCA do not appeal to minority citizens. Although about one delegate in three was female, hostility to social change among the delegates focused on changes to the status of women and extended to changes in the racial status quo ante. In my interviews, two respondents spontaneously drew a parallel between efforts to secure equal treatment for women and similar changes for African Americans; they objected to both. Some delegates to the OCA convention supported the reimposition of a broad range of social controls restricting minorities (particularly blacks) and women.

As table 12-2 shows, every delegate surveyed opposed legal abortion, and forty-two of forty-six respondents also opposed the Equal Rights Amendment (ERA) then under consideration by state legislatures. All but one of the delegates surveyed were opposed to affirmative action programs. None of those findings were unexpected. Their views parallel those of the lifestyle group the *Los Angeles Times* polling organization has called the "moralists" in national surveys. In 1987, 78 percent of the moralists surveyed by the *LA Times* agreed that "school boards should have the right to fire teachers who are known homosexuals," and 77

Table 12-2
OCA Activists Oppose Weakened Social Controls

Aspect of Change	Activists Opposed
Legal abortion	100%
Equal Rights Amendment	90%
Affirmative action	98%
Civil Rights Act	80%
Voting Rights Act	57%

Source: Author's survey of delegates to the 1987 OCA state convention.

percent of them agreed that "books containing dangerous ideas should be banned." Eighty percent favored mandatory drug testing for government employees, and 88 percent favored a constitutional amendment to restore school prayer. Only 25 percent of the moralists accepted interracial dating (Kohut 1987, 35–38). Even in this national context of support by the Christian Right for reimposition of a wide variety of social controls, it was striking that 80 percent of the delegates to the OCA convention opposed the Civil Rights Act of 1964 and 57 percent opposed the Voting Rights Act of 1965.

These findings were put in context, at least in part, by the comments of the eight delegates I interviewed. They all drew connections between social change and undesirable developments in society, notably increased crime rates. Beyond the specifics, OCA activists communicated a broader sense of distress at a world they saw turned upside-down. The activists were deeply upset by social and economic changes that, in their view, have disrupted the natural, God-given order of things. Although homosexuality was relatively far down the list of topics during my interviews, it was sometimes mentioned as yet another symbol of immoral behavior condoned, if not encouraged, by a decadent modern society. References to Sodom and Gomorrah were common among these activists.

I asked what had motivated them to become politically active. In every instance, some aspect of the changing status of women was mentioned. Most commonly, the delegates said that they were motivated to become active by their opposition to legal abortion, but a number placed this in a broader context, disapproving of all the social and political changes that have allowed women to compete with men in higher education and the workforce, delay childbearing, control their reproductive lives (opposition to legal abortion extended to opposition to legal contraception in most cases), and participate in other traditionally male-dominated activities, such as college sports.

For both of these groups, it appears, the relaxation of social controls since the decade of the sixties has been perceived as not only wrong but positively immoral. Frequently in my interviews, OCA activists expressed something approaching horror at changes in society that were, for them, both confusing and threatening. They saw reassuring rules that once governed both individual and collective behavior becoming unhinged and unenforced. In interviews I was repeatedly told that "God's will"—the natural order—has been violated by recent political and social changes. From the perspective of an activist who sees the Civil Rights Act, the Voting Rights Act, and changes that have established the legal equality of women with men as profoundly wrong, the emergence of open homosexuality must appear as further evidence of decadence in society.

The National Connection: The Future of Social Control Politics?

Social control issues are, in the post–cold war era, very significant—arguably becoming *the* central issues in our politics. As neoconservative scholar Nathan Glazer put it, ". . . the social agenda . . . brings to the Republican coalition a kind of strength it has not had for sixty years. Through the social agenda it reaches into low-income and low-status occupation groups. . . . Republicans can now make an appeal to low-status Evangelicals and Fundamentalists who were once solidly in the Democratic camp" (Glazer 1986, 28).

But pollster Andrew Kohut adds a warning for the GOP that:

> The Republican Party's current problems are rooted in its recent success. In the process of expanding its base, the GOP has moved further to the right and is beginning to show signs of fragmentation. The near doubling in size of the Moralist group—from 10% of all adults in 1987 to 18% today—illustrates the GOP's gains among white Southerners and Evangelical Protestants. . . . [But] the issues likely to mobilize the Moralists tend to drive the Libertarians away from the party, and vice-versa. . . . these groups come into direct conflict on social tolerance and business attitudes. (Kohut 1994, 66)

Kohut notes that the moralists are now the dominant Republican Party faction in the South and in rural areas of the nation, but that on the east and west coasts, the moralists—OCA supporters in Oregon—are weaker, both within the Republican Party and in politics in general. So in the Northwest, as in much of the most heavily populated areas of the nation, the GOP runs the risk of alienating its traditional supporters if it adopts moralist positions. Recent events in Oregon, as throughout much of the nation, evidence a split within the Republican Party over whether, and to what extent, the GOP should embrace the social control agenda of the Christian Right.

Notes

1. In addition to sources cited here, I have drawn upon information gathered as Political Analyst for Oregon Public Broadcasting (OPB). Since 1988, I have

written and broadcast a number of reports and analyses on the OCA and its activities.

2. The cities were Portland, Corvallis, and Ashland.

3. Originally named the Oregon Conservative Alliance, the name was shortly changed to make the OCA seem more inclusive. I attended one of the first OCA state conventions on September 26, 1987, in Portland. Some of the account here is taken from interviews conducted there.

4. The tenor of these efforts may be captured in the comment of one new right strategist who suggested that believers "don't want to think for themselves. They want to be told what to think. . . ." Quoted in Guth, p. 37.

5. I base this calculation on the fraction of the vote received by Joe Lutz in the Republican primary in 1986, and by Al Mobley, running for governor in the general election in 1990.

6. I am indebted to Jeff Mapes of *The Oregonian* for identifying this distinction between states with direct democracy measures.

7. This was the phrase used by Mobley in an interview with me when he described his perception of the attitudes of mainstream Republicans regarding the OCA.

References

Baker, Ross K. 1993. "Sorting Out and Summing Up: The Presidential Nominations," in *The Election of 1992*, ed. Gerald M. Pomper. Chatam, N.J.: Chatham House.

Barone, Michael, and Grant Ujifusa. 1987. *The Almanac of American Politics, 1988*. Washington. D.C.: National Journal.

———. 1993. *The Almanac of American Politics, 1994*. Washington, D.C.: National Journal.

Barone, Michael, Grant Ujifusa, and Douglas Matthews. 1973. *The Almanac of American Politics, 1974*. Boston: Gambit.

Bell, Daniel, ed. 1964. *The Radical Right*. Garden City, N.J.: Doubleday.

Berke, Richard L. 1994. "In Oregon, Christian Right Raises Its Sights and Wins," *New York Times* (18 July): 6.

Church, Foster. 1992. "Poll Finds Measure 9 Divides Oregonians in Many Ways." *The Oregonian* (11 October): 1ff.

Esteve, Harry. 1992. "No. 9 Supported on Moral Grounds." Eugene *Register-Guard* (5 November): B6.

Glazer, Nathan. 1986. "The 'Social Agenda.' " In *Perspectives on the Reagan Years*, ed. John L. Palmer. Washington, D.C.: The Urban Institute.

Greenhouse, Linda. 1995. "Supreme Court to Decide on Law That Bars Gay Rights in Colorado." *New York Times* (22 February): 1.

Guth, James L. 1983. "The New Christian Right." In *The New Christian Right*, ed. Robert C. Liebman and Robert Wuthnow. New York: Aldine Publishing Co.

Hill, Gail Kinsey. 1994. "Voters Show Caution In Spite of Anti-Government Mood." *The Oregonian* (11 October): 1ff.

Kohut, Andrew. 1987. *The People, The Press, and Politics.* Washington, D.C.: Times-Mirror.

———. 1994. *The New Political Landscape.* Washington, D.C.: Times-Mirror.

Lipset, Seymour Martin, and Earl Raab. 1970. *The Politics of Unreason.* New York: Harper & Row.

Luker, Kristen. 1984a. *Abortion and the Politics of Motherhood.* Berkeley: University of California Press.

———. 1984b. "The Wars Between Women." *Washington Post* (26 August): C4.

Lunch, William. 1995. "Oregon Politics, Upstate and Down." *Oregon Humanities* (Winter): 2–5.

Mapes, Jeff. 1989. "Frohnmayer Quick to Establish He's Pro-Choice," *Oregonian,* November 19. Forum section, p. 3.

———. 1992. "Poll Finds Measure 9 Losing, Packwood-AuCoin Race Close." *The Oregonian* (29 October): 1ff.

———. 1993a. "OCA Creates Activists." *The Oregonian* (22 June): B1.

———. 1993b. "Compromise Bill on Gays May Bring Confusion." *The Oregonian* (8 July): B1ff.

Neville, Paul. 1993a. "Money, Power & the OCA." *Eugene Register-Guard* (24 October): 1ff.

———. 1993b. "Doing Business on the Brink." Eugene *Register-Guard* (25 October): 1ff.

Ota, Alan K. 1988a. "Alliance Works to Shift Oregon Political Balance." *The Oregonian* (1 May): E6.

———. 1988b. "Politicians on Right Find New Power." *The Oregonian* (1 May): 1ff.

Rubenstein, Sura. 1992. "OCA Head Pledges Stripped-Down Version of Measure 9 for 1994." *The Oregonian* (8 November): 1ff.

———. 1993a. "Increasingly, Christian Right Becomes a Power in Politics." *The Oregonian* (20 June): 1ff.

———. 1993b. "Five Anti-Gay-Rights Measures Pass." *The Oregonian* (30 June): 1ff.

———. 1993c. "Anti-Gay-Rights Measures Win Handily." *The Oregonian* (22 September): C1ff.

———. 1994a. "OCA Claims That Gays Were Behind Holocaust." *The Oregonian* (19 October): B1.

———. 1994b. "OCA Leader Softens Stance on Gay-Holocaust Link." *The Oregonian* (20 October): D4.

Rubenstein, Sura, and Tom Bates. 1994. "Measure 13 Unscathed by Colorado Gay Ruling." *The Oregonian* (12 October): 1.

Schlesinger, Arthur M. 1986. *The Cycles of American History.* Boston: Houghton-Mifflin.

Schmalz, Jeffrey. 1993. "Poll Finds an Even Split on Homosexuality's Cause." *New York Times* (5 March): 1.

Strinkowski, Nicholas. 1993. "Oregon's Ballot Measure 9: Religious Fundamentalism, Gay Activism, and the Political Center." Paper presented at the Annual Meeting of the American Political Science Association, Washington, D.C., September 4.

Suo, Steve. 1994. "OCA Hopes Third Time Will be the Charm." *The Oregonian* (16 December): 1ff.

Turque, Bill. 1992. "Gays Under Fire." *Newsweek* (14 September): 34–41.

13

The Past as Prologue: The Christian Right in the 1996 Elections

Mark J. Rozell and Clyde Wilcox

The various case studies in this book show that the Christian Right was alive and vibrant in 1994. Christian conservatives controlled the party machinery in a number of states, and represented a sizable faction of Republican primary election voters. The second-generation groups are busy building broader, more inclusive religious coalitions, and the elites of groups such as the Christian Coalition almost universally are adopting moderate rhetoric. Based on these case studies, it seems safe to predict that the Christian Right will be a very active element of the Republican coalition in 1996.

Yet predicting the future of the Christian Right has proven difficult. In 1989, many journalists and a few scholars celebrated the demise of the New Christian Right. The Moral Majority was bankrupt and disbanded, and Pat Robertson's presidential campaign had been the most expensive in history but had failed to win a single presidential primary. It appeared to many that the Christian Right would once again fade into obscurity, as it had after its earlier manifestations in twentieth-century America.

Moreover, most scholars deemed the Christian Right of the 1980s a failure. Although Christian Right leaders had worked hard to elect Ronald Reagan in 1980 and 1984, as president Reagan had delivered policies to the economic and foreign policy conservatives, and only symbols to Christian conservatives. In 1989, after more than a decade of Christian Right activism, abortion remained legal, public schools could not begin their days with a prayer, and gays and lesbians continued to make slow, halting progress toward political and social equality (Moen 1992; Wilcox 1994).

In hindsight, many scholars saw the failure of the New Christian Right

as inevitable (Bruce 1994). The evangelical community was badly fragmented into different doctrinal groups, and fundamentalists, evangelicals, pentecostals, and charismatics all had relatively negative opinions
of the other groups (Jelen 1991). The Moral Majority never reached far
beyond Jerry Falwell's base denomination in the Baptist Bible Fellowship
(Georgiana 1989), and Robertson's campaign appealed primarily to
pentecostals and charismatics (Green and Guth 1988; Smidt and Penning 1990). Even if white evangelicals, fundamentalists, pentecostals,
and charismatics could unite in a single Christian Right movement, however, they would still be far short of constituting a real "moral majority":
to do so they would need to incorporate conservative Catholics, mainline Protestants, and perhaps even African Americans.

To many journalists the New Christian Right seemed an anachronism,
and its crusade to restore "traditional" moral values in a nation that was
steadily becoming better educated and somewhat more secular seemed
quixotic. Evangelical Christians were seen as dragging their feet to slow
the inevitable course of history—watching Christian television that
broadcast reruns of programs that showed married couples sleeping in
twin beds, while their children watched Madonna on MTV.

Yet rumors of the death of the Christian Right proved to be prema-
ture. And predictions of the death of the movement were not the first
failures of prescience. In 1980, academics and some scholars saw the
movement as a juggernaut in American politics, and by 1984 it was
deemed to be anemic and overrated. Some sociologists predicted that
Pat Robertson would win the presidency in 1988, and after his defeat
others predicted that the Christian Right would disappear.

The Constancy of the Christian Right

These wildly divergent predictions have missed an important underlying
point. From the 1970s into the 1990s, surveys have shown that between
11 percent and 15 percent of Americans have supported Christian Right
organizations. A somewhat larger number have supported various portions of the Christian Right platform, although the magnitude of this
support has been the subject of some debate (Simpson 1983, 1994; Sigelman and Presser 1988; Wilcox 1992). A much smaller number have
been *active* participants in Christian Right groups.

The political fortunes of the Christian Right have waxed and waned
in the past two decades because of institutional and political factors.
The Moral Majority went bankrupt not because it lost the support of

its fundamentalist base, but because the direct-mail fund-raising market became saturated, and three consecutive Republican presidential victories made it difficult to persuade the older women who constituted the financial base that it was important to send money to fight liberal, secular Democrats. Pat Robertson's defeat sent him back to his television show because we do not have a parliamentary system: in some European countries, Robertson would head a small religious party. When Robertson left the campaign trail to take up his seat on the "700 Club," he formed the Christian Coalition. The goal of the organization was to build at the grass roots—to establish precinct-level organizations throughout the country. Unlike the Moral Majority, the Christian Coalition has sought to build a truly ecumenical movement, incorporating not only the divergent and often warring elements of the evangelical community but mainline Protestants and Catholics as well. Other organizations, especially the state groups affiliated with Focus on the Family and the state chapters of Concerned Women for America, have also tried to build broader coalitions.

What has changed, then, is not the numbers of Christian Right supporters, nor the size of the potential constituency. Instead, the groups of the 1990s are better organized, and better able to bridge theological divides, than the organizations of the 1980s. Fundamentalists may still dislike Catholics, but they can put aside for now the question of who will get to heaven and concentrate instead on who will win the next election. Thus it seems likely that there are more Christian Right *activists* today than in the early 1980s, because the organizations of the "second coming" of the New Christian Right have built inclusive organizations that more broadly solicit participation.

The Christian Right in the Republican Party

The conventional wisdom is that the Christian Right hurt the Republican Party in 1992, but did not cost the GOP the election. Our own estimates are that the heated rhetoric of "Family Values Night" at the Republican convention, with its attendant news coverage, and the pro-life plank in the platform probably cost Bush 2 percent of the general election vote (see also Abramowitz 1995). Bush lost because the public decided not to renew his contract, but Clinton's margin was increased somewhat by public perceptions that the Republican Party was too closely linked to a radical religious right agenda. The 1994 elections have been described as a tsunami, an earthquake, and a meteor strike, among other cataclysmic events (Wilcox 1995). Explanations for the Republican landslide vary, but many Christian Right leaders claim credit for swinging a number of key elections.

How could the Christian Right be an albatross in 1992, then rise like the phoenix in 1994 to be the savior of the party? Again these wildly divergent interpretations miss the underlying regularity. The Christian Right represents 10 to 15 percent of the public, and its natural constituency among white evangelicals is an even larger segment. When this constituency is mobilized, it can swing close elections. Yet those who oppose the Christian Right are generally at least as numerous as those who support it, and if *they* are mobilized, the Christian Right usually loses. So in 1992 when large numbers of Americans saw "Family Values Night" at the Republican convention, the countermobilization was important. In 1994, in a set of low-salience elections, the Christian Right mobilization was greater and therefore helped the Republicans.

Whatever the role of the Christian Right in the Republican victories, the 1994 elections provided the movement with its greatest opportunity to date to influence public policy. According to the Christian Coalition, as many as forty of the GOP freshmen elected to the House were prolife, conservative Christians. The Coalition's executive director, Ralph Reed, characterized the election results as "a watershed moment for the Christian Coalition, much like the 1936 election was for labor unions and blacks" (Geroux 1994, A8).[1] Clearly, the Christian Right expects to have more influence in policy in 1995 than it had the previous year.

Yet the Republican "Contract With America" ignores the social agenda of the Christian Right, emphasizing instead federal budgetary and tax issues and political and welfare reform. House Speaker Newt Gingrich has promised to vote on a proposed constitutional amendment on school prayer, but the amendment appears to have little chance in the Senate, where even some conservative Republicans oppose the measure. And as numerous Republican presidential candidates position themselves to challenge President Bill Clinton, many in the party are advising that candidates take moderate positions on divisive social issues, or at least that the party obscure its language on abortion.

For example, William Kristol, chairman of the Project for the Republican Future, has warned of the consequences of the GOP focusing its attention during the presidential campaign on the abortion issue. Responding to high-profile sniping between rivals Senator Arlen Specter (R-Pa.), who is pro-choice, and conservative commentator Pat Buchanan, who is pro-life, Kristol said that the party could not afford to allow these candidates "to succeed" at controlling the debate. William

Bennett warned that the GOP's abortion plank had the effect of "hurting the Republican Party and the conservative cause with a lot of voters in the middle" (Edsall 1995).

Yet pro-choice candidates such as Arlen Specter and Pete Wilson will want an open debate on abortion, because a number of surveys show that there are many more pro-choice Republicans than pro-life ones (Wilcox 1994). Soon after the "watershed" election, Republican presidential candidates will be forced to confront directly the role of the Christian Right and to determine what parts of its agenda, if any, they will support. This will provide an acid test of the "new pragmatism" of the Christian Right.

The New Pragmatism: Implications and Limits

The preceding chapters make it clear that the leadership of the Christian Right has changed its strategy and tactics. In the 1970s and throughout much of the 1980s, Christian Right elites and activists alike openly talked of a takeover of the Republican Party, and made uncompromising demands on GOP candidates as a condition for their support. Now they more commonly say that all they want is to be included in the party's broad coalition—to get "a seat at the table." In order to gain an invitation to that table, Christian Right leaders have focused on a variety of strategies: moderate rhetoric, broader issue concerns, more inclusive coalitions, and compromise on key issues.

One Virginia Christian Right leader, Anne Kincaid, told us that she had learned "the hard way" to stop using rhetoric that the public finds inflammatory. She emphasized that she can be more effective by using the secular language of politics to convince people of the correctness of her views.

> "Onward Christian soldiers" scared people. Some still talk about witchcraft and the feminist movement. Yes, the Bible says that "rebellion against men is of witchcraft." It's all Biblical tenets, but the layman doesn't understand that. So it makes you sound like you've lost your marbles. The point is, you have to know your audience. (Kincaid interview)[2]

Christian Right leaders also emphasize the necessity of broadening their agenda beyond the controversial social issues. Although the GOP "Contract" ignores the social agenda of the Christian Right, Reed and others argue that items such as the balanced budget amendment and welfare reform are pro-family, and therefore appealing to conservative Christians. Consequently, rather than complaining about the lack of emphasis on social issues—the posture adopted by many conservative Christian leaders in 1981 in response to President Reagan's economic recovery plan—the Christian Coalition has committed itself to spending a million dollars to lobby Congress in an effort to help the GOP succeed at reshaping the federal budget. Even Arthur Kropp, president of People for the American Way, an anti–Christian Right organization, admits that "Ralph Reed is demonstrating that the Coalition can be a team player. . . . I think he'll make a lot of friends in Congress that way" (Geroux 1994, A1, 8). Indeed, if the Christian Coalition can succeed at being perceived as helping Republicans promote the "Contract," then it can claim the right later on to expect reciprocal support for its agenda from the GOP.

Christian Right leaders also urge the necessity of building coalitions with both secular and religious conservative groups. The Christian Coalition training manual lists various groups that are potential allies with the movement: antitax, pro-business, educational reform, pro-family and pro-life, veterans, right-to-work, gun owners, home educators, and antipornography, among others. Throughout much of the 1980s, Christian Right groups did not do so well at forming broad-based coalitions. By emphasizing social issue purity and religious differences, those groups were either unwilling or unable to work with other interests. Christian Right groups today emphasize political similarities, or at least common political interests. Consequently, even though the gun enthusiasts who supported Oliver North at the 1994 state party convention in Virginia were hostile to the social issues agenda of the Christian Right, these two groups of delegates came together to support candidates who backed their separate issues. Ralph Reed told us that he now sees the Christian Coalition's role in part to be one of encouraging activists who may disagree on some issues to form temporary coalitions to support common conservative goals (Reed interview).

Another strategy is to compromise on controversial social issues, including abortion. Many of the candidates endorsed by the Christian Right in these case studies do not support an outright ban on abortion, but instead favor parental notification and waiting periods and oppose taxpayer funding of abortions for poor women. Although only a minority of Americans favor banning abortion, large majorities support additional restrictions, making these good issues for Christian conservatives. The goal is either to paint the pro-choice candidate as an extremist opposing "reasonable" limitations on abortion, or to neutralize the abortion issue by forcing the pro-choice candidate to drop it altogether.

These mainstream appeals come with a price: when candidates campaign only to impose waiting periods or parental notification on abortion, they are unlikely to seek greater restrictions in office. Although some activists may believe that parental notification is better than no parental notification, others express discomfort with compromise on the abortion issue.

It is clear that moderate rhetoric, a broader issue agenda, and a willingness to compromise on key issues will win Christian Right leaders friends among Republican leaders. It is less clear that Christian Right leaders can maintain their mobilized base while using moderate rhetoric, emphasizing budgetary issues, and compromising on key issues such as abortion. Christian Right publications in 1993 featured articles on the evils of the gasoline tax, but nearly all of the letters focused on abortion and gays in the military (Wilcox 1994).

The Christian Right therefore finds itself torn between the pragmatism of its leaders and the purism of its followers. Movement leaders may find it difficult to convince the movement's activist core to volunteer on behalf of moderate Republicans year after year, especially if they receive no more policy payoffs than were offered by Reagan. Conversely, if the movement resorts to the purist strategies of nominating candidates who are closely associated with or members of the Christian Right, it is almost certain to lose. For the moment, many Christian Right leaders appear to have adopted a two-track strategy of moderate rhetoric when dealing with Republican leaders and extremist language when mobilizing the faithful.

After the Apocalypse: The Christian Right in the 1996 Elections

Indeed, the Christian Coalition appears to have adopted a two-pronged strategy for the 1996 presidential election: publicly signal to the activists that the GOP will lose the support of a core constituency if it nominates a pro-choice presidential or vice presidential candidate, while working behind the scenes with party leaders to moderate GOP positions on contentious social issues. Reed told a conservative gathering that "prolife and profamily voters, one-third of the electorate, will not support a party that retreats from its noble and historic defense of traditional values and which has a national ticket or a platform that does not share Ronald Reagan's belief in the sanctity of human life." Yet Reed and the Christian Coalition are willing to agree to remove from the GOP's platform language that advocates a human life constitutional amendment in order to replace it with a more moderate plank extolling the choice of life instead of abortion (Edsall 1995).

Of course, the platform is usually written by those who backed the winning candidate. In July 1995, what is surprising is the number of candidates who might have appealed to the Christian Right who have announced that they will *not* seek the presidency. With both former vice president Dan Quayle and former drug czar William Bennett declining to run, Christian conservatives have lost two of their strongest advocates. With former congressman Jack Kemp also taking a pass on a presidential campaign, Christian conservatives have lost the candidate with potentially the most broad-based electoral appeal.

At this point three pro-life Catholics—Pat Buchanan, a controversial talk-show host; Robert Dornan, a fiesty conservative who emphasizes his opposition to gay rights; and Alan Keyes, an African American social conservative—best represent the viewpoint of Christian conservative activists. None of these candidates has much of a chance to win the nomination. Keyes, a twice-defeated U.S. Senate candidate, is not a proven vote getter, and Buchanan's undiluted nativism and Dornan's frequently vitriolic rhetoric place them outside the mainstream of the party. A more viable possibility might be Texas senator Phil Gramm, who has thus far devoted greater attention to economic issues than to social policy. Many Christian social conservatives express suspicion of economic conservatives who try to make appeals on the social issues during a nomination campaign. Yet if Gramm is the nominee, it is likely that he would get enthusiastic support from the Christian Right.

Senate Majority Leader Robert Dole, once vilified as the GOP "hatchet man," is now in the unaccustomed position of running as the respectable moderate conservative—more of a commentary on the GOP's shift to the right than an indication of a change in his own political ideology. Most Christian conservatives would prefer Dole to Clinton, but in the primary elections his image of elder statesman and his more moderate policy views may hurt his chances to appeal to the more fervent party activists who prefer the firebrand style of a Buchanan or the unrepentant conservatism of a Gramm.

Of the candidates to announce to date, probably only Arlen Specter is so objectionable to Christian conservatives that many might actually choose not to support him should he prevail as the party's presidential nominee. Although party moderates will claim that Christian social conservatives have "nowhere else to go" should the GOP nominate Specter, he has so openly targeted the Christian Right agenda for criticism that there is no doubt that his candidacy would dispirit many of the more fervent party activists and cause some of them not to participate in the general election campaign at any level. A vice presidential nomination of Lynn Martin could potentially also alienate Christian social conservatives, although she has not been so blunt as has Specter in criticizing the Christian Right agenda.

California governor Pete Wilson might be the kind of moderate conservative who could both rebut any Democratic charges of being beholden to the "radical right" and be willing to deliver some policy payoffs to the Christian Right as president. Christian Right leaders who back a strategy of political pragmatism might find his candidacy attractive for that reason, although it is difficult to believe that the movement activists would be enthusiastic about an openly pro-choice candidate.

Although what John Kessel has called the "structure of the competition" is not clear in July 1995, it is obvious that Christian conservatives will be key players in the Republican nomination process. Many conservatives hope for a relatively quiet primary season, and in that event the Christian Right may be an important asset for Republicans, mobilizing their core constituency against their nemesis Bill Clinton. But Republican candidates have many times in the past fought heated battles for the hearts and minds of the GOP rank and file. If the 1996 contest is an ideological one like 1964, 1976, or 1980, then the Christian Right itself may become an issue, and candidates may openly debate school prayer, abortion, and other elements of the social agenda. If so, that may spark a countermobilization against the Christian Right.

Conclusion

The case studies in this volume make it clear that the Christian Right is capable of compromising and working within the GOP to support nominees who back some but not all of the Christian conservative agenda. In the statewide races, when given a choice between a pro-choice Democrat and a moderate-conservative Republican who supported marginal abortion restrictions, for example, Christian social conservatives worked fervently for the GOP candidates. That strategy paid substantial dividends, as numerous GOP candidates were elected in 1994 feeling some obligation to the different elements of their electoral constituency. Governor Pete Wilson may be pro-choice, but his strong support for issues of secondary concern to Christian social conservatives has meant real progress for the Christian Right agenda in California.

Yet there are still those instances in which Christian Right activists and leaders in the nominating process back a candidate such as Oliver North, whose general election defeat meant the reelection of a staunch pro-choice Democrat. In states where the party system is vulnerable to a short-term takeover by ideological activists, it is not clear that a Christian Right strategy of pragmatism will prevail.

Should Christian Right activists continue to succeed at nominating candidates who lose general elections, GOP centrists may either begin to leave the party or try to work within it to change the nomination procedures. Moderate Republicans may find Christian conservative candidates unpalatable and vote for moderate Democrats. If this leads to the defeat of the candidates backed by the Christian Right, this continual electoral defeat may dispirit Christian Right activists, causing many to leave the party to the centrists.

Alternatively, the Christian Right could pursue an across-the-board strategy of pragmatism, backing mainstream candidates rather than "fellow travelers" both for the GOP nomination and in the general election. The danger with this approach is that once again the core activists may find it difficult to get excited about always supporting mainline Republicans who offer primarily symbolic concessions to the Christian Right. To lose the fervent support of the Christian Right activists would be harmful to both the Christian Right and the Republican Party. Indeed, short of a third party, there is no real alternative for the Christian Right should the movement lose its enthusiasm for the GOP. And the Republican Party surely needs the grassroots support of Christian social conservatives who continue to distribute millions of voters guides in election years and to lobby for GOP causes.

It is most likely that the Christian Right will pursue both strategies—backing fellow travelers and being more pragmatic—because it is a movement with multiple leaders and competing organizations, not a monolithic enterprise. Although there is considerable evidence that the Christian Right is playing the political game smarter than ever before, its long-term success will depend a great deal on the ability of many of its leaders to convince activists that a long-term strategy of pragmatism promises the greatest payoff for the movement.

Notes

1. Reed probably meant the 1932 elections.
2. Kincaid is a former lobbyist for the Virginia Family Foundation and serves as the head of constituent services in the George Allen administration.

References

Abramowitz, Alan. 1995. "It's Abortion, Stupid: Policy Voting in the 1992 Presidential Election." *Journal of Politics* 57: 176–86.

Bruce, Steve. 1994. "The Inevitable Failure of the New Christian Right." *Sociology of Religion* 85: 229–42.

Edsall, Thomas B. 1995. "GOP Debates Compromise on Abortion." *Washington Post* (27 February): A6.

Georgiana, Sharon Linzey. 1989. *The Moral Majority and Fundamentalism.* Lewiston, N.Y.: Mellon.

Geroux, Bill. 1994. "The Christian Coalition Contracts with Majority." *Richmond Times-Dispatch* (30 January): A8.

Green, John C., and James L. Guth. 1988. "The Christian Right in the Republican Party." *Journal of Politics* 50: 150–65.

Jelen, Ted G. 1991. *The Political Mobilization of Religious Belief.* New York: Praeger.

Kincaid, Anne. 1993. Author interview, Richmond, Va., 17 November.

Moen, Matthew. 1992. *The Transformation of the Christian Right.* Tuscaloosa: University of Alabama Press.

Reed, Ralph. 1994. Author interview, Washington, D.C., 29 September.

Sigelman, Lee, and Stanley Presser. 1988. "Measuring Support for the New Christian Right." *Public Opinion Quarterly* 52: 325–37.

Simpson, John H. 1983. "Moral Issues and Status Politics." Pp. 188–207 in *The New Christian Right,* ed. R. Liebman and R. Wuthnow. New York: Aldine.

———. 1994. "The Mood of America in the 1980s." *Sociology of Religion* 85: 291–305.

Smidt, Corwin, and James M. Penning. 1990. "A Party Divided?" *Polity* 23: 129–38.

Taylor, Joe, 1992. "Christian Coalition Revamping Image." *Richmond Times-Dispatch* (7 December): B4.

Wilcox, Clyde. 1992. *God's Warriors: The Christian Right in 20th Century America.* Baltimore: Johns Hopkins University Press.

———. 1994. "Premillennialists at the Millennium: Some Reflections on the Christian Right in the Twenty-first Century." *Sociology of Religion* 85: 243–62.

Index

About the Contributors

Nancy L. Bednar is a graduate fellow at the Carl Albert Center, University of Oklahoma. Her dissertation is on the Christian Right in Congressional elections.

John M. Bruce is an assistant professor of government at Georgetown University. His work has been in the areas of mass behavior and political parties.

Charles S. Bullock III is the Richard B. Russell professor of political science at the University of Georgia–Athens. His latest book (coauthored with Loch Johnson) is *Runoff Elections in the South*.

Christopher P. Gilbert is assistant professor of political science at Gustavus Adolphus College, St. Peter, Minnesota. He is the author of *The Impact of Churches on Political Behavior* and has specific research interests in religion and politics. In 1991 he received the E. E. Schattschneider Award of the American Political Science Association for best dissertation in American government and politics.

John Christopher Grant is a Ph.D. candidate at the University of Georgia–Athens. His dissertation is on education innovation in the South.

John C. Green is director of the Ray C. Bliss Institute and professor of political science at the University of Akron. He has done extensive research on religion and politics and is coeditor (with James L. Guth) of *The Bible and the Ballot Box*.

James L. Guth is professor of political science at Furman University. He is coeditor (with John C. Green) of *The Bible and the Ballot Box: Religion and Politics in the 1988 Election*.

Allen D. Hertzke is associate professor of political science and assistant director of the Carl Albert Center, University of Oklahoma. He is the author of *Echoes of Discontent*.

William M. Lunch is a professor in the political science department at Oregon State University and the Political Analyst for Oregon Public Broadcasting.

Jeremy D. Mayer is a Ph.D. candidate at Georgetown University. His dissertation is on the politics of race.

Bruce Nesmith is assistant professor of political science at Coe College in Cedar Rapids, Iowa. He is the author of *The New Republican Coalition: The Reagan Campaigns and White Evangelicals.*

James Penning is professor of political science at Calvin College, Grand Rapids, Michigan. He is coauthor of *Christian Political Action* and has published articles in numerous professional journals and edited volumes.

David A. Peterson is a 1995 graduate of Gustavus Adolphus College, majoring in political science. He is presently a graduate student in political science at the University of Minnesota, working towards his Ph.D. with special interests in political behavior, religion and politics, and media influences on public opinion.

Mark J. Rozell is associate professor of political science at Mary Washington College. His latest book is *Executive Privilege: The Dilemma of Secrecy and Democratic Accountability.*

Corwin Smidt received his Ph.D. in political science from the University of Iowa. He has authored or coauthored a variety of chapters and articles related to the ways in which religious attitudes, identifications, and affiliations are manifested politically in contemporary American politics.

J. Christopher Soper is assistant professor of political science at Pepperdine University. His latest book is *Evangelical Christians in the U.S. and Great Britain.*

Kenneth D. Wald is professor of political science at the University of Florida. He is the author of *Religion and Politics in the United States* (2nd edition).

Clyde Wilcox is associate professor of government at Georgetown University. He is the author of *God's Warriors: The Christian Right in 20th Century America.*